AF901794

LITIGANTS IN PERSON IN THE CIVIL JUSTICE SYSTEM

Why do people represent themselves?

What works and what doesn't for self-represented parties?

And how can we improve Litigant in Person (LiP) experiences to make the civil justice system fairer?

Based on in-depth interviews with individuals who have acted as Litigants in Person in the civil courts, the book provides the first full-length account of LiP experiences. The author shines a light on how much we don't know about LiPs, the civil justice system, and LiPs' place within it, as well as the kinds of things we ought to be doing to improve access to justice for unrepresented parties.

Perfect for scholars of administrative justice, access to justice, court reform and legal aid, as well as government bodies and non-profit organisations, this book generates insight into meaningful methods of what works and what doesn't work for self-represented parties, based on the real-life experiences of LiPs.

Litigants in Person in the Civil Justice System

In Their Own Words

Kate Leader

•HART•

OXFORD • LONDON • NEW YORK • NEW DELHI • SYDNEY

HART PUBLISHING

Bloomsbury Publishing Plc

Kemp House, Chawley Park, Cumnor Hill, Oxford, OX2 9PH, UK

1385 Broadway, New York, NY 10018, USA

29 Earlsfort Terrace, Dublin 2, Ireland

HART PUBLISHING, the Hart/Stag logo, BLOOMSBURY and the Diana logo are trademarks of Bloomsbury Publishing Plc

First published in Great Britain 2024

Copyright © Kate Leader, 2024

Kate Leader has asserted her right under the Copyright, Designs and Patents Act 1988 to be identified as Author of this work.

All rights reserved. No part of this publication may be reproduced or transmitted in any form or by any means, electronic or mechanical, including photocopying, recording, or any information storage or retrieval system, without prior permission in writing from the publishers.

While every care has been taken to ensure the accuracy of this work, no responsibility for loss or damage occasioned to any person acting or refraining from action as a result of any statement in it can be accepted by the authors, editors or publishers.

All UK Government legislation and other public sector information used in the work is Crown Copyright ©. All House of Lords and House of Commons information used in the work is Parliamentary Copyright ©. This information is reused under the terms of the Open Government Licence v3.0 (http://www.nationalarchives.gov.uk/doc/open-government-licence/version/3) except where otherwise stated.

All Eur-lex material used in the work is © European Union, http://eur-lex.europa.eu/, 1998–2024.

A catalogue record for this book is available from the British Library.

A catalogue record for this book is available from the Library of Congress.

Library of Congress Control Number: 2023951830

ISBN: HB: 978-1-50994-832-1
ePDF: 978-1-50994-834-5
ePub: 978-1-50994-833-8

Typeset by Compuscript Ltd, Shannon

To find out more about our authors and books visit www.hartpublishing.co.uk. Here you will find extracts, author information, details of forthcoming events and the option to sign up for our newsletters.

For Dom and Avi (even though he can't read)

ACKNOWLEDGEMENTS

There are many people who played an important role in bringing this book to life. First, Linda Mulcahy and Nicola Lacey, my PhD supervisors, where this project began and who have always generously and tirelessly supported me. I am so fortunate to have such extraordinary scholars and women looking out for me. Thanks also to my PhD examiners, Coretta Phillips and Hazel Genn, whose insightful feedback improved this work no end. Thanks to Kate Whetter and Verity Stuart at Hart Publishing, as well as to Catherine Minahan, whose exceptional attention to detail has made this book far, far more coherent than it would have been. Thank you to my generous friends and colleagues who read and gave feedback on my work-in-progress: Lucy Welsh, Jessica Shurson, Tara Mulqueen, Matt Matravers and Grainne McKeever. I also want to thank my fellow litigant-in-person researchers for their solidarity and support: Tania Grieshofer, Jess Mant, Bridgette Toy-Cronin and Grainne McKeever, who has been such a generous reader and supporter that it is only right that she gets thanked twice. Thank you to all my friends and colleagues at LSE Law, Birkbeck and York Law School throughout my time at these places. Thanks to Dom for the love and support, and to Avi for the joy that more than makes up for the (relentless, endless) sleeplessness. Finally, the most important thank you in this book goes to my interviewees, who generously shared their stories with me. Without them, this book would not be possible.

CONTENTS

Introduction

> Basically, you are sold a myth that the British judicial system is the finest in the world, that it is fair, just, reasonable and concerned with finding out the truth. That is a load of fucking bollocks, pardon the French.
>
> *Eleanor*

> No disrespect to your colleagues or solicitor friends and stuff [laughing] … All college, no knowledge? Where's the common-sense element? I mean, there's very little common sense in law. You know it doesn't, it just doesn't make sense, does it? A lot of law.
>
> *Neil*

> It seems to me you're trying to save money in something that, where actually, you can't really save a lot of money. All you can do is make things less fair, less right, and then you save money but then you don't get the right result. So, that's what I think about the court system from my experience.
>
> *Trevor*

I. Introduction

This book is about litigants in person (LiPs) in the civil justice system. It is both about how LiPs experience the law, and about how the law 'experiences' LiPs. To find out what it was like to be a LiP today, I asked some.[1] This book is the result of those conversations. What I learned is that for most LiPs, the experience of going to law is far worse than we have previously understood. We know that representing oneself is difficult, but what this book shows is that it is also frustrating, exhausting and traumatic. Its impact can be life-changing, destructive and destabilising. The LiPs in these pages report relationship breakdowns, mental health crises, loss of jobs, income and homes, as well as a deep alienation from law and legal proceedings. Most find going to law to be so far from what they expected as to have a profoundly disillusioning effect on their trust in legal professionals and legal institutions.

[1] The interviewees' names and some details have been changed to protect their anonymity.

So why does this matter? I believe it matters for a number of reasons: some are practical, some are about the law and some are about power. Practically, the number of LiPs is going up, so we have reason to learn about them and their experiences. On a happier note, some of the difficulties described in this book are administrative or minor and might be easily fixed, so we need to think about how we might do this. We also say that anyone can and should be able to represent themselves, so we need to think more about how this ideal might be realised more fully.[2]

In terms of the law, the experience of LiPs in these pages shows that legal proceedings, despite paying lip service to 'access to justice', remain inaccessible, complex and exclusionary. We need to think about how this might be addressed in a more meaningful way: through providing greater practical access to up-to-date legal materials, and through directly assisting LiPs in understanding and navigating legal process. We also need to realise the limits of these kinds of interventions and the extent to which LiPs will always labour under a disadvantage. How can this be accommodated more fairly through systemic change to ensure greater equality of arms, particularly in situations where (as is most common) LiPs are facing represented opponents?

In terms of power, one of the most important things this book shows is that encounters with legal professionals are at the heart of the nature of LiP experiences, in particular the way in which professionalism, including professional norms and the languages of professions, functions to exclude them. One of the biggest mistakes we make when thinking about LiPs is to consider them in isolation. But LiP difficulties are not always (or even often) problems inherent to LiPs; instead, they are indicative of systemic inadequacies in the civil justice system itself, a system that theoretically provides access for LiPs but which functionally excludes them. As Lord Woolf put it:

> Only too often the litigant in person is regarded as a problem for judges and for the court system rather than the person for whom the system of civil justice exists. The true problem is the court system and its procedures, which are still too often inaccessible and incomprehensible to ordinary people.[3]

So, learning about LiPs allows us also to learn some important things: how we treat laypersons in the law; the law's exclusionary complexity; and, perhaps most importantly, the profound undermining of trust and faith in legal processes that can result from negative experiences of going to law.

Finally, as this book will show, we tend to divide LiPs in our mind into 'worthy' and 'unworthy', based on a division between who *has* to go to law versus those who 'choose' to. This distinction does not parallel LiPs' *right* to go to law but instead

[2] Not everyone agrees with this, of course, as I will explore in chs 1 and 2 when I think about how the law 'experiences' the LiP.

[3] H Woolf, Access to Justice: The Final Report to the Lord Chancellor on the Civil Justice System in England and Wales (London, Stationery Office, 1996) para 17.2.

reveals the ways in which LiPs are judged for decisions they make about what is sufficiently important in their own lives to mandate pursuing or defending claims. It is seemingly the expected thing that, if we are sympathetic to LiPs' plight, we should focus on how worthy LiPs are and how important their cases are: that they only go to law because they must, and that the pejorative representations of them are misleading and off the mark. This is of course true for some (it may well be for many, as it is in this group of individuals), but to do so is surely to miss the point; LiPs are LiPs in actions because they are permitted by law to be there. And if they are permitted to be there, they should not have to plead necessity; the determination to 'rehabilitate' LiPs simply draws attention to the degree to which LiPs are expected to apologise for their presence. Litigants in person are judged simply for exercising their legal rights. The stories of LiPs in this book matter, then, because they can show us that such attitudes are destructive, discriminatory and, more importantly, misconceived.

II. What is a Litigant in Person?

Who exactly is a LiP? This is less straightforward than we might think. Hazel Genn described the historical lack of data on LiPs as a 'black hole'.[4] The demographic research that does exist shows considerable diversity in gender, age, ethnicity and education.[5] On top of this, inconsistencies as to the definition of the term 'litigant in person' can be confusing. Lord Justice Peter Gibson defined a LiP as a 'party to litigation who represents himself by appearing in court himself'.[6] But this definition excludes individuals who may lack legal representation, be involved in legal proceedings and never set foot inside a courtroom (it also, incidentally, excludes women). These people are also LiPs.[7] A more comprehensive definition, then, is the one issued by the *Equal Treatment Bench Book*: 'The term [litigant in person] encompasses those preparing a case for trial or hearing, those conducting their own case at a trial or hearing and those wishing to enforce a judgment or to appeal.'[8]

[4] H Genn, 'Do-It-Yourself Law: Access to Justice and the Challenge of Self-Representation', speech delivered at lecture *Assisting Unrepresented Litigants*, Sydney (15–17 April 2014). See also H Genn, *Judging Civil Justice: The 2008 Hamlyn Lectures* (Cambridge, Cambridge University Press, 2009) 133.

[5] J MacFarlane and C Sullivan, 'Tracking the Trends of the Self-Represented Litigant Phenomenon: Data from the National Self-Represented Litigants Project 2019–2021' (Windsor, National Self Represented Litigants Project, 2021); K Williams, 'Litigants in Person: A Literature Review' (London, Ministry of Justice, 2011).

[6] *Jonathan Alexander Ltd v Proctor* [1996] 2 All ER 334, 341 per Gibson LJ.

[7] And this conversation leaves aside the question of using the term 'litigant in person' over the arguably more comprehensible term 'self-represented litigant [SRL]' used in other jurisdictions, such as Australia and Canada. This term was rejected, I think regrettably so, by Lord Dyson in 2013. See Practice Guidance (Terminology for Litigants in Person) 11 March 2013 [2013] 2 All ER 624.

[8] Judicial College, *Equal Treatment Bench Book* (London, Judicial College, 2013) 1.

But although this definition is much more helpful, confusion can arise from the assumption that LiPs are claimants who bring proceedings.[9] The association of LiP with claimant is linked to pejorative assumptions predicated on the belief that LiPs are litigious and actively (and usually unnecessarily) pursue proceedings. But LiPs act as both claimants and defendants. If anything, as Moorhead and Sefton pointed out in their 2005 study, the majority of LiPs are defendants. Indeed, 'passive defendants', whom Moorhead and Sefton define as named defendants in litigation who never actively take part in proceedings, let alone appear in court, formed 56 per cent of their sample.[10] Definitions of LiPs that are based on appearing in a courtroom or active participation limit, rather than assist, our understanding.

The term 'litigant in person' also invokes the idea that LiPs deliberately 'go it alone'. But this is almost never the case.[11] Most LiPs have intermittent, and considerably varying, degrees of representation and advice.[12] The impact of this kind of advice and representation has a meaningful influence on how and why individuals become LiPs. Cumulatively, then, many of the assumptions we make about LiPs often turn out to be wrong, and many of the ways in which we attempt to define LiPs fail to capture their true breadth. For the purposes of this book, I define LiPs as broadly as possible: individuals who are either claimants or defendants, and who do not have sustained legal representation throughout the life of their legal proceedings.

III. The Interviews

The backbone of this book is 15 oral history life-story interviews with LiPs, all of whom have initiated or defended claims in the County Courts. Oral history is distinct as a form of historiographic practice in the primacy of the interview as the method of gathering data. This is where oral history can be distinguished from autobiography because, as Michael Frisch points out, oral history depends on the interrelationship of interviewer and interviewee: it constitutes a 'shared authority'.[13] Oral history interviewing, then, relies on the importance of what interviewees *say*, and is also predicated on the relationship between interviewer and interviewee. Oral history life stories provide a unilateral perspective as a means to, 'engage directly with the litigant's social world'.[14]

[9] R Moorhead and M Sefton, *Litigants in Person: Unrepresented Litigants in First Instance Proceedings* (London, Department of Constitutional Affairs, 2005) 245.

[10] ibid 27.

[11] See J MacFarlane, 'The National Self-Represented Litigants Project: Identifying and Meeting the Needs of Self-Represented Litigants' Treasurer's Advisory Group on Access to Justice Working Group Report, 2013, 86.

[12] H Genn, *Paths to Justice* (Oxford, Hart Publishing, 1999) 83–98.

[13] M Frisch, A Shared Authority: Essays on the Craft and Meaning of Oral and Public History (Albany, NY, State University of New York Press, 1990).

[14] R Moorhead, 'The Passive Arbiter' (2007) 16(3) *Social and Legal Studies* 405, 417.

The basic structure of the interview questions in this study is shaped by my choice of a 'life stories' approach and use of oral history as a methodology. The format of these interviews was therefore essentially biographical, where interviewees' experiences as LiPs formed only one part of the account they gave. Clifford Geertz commented '[w]hatever it is the law is after it is not the whole story', and so these interviews are a means to try to find out, for LiPs, what the 'whole story' might be.[15] This strategy encourages interviewees to account for their experiences in law in a new and separate context that does not presuppose that this is the sole focus of the conversation. This lack of legalising of context also allows interviewees to give lesser or greater weight to their experiences as LiPs, as is in accordance with, as Geertz put it, 'what the devil they think they're up to'.[16] This means that while the questionnaire I developed for interviews encompasses multiple detailed questions about LiPs' litigation experience, it also spends equal time concentrating on interviewees' childhoods, backgrounds, professional experience, personal lives and beliefs. Interviewees were asked questions such as 'What is your happiest memory of school?' and 'What was your personality like as a child?' Such questions serve multiple purposes: in the first place, they allow development of a biographical narrative led by the interviewee. But, secondarily, such questioning helps develop an intimacy between interviewee and interviewer. By asking them questions about memories, desires and emotions, the interviewees are encouraged to be franker in later questioning that is more directly pertinent to my research questions and that cover topics that are potentially emotional or stressful for participants.

However, while the establishment of closeness is a key aim of such questions, they do also serve a more direct purpose. Other questions that occur early in the script involve topics such as bullying, encounters with authority figures, and attitudes towards the law, the police, politics and justice. Interviewees are asked to reflect on earlier experiences long before they acted as LiPs. This allows the interviewees to attempt to chart the origins or development of beliefs about law, what the law can or should do, and what expectations an individual might have about their relationship to the law and the legal world. These questions are a way to trace interviewees' 'horizon of expectations' about law prior to their encounter with it as a LiP.[17]

Ultimately, the script I developed contains 134 questions, ranging over the entire extent of an individual's biography. But while the questionnaire serves as a template, it is not a rigorously read-out script but instead is part of a semi-structured interviewing process. In the interviews, while I returned to the script for guidance and kept a coherent and largely chronological structure to the interviews,

[15] C Geertz, Local Knowledge: Further Essays in Interpretive Anthropology (London, Basic Books, 1983) 171.

[16] ibid 56.

[17] The term 'horizon of expectation' comes from Hans Robert Jauss in the field of Reception Studies, where he argues it describes the historically specific cultural conventions and codes that readers bring to a text. See H Jauss, *Towards an Aesthetic of Reception* (Minneapolis, MN, University of Minnesota Press, 1982) 26–30.

I let interviewees continue to speak until they had finished their train of thought, and also moved topics with them if they wanted to discuss something else, free to, as Bernard expresses it, 'follow new leads'.[18]

The shortest interview in this study was just under three hours in length in one session, and the longest interview was between nine and 10 hours over two sessions, with the average length of the interviews being around five to six hours in duration, over two to three sessions, although up to four sessions in some cases.[19] To find interviewees, I set up a website, a Facebook account and a Twitter feed called *Litigant Stories*, calling for interviews for the study and explaining the project. The interviewees in this study come from a variety of places in England and Wales, from Southampton to Yorkshire to Bristol to Grantham and beyond, with only four out of 15 being based in London. The ages of participants span from 27 to 83. In addition, I was able to capture a wide variety of legal categories, with the interviewees going to the County Courts in relation to issues including housing and possession proceedings, family matters (prior to 2014), small claims, non-money claims, negligence claims, bankruptcy claims and more.

The interviewees consist of both claimants and defendants, and they have a mixed background in terms of obtaining advice and representation, with some using the Personal Support Unit (now Support Through Court) and the Citizens Advice Bureau (CAB), and others not, and some being legally represented for parts, and others not. Some also faced represented opposition and others faced LiPs. In addition, at the time of interview some were still in the midst of litigation, others had completed litigation and others were contemplating further litigation.

The reason I chose to focus on the County Courts is because they are theoretically designed to facilitate access for LiPs.[20] Consequently, the experiences LiPs have with these proceedings allow us to test whether the current procedures in place to help LiPs are represented in the experiences LiPs have, or whether (as I will argue) there remain significant barriers to access. But when I say that I am looking at County Court proceedings, I do not mean that my research is limited to this court alone. One of the significant findings of this study is that almost all the LiPs interviewed had been involved in other court proceedings as well; so while the County Courts form a baseline of shared experience, the interviews take us to many different courts, including tribunals, higher civil courts, criminal proceedings and the European Court of Human Rights (ECtHR).

In addition, although I have so far talked about different kinds of *courts* with which LiPs are involved, these interviews do not focus only on what happens in the courtroom. This would give a misleading weight to these kinds of appearances,

[18] HR Bernard, Research Methods in Anthropology: Qualitative and Quantitative Approaches (Lanham, MD, Rowman Altamira, 2011) 157.

[19] It is important to note, of course, that this only denotes recording times. This does not include the time spent before the interview recording began, any breaks and the time afterwards.

[20] Even the *Handbook for Litigants in Person*, though, written by six judges for LiPs in civil proceedings, prefaces the guide with a warning that no court is designed for a LiP. See HHJ Edward Bailey et al., *A Handbook for Litigants in Person* (London, Courts and Tribunals Judiciary, 2012) ii.

when the reality of legal proceedings is that attending hearings is a minor part of the process. Most litigation involves far more time spent behind the scenes in negotiations, discussions, settlements and mediation.[21] Consequently, this book pays equal attention to LiP experiences before, during and after appearing in court, and includes LiPs who never set foot in a courtroom.

Finally, due to the intensive nature of the interviews, which require self-identification as a LiP and repeated long interviewing sessions, this sample is dominated by individuals who have repeated experience as LiPs, in some cases over the course of more than 15 or 20 years. In the course of the research, I began to realise that this apparent sample limitation was in fact a strength, and one of the most revealing aspects of the study. Research into LiPs is usually predicated on their pursuing or defending a single claim. But how frequent are 'one-off' LiPs? What if far more LiPs than we realise have a more complex and protracted encounter with legal proceedings? In addition, the fact that we have concentrated on single claims means we know very little about the experiences of those who *are* involved in multiple claims. This book therefore thinks in detail about how and why individuals may become serial litigants, and what this experience can tell us about the LiP landscape.

IV. Conceptual Framework

This book takes its conceptual framework from the idea of exploring different 'ways of seeing' when it comes to LiPs.[22] Instead of only focusing on how LiPs are seen *by* the legal profession, through using oral history techniques in the form of life stories interviews, this book seeks to understand how LiPs see the legal profession, the law and themselves. What emerges from this analysis is a very different story from what we are used to hearing; LiPs' ways of seeing are radically different from those of legal professionals, and the result of this is that these groups largely talk across one another. The failure of understanding one another's ways of seeing is central to explaining many of the difficulties that arise in practice.

A key focus in this book is the attempt to elaborate on different 'ways of seeing' communicated by both LiPs and by legal professionals, and the gaps between the two (loosely definable as 'lay' and 'law'). In Moorhead and Sefton's 2005 study into unrepresented litigants, for example, they observe that 'With unrepresented litigants, judges and court staff pointed out there was a much stronger possibility of cases being entirely misconceived, or being expressed solely in social, non-legal terms.'[23] What Moorhead and Sefton draw attention to is a collision between

[21] Genn (n 12) 2 describes this as the 'centrality of out of court settlement' to the civil justice system.

[22] I have borrowed the term 'ways of seeing' from John Berger's pioneering work of images and visual arts, where he explores how the way in which we see is affected by what we know and believe. See J Berger, *Ways of Seeing* (London, Penguin, 1972).

[23] Moorhead and Sefton (n 9) 154.

what they term 'social' (non-legal) understanding and legal understanding. This conflict is one of the primary problems LiPs face when representing themselves, as what they perceive to mean by 'common sense', 'justice', 'relevance' or 'fairness' may bear little resemblance to legally understood meanings of these terms. This book will contend that this kind of knowledge gap is a crucial means by which LiPs are excluded from meaningful participation in legal process.

In analysing these different ways of seeing, I use the term discourse in the sense that Michel Foucault meant; not as a formalistic analysis of language, but rather as an interrogation into the specific conditions under which a way of seeing is constructed and deployed, and the effect that this has.[24] As Foucault points out,

> we must grasp the statement in the exact specificity of its occurrence; determine its conditions of existence, fix at least its limits, establish its correlations with other statements that may be connected with it, and show what other forms of statement it excludes.[25]

In this respect, to analyse discourses, and to think about the discourse of legal practitioners and LiPs is to fundamentally consider the network of power relations within which such discourses take place.[26] Importantly, this kind of discourse is not limited to language, but also encompasses embodied behaviours, procedure and habituated practice, which may be gathered under the rubric of the performative aspects of law, all of which play an important role in constituting ways of disadvantaging and excluding LiPs.[27]

However, in describing the relationship between 'lay' and 'law', while I believe that certain themes of practice and certain behaviour may be *generally* apparent in the behaviour of legal practitioners, I am not claiming that all legal practitioners think or behave in a uniform way – of course they do not. It is at this point that Pierre Bourdieu's work is valuable. Bourdieu follows Foucault in seeing discourse as constituting and defining power relations, but he is particularly interested in how individuals absorb and reproduce such discourses, or what he terms 'field specific knowledge', arguing that this is largely through unconscious habits and practice, or what he terms *habitus*.[28]

For Bourdieu, *habitus* is a dynamic idea that seeks to describe an individual's predispositions and belief systems, based on what individuals learn to value from

[24] M Foucault, The Archaeology of Knowledge and the Discourse on Language (New York, Pantheon Books, 1972) 27.

[25] ibid 28.

[26] ibid 29.

[27] The role of performance theory in helping illuminate legal process as constituting far more than speech is dealt with in ch 5.

[28] Bourdieu's 'field theory' emerges from his analysis of different 'fields' of cultural production where he investigates how field-specific concepts develop and how individuals working within these fields seek to establish a specialised identity. See P Bourdieu, *The Field of Cultural Production: Essays on Art and Literature* (New York, Columbia University Press, 1993) 162–64.

early childhood onwards. This acquisition of values comes through the drive of all humans to seek recognition and validation from others.[29] This drive continues into our professional lives, and any individual working within a field, such as the legal field, will naturally seek recognition within that field: we are all in pursuit of what Bourdieu termed symbolic capital, whether that be prestige, advancement or explicit financial gain.[30] To be successful within a field, individuals (or what Bourdieu termed 'agents') will internalise and naturalise the logics of that particular field or, more informally, they will learn the 'rules of the game' in their effort to get on. But in the process of learning the rules of the game, Bourdieu argues that these individuals end up misrecognising the 'social conditions under which it [the juridical field] is manifested' as being 'natural'. This is something apparent in all fields:

> The tendency to conceive of the shared vision of a specific historical community as the universal experience of a transcendental subject can be observed in every field of cultural production. Such fields appear as sites in which universal reason actualises itself, owing nothing to the social conditions under which it is manifested.[31]

So, like Foucault, Bourdieu is arguing that discourses or practices that emerge within specialist fields present themselves as timeless or 'eternal', but in so doing disguise the specific historical conditions, and power relations, under which they are constituted to the point that even those working within these fields may not necessarily recognise the inequality on which such practices are founded.

For Bourdieu, misrecognition is essential for establishing the relative autonomy of any specialist field. So, the gap between lay and law for Bourdieu is reproduced through agents' unconsciously learning and playing out the rules of the game in that field. But this gap is not accidental; instead, the gap is the border between laypersons and law that emphasises the necessary skills *possessed by the legal profession alone*. As Bourdieu comments:

> The institution of a 'judicial space' implies the establishment of a borderline between actors. It divides those qualified to participate in the game and those who, though they may find themselves in the middle of it, are in fact excluded by their inability to accomplish the conversion of mental space – and particularly of linguistic stance – which is presumed by entry into this social space.[32]

Bourdieu's theory is critical for this research, as it helps to explain how LiPs' failure to achieve the requisite skills demanded of them in the courtroom (and elsewhere) is a necessary and deliberate consequence of entry into juridical space. The 'conversions' required of language and behaviour cannot be accomplished by LiPs because *they are not meant to be*. A LiP's failure is therefore a means of maintaining

[29] P Bourdieu, *Pascalian Meditations* (Stanford, CA, Stanford University Press, 1997) 166.
[30] ibid 166.
[31] P Bourdieu, 'The Force of Law: Towards a Sociology of the Juridical Field' (1987) 38 *Hastings Law Journal* 814, 819.
[32] ibid 828.

the specialist legal profession: it sustains dependence on legal representation to navigate legal process.[33] Legal practitioners will not necessarily be fully cognisant of the difficulties for LiPs, though, because they have naturalised what is in fact a very specifically legally produced form of understanding and knowledge.[34]

This is evidenced by Moorhead and Sefton, who noted in 2005:

> There was some evidence of a broader, and understandable, confusion of law with social or moral notions of 'justice'. Unrepresented litigants frequently sought to introduce evidence of facts relevant to their own perceptions of fairness but irrelevant to the legal adjudication of their dispute.[35]

I suggest that what Moorhead and Sefton term 'confusion' is better understood as a conflict of concepts produced by the gap between lay and law. This gap is productive because it allows the legal field to redefine ordinary concepts into a hierarchy of meaning that privileges legal understanding and undermines social meaning. As Bourdieu expresses it, '[t]he professionals create the need for their own services by redefining problems expressed in ordinary language as *legal* problems, translating them into the language of the law'.[36]

Alongside Foucault's work on discourse and Bourdieu's field-theory, another important theoretical building block for this research is the work of Magali Sarfatt Larson, whose 1977 work, *The Rise of Professionalism: A Sociological Analysis*, outlines what Larson terms the 'professional project'. For Larson, the professional project is

> the process by which producers of special services sought to constitute and control a market for their expertise. Because marketable expertise is a crucial element in the structure of modern inequality, professionalization appears also as a collective assertion of special social status and a collective process of upward social mobility … professionalization is thus an attempt to translate one order of scarce resources – special knowledge and skills – into another – social and economic rewards.[37]

Larson's work also emphasises the gap between lay and law, arguing that this gap is a deliberate consequence of this professional project. Like Bourdieu, Larson does not claim that such a project is necessarily a conscious undertaking.[38] But Larson's work also helps us to understand that critical to the development of a profession is attention to standardisation of practice, the development of a 'cognitive commonality' and the move to eliminating any competition from unregulated actors. All these tendencies, Larson argues, are orientated towards the ultimate goal, which is the social distancing of professionals from non-professionals, and

[33] I elaborate on this idea in more detail in ch 2.
[34] Bourdieu (n 33) 831.
[35] Moorhead and Sefton (n 9) 256.
[36] Bourdieu (n 33) 833–34.
[37] MS Larson, *The Rise of Professionalism: A Sociological Analysis* (Berkeley, CA, University of California Press, 1977) xvii.
[38] ibid 6.

the consequent status that arises from this distinction.[39] I draw on Larson's work to argue that many of the difficulties that LiPs experience are a by-product *of* this professional project. Seen through this lens, LiPs are not educated, regulated, licensed or trained to be doing legal work, and are replacing a professional. This analysis opens up another possibility as to why LiPs are talked about pejoratively: because they are replacing lawyers.

In addition to the literature that seeks to understand and approach talking about legal practitioners and 'the law', this book also draws on socio-legal scholarship to talk about 'the lay'. For this, scholars working within the ideas of 'legal consciousness' are particularly pertinent here.[40] In this respect, the work of Ewick and Silbey in *The Common Place of Law* is of particular value.[41] It concentrates on what the law means to those outside of the legal profession and how ordinary people understand their connection with the law. As such, the authors' work focuses on conceptions of law as conceived outside of a legal framework, and provides insight into lay meanings of terms such as 'justice' or 'fairness'. In addition, the scholarship of Sally Engle Merry in the United States (US) and Hazel Genn's landmark *Paths to Justice* in the United Kingdom (UK) are important reference points in this research. Merry's work concentrates on the experience of lower-value litigants or defendants, noting that such individuals frequently perceive themselves as disdained by a system that determines the claims that are important to them to be 'garbage' or 'junk'; such experiences were also commonplace in this study.[42]

Genn's work outlines 'justiciable problems' and what people do about them. Genn's emphasis on litigant perceptions and experiences, and on the impact of going to law, has been of considerable influence in developing my own questions for interview.[43] However, while such socio-legal scholarship is of great value in exploring the lay, to understand LiPs it is also essential to think about them outside of the frames and categories into which legal research tends to place them. In this respect, it is useful to draw on disciplines outside *of* law to try to understand these individuals who are outsiders *to* the law. Because of this, this book draws on materials and practices from theatre and performance studies, oral history, and anthropological and ethnographic theory to think about LiPs differently.

Finally, while this research is predicated on exploring the distinction between lay and law, what this book ends up doing is disrupting these categories. Reducing 'the law' to a uniform position, rather than a site of contestation and disagreement,

[39] ibid 77.

[40] Halliday and Morgan define legal consciousness as 'the background assumptions about legality which structure and inform everyday thoughts and actions'. S Halliday and B Morgan, 'I Fought the Law and the Law Won? Legal Consciousness and the Critical Imagination' (2013) 66 *Current Legal Problems* 1.

[41] P Ewick and S Silbey, *The Common Place of Law: Stories from Everyday Life* (Chicago, IL, University of Chicago Press 1998).

[42] SE Merry, Getting Justice and Getting Even: Legal Consciousness Among Working Class Americans (Chicago, IL, University of Chicago Press, 1990).

[43] Genn (n 12)17.

is misleading and counterproductive. Similarly, calling LiPs 'laypersons' can also be unhelpful. Many LiPs in this study have repeat experiences as claimants and defendants, with some ending up being engaged in multiple kinds of legal proceedings over decades.[44] As such, these LiPs are involved in their own kind of repeat practice, and evolve techniques and skills that mirror the acquisition of specialist skills. So, while LiPs do not acquire *legal* skills (and indeed, how they fail to do so is critical to this research), the attempt by LiPs to acquire what they *perceive* to be legal skills and knowledge means they end up being not quite laypersons either. While their expertise does not constitute legal expertise, it is a form of specialism, if a peculiar one, and it is an integral part of how LiPs understand themselves.

V. Book Overview

This book is divided into three parts. Part I, 'Before Litigation' provides an overview of the context in which LiPs operate and the historical backdrop to their existence, before finally looking at the lives of the LiPs in this study prior to coming to law. While the purpose of this book is to hear from LiPs, we need to know a bit about the environment in which they operate and how they are perceived. And so, before I examine how the LiP experiences the law, I begin with how the law 'experiences' LiPs. In chapter 1, I think about how LiPs are understood or, as I argue, *mis*understood in writing from practitioners and some scholars, and what potential issues may flow from these misconceptions. Starting with the passage of the Legal Aid, Sentencing and Punishment of Offenders Act (LASPO) 2012, which removed the majority of civil legal aid, I analyse the literature emerging at this moment of crisis, arguing that two distinct discourses become apparent. First, there is an alarmist discourse that emphasises the coming 'flood' of LiPs and the potentially disastrous impact this will have on the courts. As I will demonstrate, this discourse conceptualises LiPs as a problem for the courts, and in doing so draws on a rich history of scholarship that depicts LiPs as, at best, nuisances and, at worst, pathological. The other discourse that emerges is one that argues that legal aid changes will lead to disadvantageous outcomes for LiPs, as a concomitant result of the loss of the assistance of legal professionals. This way of talking about LiPs does not position LiPs as inherently difficult, in fact it is far more well-meaning; however, I will argue that both discourses, through confining themselves to a 'legal lens', limit the ways in which we see LiPs. I conclude by arguing that our inability to see LiPs outside of the frames we impose on them significantly limits our understanding.

Having considered how LiPs are often misunderstood or neglected by legal practitioners and scholars, chapter 2 seeks to understand how we came to acquire these attitudes: have we always felt this way about those who represent themselves? And if

[44] In considering repeat experiences, this work also engages with Marc Galanter's work on 'One Shotters' and 'Repeat Players', Galanter (n 23) 98–99.

not, when and how did this start to happen? I pursue this inquiry through the critical investigation of the term 'litgant in person' itself, studying the moment when the term first appears and the context in which this takes place. I argue, drawing on Larson, that the term 'litigant in person' emerges as a by-product of the broader development of the law's 'professional project' over the course of the nineteenth century, starting with the founding of the new County Courts and ending when these new courts become fused with the higher courts. As I will show, in this period, self-represented parties become caught up in wider developments occurring within the profession: the ongoing conflict between the 'higher' and 'lower' branches of the profession, the emphasis on increasing standardisation, and concerted attempts to stamp out unregulated practitioners. As the professional project develops, courts become less and less accessible for laypersons. Ultimately chapter 2 argues that being a LiP is not simply self-representation; it is self-representation that only occurs in a standardised and formalised environment. As I conclude, when the term 'litigant in person' first appears in the literature, then, it does not indicate a greater participation of laypersons in the legal system; instead, it symbolises their aberrance from what has become the norm of legal representation.

Chapter 3 looks more closely at who LiPs are, at what they think about law before they get there and why they became LiPs: it offers insight into their stories; how they see themselves and the issues that lead them in different ways to contact with legal proceedings. It demonstrates that, even within a small sample, the variety of backgrounds, education, beliefs, issues and reasons to go to law problematise any simplistic assumptions of LiPs as litigious, anti-authority or distrustful, and allows a richer and more complicated picture to emerge.

Part II of this book (chapters 4 and 5) constitutes the 'During Litigation' section of the findings and looks at what it is like to go to law as a LiP. As I will show, this experience is far more difficult than we have understood previously, and the narratives here tell us of the significant negative impact of litigation: loss of houses, marriages, family contact, jobs and income, as well as experiences of depression, institutionalisation and incarceration. This section of the analysis is also critical to considering how serial litigants emerge, looking in detail at how failed attempts at litigation tend to 'snowball' and lead to further and more desperate efforts to rectify a situation that is now almost always unable to be resolved. Whilst this may be read as 'litigious' or even 'vexatious', when seen from the perspective of the individual involved, a better descriptor might often be 'desperate' or 'tragic'. I also focus in this part on why going to law is so difficult for LiPs. Ultimately, what emerges from the stories here is that LiPs face highly unclear performative demands, which are discriminatory in practice and a clear source of disadvantage. As chapter 5 concludes, there is no *place* for LiPs in legal process, which means that there is no clearly defined role for a LiP: we do not know what a good LiP looks like. But this does not stop us from seeing LiPs as incompetent. Rather than viewing LiPs as failing, though, we ought to consider that as long as they are treated as anomalous or exceptional, there is perhaps no way for them to be good.

Part III of this book encompasses chapter 6, which considers the afterlife of litigation, thinking specifically about what effect the experience of going to law has on LiPs. As this study reveals, in several cases, such individuals become motivated by their negative experiences to assist others in navigating going to law. This generates insight into how particular kinds of attitudes and beliefs become passed on through LiP networks of both information and disinformation in the absence of access to formal legal advice. The destruction of the advice sector in tandem with the withdrawal of legal aid has been calamitous in many ways for LiPs, most of whom relied on pre-action assistance and many of whom can no longer access it. This final part of the book also considers the effect of loss of trust in legal proceedings for many LiPs in this study, resulting from their experiences of failure. The profound negative impact of failed or protracted litigation for some also results in a belief in conspiracy theories. Such conspiracies can be shared amongst informal advice networks, sustaining and perpetuating hateful beliefs and ideas. Ultimately, chapter 6 argues that these deeply negative experiences of litigation are frequently the result of the fact that what LiPs may want or value is rendered almost impossible to translate into the policy and practice of the civil justice system in which they seek to pursue or defend their claim. This can lead to emotionally devastating experiences and loss of faith in legal institutions. Whilst such individuals may indeed end up serially litigious and potentially involved in vexatious proceedings, *their* perspective shows us a far more ruinous narrative.

In the end, all the stories told in this book reveal the complex, impactful and emotional experiences of legal proceedings of which we do not hear enough; as this volume argues, litigant voices and experiences warrant far greater consideration.

PART I

Before Litigation

1

How the Law Sees the Litigant in Person

I. Introduction

Before we get to the litigant stories, we need to understand what they are up against. And that is what this chapter starts to think about. This chapter considers how LiPs are talked about, and what this can tell us about what legal professionals say and think about them. This is important in understanding the kind of environment these individuals are entering when they pursue or defend legal claims. I argue that we can roughly divide this literature into two camps. First, there is the writing that is explicitly pejorative about LiPs. This kind of material is part of a longer history of negative attitudes towards LiPs that talks about them as time-wasting, incompetent, psychologically disturbed, threatening and more.[1] As I will demonstrate in section II of this chapter, these kinds of attitudes remain commonplace and can inform basic assumptions about LiPs that affect how they are perceived even before they enter a room.

But while this material can obviously be damaging, what is perhaps surprising is the problems we also encounter with the second camp of literature – the seemingly more positive one. This writing is all about helping the LiP, and is reflective of a genuine and widespread effort by the profession to assist LiPs and to mitigate the more negative experiences they have of going to law. Third-party support organisations, the judiciary, the Ministry of Justice and others have all considered what we can *do* about LiPs. But, for all their good intentions, there are still problems: first, these writings often are not based on a very good understanding of who LiPs are and what they are about; and, second, this means the solution is almost always to get a lawyer.[2] What this chapter suggests, then, is that we are still missing something: for LiPs to genuinely have better experiences when going to law, an explicit commitment needs to be made both to understand them more and to think about how they can navigate legal proceedings *without* legal professionals. Ultimately, that is why we need the stories in this book: because we need to bring LiPs into focus outside of the limiting lens of how legal professionals see them.

[1] I think in more detail about how and why these attitudes exist in ch 2.

[2] Or not to come at all: to 'lump it' in Marc Galanter's influential terms. See M Galanter, 'Why the "Haves" Come out Ahead: Speculations on the Limits of Legal Change' (1974) 9 *Law & Society Review* 95.

II. Litigants in Person as a Problem

'Shut the Flood-Gates: The Litigants are Coming!' cries the headline of a 2013 short comment piece in the *Alternative Law Journal*.[3] The alarmist tone of the article is generated by the possible changes to administrative law in Australia that would lead to more LiPs.[4] While this article may be Australian, this dramatic tone has become familiar in the UK since the coming into force of the Legal Aid, Sentencing and Punishment of Offenders Act (LASPO) 2012 in April 2013, and the resultant £350m in cuts to civil legal aid that transformed the legal landscape, leaving many more people unable to access legal representation in the civil justice system. During this period, LiPs went through a strange transition too, from being mostly ignored (if occasionally complained about), to becoming the harbingers of the potential downfall of the civil justice system. While this may seem an overly sensationalist analysis, it does not overstate just how alarmist the tone of much of this output was, with an emphasis on a surge in LiPs, flooding and overwhelming the courts.[5] This was based on the presumption that the effect of LASPO 2012 would be a dramatic rise in LiP numbers and a permanent decline in the availability and provision of legal representation for civil litigants, which has now been borne out from the evidence of over 10 years of operation.[6]

The passage of LASPO 2012, and the literature that emerged at this moment of crisis, is useful as a way in which to think about how law views the LiP for two reasons: first, because the introduction of the 2012 Act provoked one of the few explicit conversations the law has ever had about LiPs; and, second, because the interviews conducted and discussed in this book took place in the years following LASPO 2012, as the legal aid cuts bedded in, and are an important part of their context. The alarmist discourse emerging at this moment, which emphasises the coming 'flood' of LiPs and the potentially disastrous impact this will have on the courts, conceptualises LiPs as a problem for the courts, and in doing so links to a rich history of scholarship that depicts LiPs as, at best, nuisances and, at worst, pathological. This is perhaps the best-known way

[3] E Lee, 'Shut the Flood-Gates: The Litigants are Coming!' in 'Downunder All Over' (2013) 38(3) *Alternative Law Journal*, 190.

[4] Or Self-Represented Litigants (SRLs), as they are known in Australia. Australia has been facing similar questions when it comes to coping with unrepresented parties.

[5] See, eg, J Hyde, 'Judges call for urgent overhaul to cope with surge of LIPs' *Law Society Gazette* (London, 5 July 2013); E Reyes, 'Litigants in Person Numbers Soar' *Law Society Gazette* (London, 13 October 2011). These articles will be explored in section III.

[6] See Judiciary of England and Wales, *Judicial Working Group on Litigants in Person Report* (London, July 2013), s 2.3. See also C Bevan, 'Self-Represented Litigants: the Overlooked and Unintended Consequence of Legal Aid Reform' (2012) 35(1) *Journal of Social Welfare & Family Law* 43; G Cookson, *Unintended Consequences: The Cost of the Government's Legal Aid Reforms: A Report for the Law Society of England & Wales* (Department of Management, School of Social Science and Public Policy, November 2011); M MacLean and J Eekelaar, 'Legal Representation in Family Matters and the Reform of Legal Aid: A Research Note on Current Practice' (2012) 24 *Child and Family Law Quarterly* 223; Civil Justice Council, *Access to Justice for Litigants in Person: A Report and a Series of Recommendations to the Lord Chancellor and to the Lord Chief Justice* (London, CJC, 2011).

in which law 'experiences' LiPs: where they are framed as difficult, litigious or troublesome.

In October 2011, the *Law Society Gazette* published an article entitled 'Litigants in Persons Numbers Soar'. In it, author Eduardo Reyes discloses a 'dramatic increase' in LiPs, based on data from the Personal Support Unit [now Support Through Court] at the Royal Courts of Justice showing that it received a 19 per cent increase in applications to assist LiPs appearing in the Principal Registry of the Family Division in the eight months running up to August 2011 across the country.[7] Reyes' article pre-dates the coming into force LASPO 2012. The article goes on to argue that the increase in LiPs would only be aggravated when the Act came into force: 'Many solicitors,' Reyes says, feel this will 'trigger a huge rise', and that this rise will lead to 'strain' and a 'burden' on the court system.[8]

Reyes' alarmist tone is not anomalous, nor incidental. Numerous articles and letters appear in the *Law Society Gazette* and elsewhere from 2011, discussing the expected rise of LiPs in the face of legal aid changes, many of which tend to reproduce to a greater or lesser extent this tone. In January 2012, for example, Grania Langdon-Down writes of an expected 'huge increase' in LiPs, resulting in 'dire warnings' from the judiciary due to the potential risk of 'chaos'.[9] In July 2013, John Hyde's article refers to an oncoming 'surge of LiPs'.[10] A published letter from an occasional contributor in July 2013 is entitled 'Legal Aid: Children Suffer' and claims that 'Litigants in person are the scourge of the courts – ask any judge.'[11] Similarly, Catherine Baksi's October 2013 article is memorably titled 'Litigant in Person Punches Wife During Hearing'.[12] This refers to an incident in a Family Court proceeding in Essex, where the father, a LiP, crossed the floor to the witness box and repeatedly hit his wife. A Ministry of Justice spokesperson, when asked about this event, pointed out that, regardless of legal aid changes, about half the parties in Family Court proceedings were usually LiPs, and went on to observe that lawyers representing a party would not usually 'play a role in court security matters, and we have no evidence to suggest any increase in this type of incident since April'.[13] Nevertheless, the article's author argues that this incident highlights 'security concerns as more people appear in court without a lawyer'.[14]

[7] Reyes (n 5). Support Through Court, formerly the Person Support Unit, provides non-legal assistance and support for self-represented litigants. Volunteers assist litigants in non-legal tasks, including typing up information, providing forms and templates, and signposting them to legal assistance. In addition, they will also accompany a litigant into the court if the litigant chooses this.

[8] ibid.

[9] G Langdon-Down, 'Litigants in person could struggle to secure access to justice' *Law Society Gazette* (London, 19 January 2012).

[10] Hyde (n 5).

[11] J Greenwood, 'Letters: Legal Aid: Children Suffer' *Law Society Gazette* (London, 22 July 2013).

[12] C Baksi, 'Litigant in Person Punches Wife During Hearing' *Law Society Gazette* (London, 21 October 2013).

[13] ibid.

[14] ibid.

While Baksi's reference to the direct physical threat of the LiP might seem extreme, Langdon-Down's article in fact treads similar ground, citing District Judge Nick Crichton on the security threat posed by LiPs:

> We are getting more and more people coming to court in private law cases without the benefit of sensible, structured legal advice, wanting to spill blood on the court carpet. Angry with each other, they shout across the court, they refuse to listen when you try to calm them down and it is very difficult to find a solution that they will go away and work with.[15]

These articles demonstrate two overarching beliefs: first, because of legal aid changes, the numbers of LiPs will rise; second, more LiPs are not a good thing. In these articles, LiPs are presented as difficult to manage, disruptive and potentially violent.[16]

Alarmist ideas relating to LiPs have a long and rich history, both in the UK and abroad. Pejorative characterisations of LiPs abound in twentieth- and twenty-first-century scholarly literature. Litigants in person (or their overseas equivalents, such as *pro se* in the US and SRLs in Australia) have been described, variously, as 'mavericks',[17] obsessive and difficult,[18] 'cranks' and 'pests',[19] ignorant,[20] naive,[21] disruptive,[22] crafty,[23] time-wasters,[24] delusional,[25] 'injustice collectors'[26]

[15] District Judge Nick Crichton quoted in Langdon-Down (n 9).

[16] It is important to emphasise that this is a selection in a broader context, where other articles published in the same publications are broadly sympathetic and attempt to help, such as R Chapman, 'Solicitors can help litigants in person prepare for their day in court' *Law Society Gazette* (London, 5 April 2012). The selectivity is meant to illustrate the underlying tone, however, which reveals that negative attitudes towards LiPs are still deeply embedded in how we approach thinking about them. This negativity and unease can, and does, easily co-exist with the desire to assist such parties. For example, Lucy Reed refers to 'hordes of plastic bag wielding LiPs' in her blog, but also recently published a guide to assist LiPs in Family Court. See L Reed, 'Pink Tape' blog at http://pinktape.co.uk/2013/05/page/2/ (accessed 14 April 2023); and L Reed, *The Family Court Without a Lawyer: A Handbook for Litigants in Person* (Bath, Bath Publishing, 2023).

[17] S Smith, Maverick Litigants: A History of Vexatious Litigants in Australia 1930–2008 (Melbourne, Maverick Publications, 2009).

[18] T Sourdin and N Wallace, 'The Dilemmas Posed by Self-Represented Litigants – The Dark Side' (2014) 24(1) *Journal of Judicial Administration* 61.

[19] M Taylor, 'Querulent Behaviour, Vexatious Litigants and the Vexatious Proceedings Act 2005 (Qld)' conference paper delivered at the Australasian Institute of Judicial Administration, *Assisting Unrepresented Litigants –A Challenge for Courts and Tribunals Conference*, Sydney, 15-17 April 2014.

[20] *People v Sharp*, 7 Cal 3d 448 (1972); California Secretary of State, *Proposed Amendments to Constitution Primary Election*, 6 June 1972: 8; Judicial College, *Equal Treatment Bench Book* (London, Judicial College, 2013).

[21] IP Robbins and S Herman, 'Pro Se Litigation – Litigating Without Counsel: Faretta or For Worse' (1975) 42 *Brook Law Review* 637; MK Ridley, 'The Right to Defend Pro Se: Faretta v California and Beyond' (1975) 40 *Alabama Law Review* 425.

[22] *Argersinger v. Hamlin*, 407 US 25 (1972).

[23] BR Dryden, 'Technological Leaps and Bounds: Pro Se Prisoner Litigation in the Internet Age [comments]' (2008) 10 *University of Pennsylvania Journal of Constitutional Law* 854.

[24] *People v Sharp* (n 20) 463.

[25] E LeCluyse, 'The Spectrum of Competency: Determining a Standard of Competence for Pro Se Representation' (2015) 65 *Case Western Reserve Law Review* 1239.

[26] Taylor (n 19). See also D Herman, 'Hopeless Cases: Race, Racism and the Vexatious Litigant' (2012) 8 *International Journal of Law in Context* 27.

and, importantly, 'nuts'.[27] The *New York Law Society Journal* memorably dubbed them as 'a society of losers'.[28] Negative characterisations of LiPs are never just abusive epithets, of course. They are always revealing in terms of what they tell us about how LiPs are understood, or indeed misunderstood, by many people in the legal profession and others. This can mostly be categorised as an historical tendency in the literature to assume that all LiPs are potentially high-risk, querulous or vexatious litigants. This manifests in using terminology that identifies a systemic issue, but which then blames the LiP for this.

For example, there is the issue of delay and disruption. At first glance, accusing a LiP of delay does not necessarily seem a personal attack. There is indeed some evidence that LiPs take longer to pursue claims, although this is not conclusive, with some evidence also suggesting that full representation is equally likely, or more likely, to draw out proceedings.[29] However, the term 'time-waster' suggests a deliberate decision on the LiP's part to draw out proceedings, rather than it being the case that it may simply take a LiP longer to accomplish tasks compared to trained professionals. It also implies a lack of merit in LiPs' cases. Similarly, there is also evidence that LiPs' presence in courts and tribunals disrupts normal procedures: however, while this is factually accurate, calling LiPs disruptive implies that they somehow bring chaos with them.[30] Finally, LiPs are indeed uneducated in legal language, procedure and behaviour, and in this respect describing them as 'ignorant' is hardly incorrect; but the term 'ignorant' can suggest that this is an inherent or wilful defect of LiPs.

My point is not to dispute that LiPs' presence in legal proceedings can cause problems, but rather to point out that LiPs tend to be blamed for any issues as indicative of their own shortcomings. Yet the delay in proceedings caused by LiPs – indeed, the trouble they may cause in general – is more indicative of a system that, on the one hand, upholds LiPs' right to self-litigate and yet, on the other hand, fails to mould proceedings to their needs and perspectives. As Moorhead and Sefton's 2005 study concludes:

> The struggles they [LiPs] have comprehending law and procedure; and the importance of ensuring that substantive justice is done in our courts suggests that unrepresented litigants need help far more than they need approbation.[31]

Turning to the other negative epithets described above, these are even more immediately recognisable as attacks based on a perception that LiPs are high-risk

[27] DA Swank, 'The Pro Se Phenomenon' (2005) 19 *Brigham Young University Journal of Public Law* 373.

[28] Editorial, *New York Law Journal* (23 November 1971) 1.

[29] Civil Justice Council (n 6) viii; R Moorhead and M Sefton, *Litigants in Person: Unrepresented Litigants in First Instance Proceedings*, Department of Constitutional Affairs Research Series 2/05 (London, Department of Constitutional Affairs, 2005) ii; H Genn and Y Genn, *The Effectiveness of Representation at Tribunals*, Report to the Lord Chancellor (London, LCD, 1989) 245. This of course leaves aside the question of how we determine how long is 'too' long.

[30] See California Secretary of State (n 20) 8.

[31] Moorhead and Sefton (n 29) 265.

or vexatious litigants. The terms 'maverick' and 'injustice collector', for instance, conjure up the archetypal vexatious litigant who goes it alone, ignoring legal advice, despite there being little evidence of such individuals.[32] Similarly, the idea that LiPs are 'nuisances' or 'pests' emphasises not only their disruptive qualities but also the idea that they repeatedly pursue frivolous issues. Finally, these negative epithets routinely – and importantly – emphasise a link between behavioural disorders, mental health and LiPs.[33] These are the LiPs described as 'delusional' or 'nuts'. In her article 'Hopeless Cases', Didi Herman notes that vexatious litigants are

> characterised as falling into one of two groups: those with histories of mental health problems who launch multiple legal actions against diverse targets; and those whose initial legal action, for example (one that recurs often) a complaint of discrimination under the Race Relations Act (RRA; now incorporated into the Equality Act 2010), was resolved against them, and who then attempt to carry on with aspects of that complaint in various ways.[34]

This tendency to blame LiPs for their shortcomings seems to result from a strong belief on the part of the legal profession that LiPs ought to have legal representation. A LiP's decision to act in person (presupposing this decision was voluntary, which, as I will outline, is often not the case) indicates a potential alarm bell. Sourdin and Wallace claim, in their 2014 study into querulous and vexatious litigants, the 'perception that these litigants [LiPs] pose a problem for courts is widespread'.[35] I would reconfigure this, however, to argue that the perception that LiPs *are* a problem is widespread. This slippage between the two – from the LiP causing problems to being *a* problem – is primarily attributable to legal distrust of anyone who would voluntarily forgo representation.

In Hazel Genn's landmark *Paths to Justice*, she critiques previous studies of legal need for focusing too much on 'the kinds of *people* who use legal services, rather than on the kinds of problems which are taken to lawyers'.[36] She goes on to say that this serves to homogenise legal problems: if one focuses on the people outside of the specific legal claim, one has no means of differentiating success or failure on the basis of legal merit. My argument pursues a related tack. Focusing on who LiPs *are* internalises shortcomings within the LiP themselves.

[32] In *Paths to Justice*, Genn notes that only 35% of her sample were 'self-helpers' who obtained no advice in dealing with their problem; however, even they were likely to have sought advice previously, and these individuals mostly do not end up pursuing litigation anyway (81%). It is also interesting to note the 5% who do not obtain any advice; as Genn notes, such individuals tend to have lower educational and income levels. One could speculate that such individuals may also be indicative of the 'passive defendants' Moorhead and Sefton identify in their 2005 research. See H Genn, *Paths to Justice* (Oxford, Hart Publishing, 1999).

[33] And the conflation of these issues is explored further in ch 6 of this volume, which looks at LiPs who rely on conspiracy theories to explain what happens to them during litigation.

[34] Herman (n 26) 28.

[35] Sourdin and Wallace (n 18) 14.

[36] Genn (n 32) 1.

This is seen in the situation above, where the difficulties that arise from the presence of LiPs are ascribed to behavioural or personality issues. The conflation of LiPs with high-risk and vexatious litigants leads to several serious misconceptions.

In the first instance, vexatious litigants form a tiny minority of LiPs. The Civil Justice Council notes that 'although a small minority of self-represented litigants behave in a way that leaves an adverse impression, the overwhelming majority of self-represented litigants are legitimate users of the system'.[37] Yet they continue to garner a disproportionate amount of attention.[38] This tends to make the problem with vexatious litigants seem much bigger than it is. However, associating LiPs with vexatious litigants is also fundamentally flawed. In law, definitions of vexatiousness hinge largely on the substance of the claim: they are *vexatious proceedings*. Lord Bingham, in *Attorney-General v Barker*, elaborates:

> The hallmark of a vexatious proceeding is in my judgment that it has little or no basis in law (or at least no discernible basis); that whatever the intention of the proceeding may be, its effect is to subject the defendant to inconvenience, harassment and expense out of all proportion to any gain likely to accrue to the claimant; and that it involves an abuse of the process of the court, meaning by that a use of the court process for a purpose or in a way which is significantly different from the ordinary and proper use of the court process.[39]

While vexatious litigation 'involves an abuse of the process of the court', this can arise only if 'the substance of the proceedings themselves can be characterised as vexatious'.[40] In other words, a distinction is made in law between a vexatious claim and vexatious conduct. If a claim is sound, the manner in which it is pursued may not be characterised as vexatious. Lord Parker noted in *Re Langton*:

> Despite the fact that it may be said that the manner in which that action was conducted was vexatious, it must be remembered that the respondent acted in person, and, not only that, but that the action itself could not be said to be a vexatious action; it was one which the respondent was fully entitled to litigate and did litigate and accordingly, so far as these proceedings are concerned, I ignore that action except as a matter of history.[41]

It therefore makes a material difference if the respondent is acting in person. Lord Parker clearly comments here that although the 'manner' in which proceedings were conducted was 'vexatious', the action itself was not vexatious: rather, the LiP was 'fully entitled to litigate', and consequently cannot be considered a vexatious litigant.

[37] Civil Justice Council (n 6) para 31.

[38] This is arguably because dealing with this minority absorbs a disproportionate amount of time and resources.

[39] *Attorney-General v Barker* [2000] 1 FLR 759, 764, per Bingham LJ.

[40] ibid.

[41] *Re Langton* [1966] 1 WLR 1575, 1758, per Lord Parker LCJ.

This distinction can be clearly seen where LiPs are most common, in places such as the Family Court.[42] As Lord Gill noted in his review of the Scottish civil courts:

> Respondents representing those who practice in the field of family law pointed out that because of the high level of emotion involved in family law cases, it would be difficult to categorise a litigant in a family action as 'vexatious'.[43]

As Lord Gill notes, given how high the stakes *always* are in family proceedings, it is difficult to imagine a scenario where any kind of litigation could be perceived as vexatious. An important point to draw from this distinction, then, is that although LiPs are often conflated with vexatious litigants, they may in fact be less likely to pursue frivolous claims, a finding that is supported by the stories in this book. Indeed, as Didi Herman notes, it seems reasonable to ask if it is even possible to make a distinction between frivolous and non-frivolous claims when it comes to LiPs.[44] Certainly, a point Herman makes in her article, and to which this book returns, is that we run into trouble as soon as we assume that legal definitions of 'meritorious' correspond in any way to the value any litigant might attach to the remedy they seek.

Seeing LiPs as 'a problem' not only forestalls questioning the structural exclusions, such as the characterisation of what they value as potentially lacking merit, it also leads to another misconception, which is overlooking the complexity of the context in which LiPs operate. Litigants in person appear in many kinds of courts and tribunals, which have differing procedures. On top of this, LiPs may face both represented and unrepresented respondents. Against whom are they standing? Does the fact that there is a LiP affect the behaviour of other participants in these circumstances? MacLean and Eeklaar's 2014 study into the Family Court found that out of 50 hearings, there were 20 where one party was not represented. Of these cases, only 10 qualified as involving an 'active' LiP in Moorhead and Sefton's terms. In two of the 20 cases where a party was not represented, the legal professional who was involved was 'of such a junior nature' that 'the judge commented to the researcher on the inequality of arms'. They went on to observe that in a further eight cases of the 20, one party did not attend at all, and their failure to do so meant the judge could not proceed. MacLean and Eekelaar consequently argue the need for the term 'absent LiPs'.[45] The sheer variety of the landscape – whether a LiP is active, passive, a claimant or a defendant; whether they face a barrister, group, corporation, LiP; whether they are in a County Court, a social security tribunal, an immigration tribunal, the High Court, and so on – could be usefully considered when attempting to

[42] Moorhead and Sefton's study found 48% of cases in the Family Court had at least one unrepresented litigant. See Moorhead and Sefton (n 29) 25.

[43] The Right Honourable Lord Gill, *Report of the Scottish Civil Courts Review* (Scotland, RR Donnelly, 2009) 240.

[44] Herman (n 26) 31.

[45] MacLean and Eekelaar (n 6) 227.

understand LiPs' experiences, but this complexity is elided when we see the LiP as *a* problem.

Finally, another key assumption made by those who see LiPs as a problem is that LiPs deliberately forgo legal representation. This results, first, from a misunderstanding on the part of some in the legal profession about accessibility *to* representation in the first place. As many lawyers who work in legal aid already know, Lord Otton's 1995 report found, many years prior to legal aid changes, that those who act as LiPs may not do so out of choice but rather because of failure to obtain legal aid or afford representation: LiPs will fail to obtain the representation or advice sought or desired due to financial difficulties, problems of time or access.[46] A simple example is a LiP who tries and fails to access a Citizens Advice Bureau due to increasingly limited opening hours and the closure of branches of the service.[47] Another is a LiP who becomes a LiP at some point during the life of their claim because of withdrawal of legal aid.[48] Cookson's 2011 research stated that

> [a]pproximately 11% of people denied legal aid will not seek alternative advice. Following this choice, people will either give up on their social justice problem or attempt to tackle it on their own … This proportion varies by area of law with 65% of people who failed to obtain family law advice tackling their problem alone compared to 83% in social welfare law. This difference may reflect the greater complexity of family law and the higher proportion of cases which end up in court.[49]

There is a danger in perceiving legal aid changes as being responsible for cutting off access to representation. Difficulties with obtaining legal representation are longstanding; the enactment of LASPO 2012 has aggravated the situation immeasurably, but it did not create it.[50]

Ultimately, for those who see LiPs as a problem, the influx of LiPs poses a significant threat. But even this fear of an influx is attributable to failure to adequately understand LiPs: in this case, the lack of accurate data regarding LiP numbers. One of the most striking features in the articles cited above is the repetition of a diluvian analogy: LiPs are going to 'flood' tribunals in a wave or a surge, or even in a 'tsunami'. Alternatively, LiPs are going to 'clog up' the courtrooms, suggesting that they are going to cause disruption to an otherwise smooth-running process.

[46] G Applebey, 'Justice Without Lawyers: Litigants in Person in the English Civil Courts' (1997) 18 *Holdsworth Law Review* 109.

[47] See J Plotnikoff and R Wilson, *A Study of the Services Provided under the Otton Project to Litigants in Person at the Citizens Advice Bureau* (London, Lord Chancellor's Office 1998); Genn (n 32) 76–77; Genn and Genn (n 29) 60–62.

[48] Although withdrawal of legal aid is in fact relatively rare, according to Moorhead and Sefton. It is more likely that those who are intermittently represented due to issues with legal aid will be unrepresented at the beginning because of the length of time it takes to process: Moorhead and Sefton (n 29) 30.

[49] Cookson (n 6) 63.

[50] See, eg, Moorhead and Sefton (n 29) from 2005; and Lord Otton, Interim Report of the Working Party Established by the Judges' Council into Litigants in Person in The Royal Courts of Justice London (RCJ, London, 1995).

As noted previously, one family law KC refers in a blog to the 'hordes of plastic bag wielding LiPs'.[51] This results in a kind of siege mentality where, due to lack of knowledge as to rising numbers, alarmist ideas about LiPs are more likely to be aired.

But, as I have previously outlined, what we know about LiPs has always been relatively limited. This is indicative of their marginal status in litigation. As Cameron and Kelly note, there has been a lack of 'any systematic effort' in common law jurisdictions to understand who LiPs are, what their legal problems are, what LiPs can do about these problems and why LiPs might choose to represent themselves.[52] Data on LiPs only began to be collected by the Ministry of Justice in 2014, and even now, data are not collected by the courts in any systematic fashion.[53] Consequently, much of the research attempting to quantify and qualify who the LiP is relies on filling in the gaps and assuming that someone is a LiP if there is no obvious evidence of representation.[54]

What we do know from the *Civil Justice Quarterly Statistics*, subject to the limitations outlined above, is the percentage of representation in different types of cases in civil matters. So, for example, the latest statistics (April–June 2022) show 95 per cent representation on both sides when it comes to unspecified money claims (such as compensation claims), and radically less in other areas. Specified money claims, for example, had at least one LiP in 68 per cent of cases.[55] Overwhelmingly, it was the claimant who was represented in this one-sided scenario, with defendants much more likely to be unrepresented, in keeping with Moorhead and Sefton's 2005 findings of 'passive defendants'. Only a quarter of specified money claims were unrepresented on both sides. This means that the likelihood of a LiP's facing represented parties is much higher than their facing another LiP, something we will hear about repeatedly in the litigant stories told in this book.[56] But this is clearly an incomplete picture.

In 2011, a Ministry of Justice literature review in the area concluded:

> Only a minority [of studies] provide robust evidence for our research questions. Few controlled for case complexity. As a result, this review should be treated as presenting evidence on the potential issues and impacts of litigants in person, rather than conclusive evidence of this.[57]

[51] Reed, 'Pink Tape' (n 16).

[52] C Cameron and E Kelly, 'Litigants in Person in Civil Proceedings: Part II Solicitors' Perspectives' (2003) 33 *Hong Kong Law Journal* 313.

[53] As from mid-2014, the Ministry of Justice has published LiP figures. However, these figures are based on the 'representation' box's being left blank in the court forms. This is the same method Moorhead and Sefton used in their 2005 research.

[54] Moorhead and Sefton (n 29) 13-14.

[55] The numbers of LiPs have been steady, if slightly higher, since 2014, when there was 97% representation in compensation claims and where 61% of money claims had at least one LiP.

[56] See Ministry of Justice, *Civil Justice Statistics Quarterly: April-June 2022* (London, National Statistics Office, 2022).

[57] K Williams, *Litigants in Person: A Literature Review* (London, Ministry of Justice, 2011) 3.

This is still the case in 2024. This means, in the context of legal aid changes, that one of the most basic questions we need to answer – 'Is there a rise in LiPs?' – can best be answered 'Probably.' To know definitively would require knowing how many LiPs there were before and how many there are now. But we do not know either number. The discourse that constructs LiPs as a problem, then, may fear LiPs, but it also does not know enough about them.

III. Litigants in Person Need a Lawyer

It would be disingenuous on my part to claim that negative writings are representative of all writing on LiPs. Of course this is not the case. While negative characterisations of LiPs persist, there is simultaneously a growing discussion by sympathetic legal practitioners and researchers on to how to include LiPs more meaningfully in legal processes.[58] Cameron and Kelly note, in their 2002 series of articles into LiPs in common law jurisdictions:

> The trend in the literature has moved from equating litigants in person with 'vexatious litigants' to considering litigants in person from the perspective of the problems they create for other stakeholders in the system (other parties and their legal advisors, judges and court administration officials) to the more recent approach of accepting them as a fact of life and identifying strategies to make it easier for them to represent themselves.[59]

I would argue, however, that the current state of affairs is less of a trajectory from the first attitude (all LiPs are potentially high-risk or vexatious litigants) past the second (LiPs cause problems for other users) to the last (LiPs are a fact of life and we must accommodate them) than a messy confluence of all three. The increased acknowledgement of the need for reform to assist LiPs exists simultaneously with the tendency to focus on LiPs *as* a problem. This is why the *Law Society Gazette* articles relating to legal aid changes that opened this chapter are so valuable for research: they offer a window into this very confusion. This confusion exists because the future of the legal profession is indelibly tied to the rise of LiPs. As Zoe Saunder's article 'How Can Lawyers Learn to Love Litigants in Person?' notes:

> The Government's evisceration of Legal Aid leaves those of us involved in the court system feeling a bit like the inhabitants of an island about to be hit by a tsunami, watching the sea recede further and further away, powerless to do anything but wonder how big the wave will be and how much damage it will cause. The tsunami will come in the

[58] See, eg, L Trinder et al, *Litigants in Person in Private Family Law Cases* (London, Ministry of Justice Analytical Series, 2014); J McFarlane, 'The National Self-Represented Litigants Project: Identifying and Meeting the Needs of Self-Represented Litigants, Treasurer's Advisory Group on Access to Justice' Working Group Report 86 (nd); MacLean and Eekelaar (n 6).

[59] Cameron and Kelly (n 52) 341.

> form of litigants in person who would previously have had recourse to public funding for advice and representation but will no longer have that resource and will have to represent themselves.[60]

The one certain effect legal aid cuts have on the profession is a reduction in legal representation in a broader range of civil proceedings.[61] Any fear of rising numbers of LiPs cannot therefore be separated from this perceived professional threat. This is not just about displacing legal professionals, but also a threat to procedures in their current form, as reform will potentially entail changes in how the courts operate as well. The problem then becomes one where LiPs are remodelled from being problems to being objects of concern, because, in a post-LASPO environment, not having representation will become the norm. Here, the concern about LiPs is that they are likely to do badly, but this is ultimately secondary to a concern about the broad-reaching changes that will occur to the legal profession and the effect on the courts of more LiPs.

In 2014, The Bar Council produced a paper, *The Legal Aid, Sentencing and Punishment of Offenders Act 2012 (LASPO): One Year On*, where it asserted:

> Although it is too early to determine the longer-term impact of the Government's transforming legal aid agenda (of which LASPO forms a central part), this early research suggests that much of what we feared has come to pass, including: A significant increase in litigants in person, especially in the family courts; increased delays in court and additional burdens on already-stretched court resources; increased and likely unsustainable pressure on frontline providers offering free legal support, advice or representation; A growing reluctance of solicitors and barristers to take on complex, low-value litigation, denying many access to legal advice and representation, and a growing number of barristers actively considering the viability of a long-term career at the Bar.[62]

As we can see from the above, although LiPs do get a look in in this report, and although LiPs are posited as representing an access to justice issue, their presence is emphasised more in the context of the impact they will have on the courts. Of more pressing concern is the long-term impact of such changes on the legal profession itself. This is of course unsurprising in a document produced by the Bar Council, however, it serves to underline that such a post-LASPO discourse prioritises the needs of the legal profession over those of the LiP, however much access to justice is raised as an issue. From this perspective, when LiPs are raised as a topic, this is usually to emphasise that more LiPs will have a detrimental impact on the court process: LiPs are not necessarily problems in and of themselves, but they will cause problems in the court and will fare

[60] Z Saunders, 'How Can Lawyers Learn to Love Litigants in Person?' *The Lawyer* (London, 11 April 2013).

[61] Cookson (n 6) 39.

[62] Bar Council, The Legal Aid, Sentencing and Punishment of Offenders Act 2012 (LASPO): One Year On (London, Bar Council, 2014) 2.

badly without professional assistance. For example, in *Unintended Consequences*, Cookson notes:

> In certain key respects a rise in litigants in person will have noticeable, material unintended consequences to Government: poorer outcomes for litigants, greater burden on HMCTS, greater legal costs for legal aid-represented litigants and for government-run organisations such as the NHS.[63]

It is important to contextualise all of this within a broader crisis of the justice system. Court closures, tendering of legal aid, poor provision of support, significant delays in hearings, and multiple other issues due to austerity measures and underfunding have left the entire apparatus of civil justice (and its criminal counterpart) struggling. In this context, legal professionals are facing multiple issues on all fronts from pay, to conditions, to delays resulting in strikes, people leaving the profession, advice deserts, high-stress environments and depression. It is not surprising, then, that legal professionals perhaps do not have much time to think about what to do about LiPs in the longer term, as they are too busy performing basic 'firefighting' to get their job done. But it does mean that this creates an environment where legal professionals are more likely to feel burdened or hostile towards any additional strain, such as more LiPs.

This question of a LiP *burden* is echoed by other LiP studies that note that LiPs are less likely to settle,[64] more likely to have their cases thrown out,[65] more likely to take up more court time than represented parties[66] and more likely to cost more money to the courts.[67] Unlike the previous assertions relating LiPs to high-risk and vexatious litigants that are, at times, highly problematic, the assumption that not having legal representation is a problem is in fact better founded. Research, such as Genn and Genn's 1989 tribunal study and Moorhead and Sefton's 2005 work, have found consistent evidence that someone with good legal representation is more likely to succeed than a LiP.[68] This is not entirely straightforward, as it has also been demonstrated that poor-quality legal representation may be significantly *worse* than no representation at all.[69] However,

[63] Cookson (n 6) 38.

[64] R Hunter, 'Adversarial mythologies: policy assumptions and research evidence in family law' (2003) 30 *Journal of Law and Society* 156; J Dewar et al, *Litigants in Person in the Family Court of Australia* (Canberra, Family Court, 2000).

[65] Advice Services Alliance, *Proposal for the Reform of Legal Aid in England and Wales*, Consultation Paper CP12/10 (London, Ministry of Justice, 2011).

[66] Williams (n 57) 6. As this report acknowledges, when *both* parties are unrepresented, the proceedings may be shorter, but when one side is unrepresented, the case can take longer. However, these findings are also subject to the type of court or tribunal and the kind of legal claim, so it is difficult to make any generalist statement.

[67] See Cookson (n 6) 40.

[68] Genn and Genn (n 29) 108; Moorhead and Sefton (n 29) 221. It is important to note that Genn and Genn refer to 'good representation', so this does not exclude the possibility that *bad* representation can lead to worse outcomes, or at least to no material difference. See DJ Greiner and CW Pattanayak, 'Randomized Evaluation in Legal Assistance: What Difference Does Representation (Offer and Actual Use) Make?' (2012) 121 *Yale Law Journal* 2118.

[69] R Moorhead, A Sherr and A Paterson, 'Contesting Professionalism: Legal Aid and Nonlawyers in England and Wales' (2003) 37 *Law and Society Review* 765.

there is widespread belief, that is at the very least to some extent supported by research, that legal representation improves outcomes.[70] Lord Pannick memorably articulated this in a House of Lords debate on the LASPO Bill: 'Do-it-yourself litigation – because that is what it is – will be as effective as a do-it-yourself medical operation'.[71]

Lord Pannick's analogy of LiPs with DIYers offers an intriguing opening into the question of why LiPs are more likely to lose: they are not qualified. Lawyers can discern what is relevant to a proceeding; they also know the form in which to present information in courts and tribunals.[72] Crucially, they also know how to behave appropriately in the subtler ways: how to address different people in the courtroom, and so on. As study after study notes, it is LiPs' ignorance – of substantive law, legal procedure and appropriate behaviour, their inability to discern what is relevant to their claim or defence – that means they lose.[73] The unavoidable implication of this discourse, therefore, is that what a LiP really needs is to either get a lawyer or to *be* one.[74] This is certainly the case being forwarded by critics of legal aid changes. As the Bar Council noted in 2016:

> The growth in the number of people who are attempting to handle often complex legal problems on their own is a particular cause for concern. The rise in court fees and the significant cuts to legal aid have put many litigants in the difficult position where they feel unable to access justice through the Courts, or through solicitors or barristers with the appropriate expertise to help them.[75]

This argument – that LiPs should have lawyers – is highly persuasive in the context of legal aid cuts post-LASPO 2012, which undoubtedly disproportionately affect vulnerable litigants.[76] Amnesty's 2016 report notes that the cuts primarily affect litigants in family cases, immigration tribunals, housing and other areas where such individuals are likely to be disadvantaged already in terms of socio-economic background, mental health or for a host of other complex reasons.[77]

[70] There is also some evidence from the US that being a *pro se* litigant causes worse outcomes due to judicial bias. See V Quintanilla et al, 'The Signaling Effect of Pro Se Status' (2017) 42 *Law & Social Inquiry* 1091.

[71] Lord Pannick, HL Deb 21 November 2011 vol 536, col 843.

[72] See Genn and Genn (n 29) 244, 246–47.

[73] See Moorhead and Sefton (n 29); Plotnikoff and Wilson (n 47).

[74] It is notable, for example, that Genn and Genn were highly critical of the idea of the tribunals that were more 'friendly' to LiPs: Genn and Genn (n 29) 248.

[75] Bar Council statement, 'Bar Council Responds to Latest LSB Report on Legal Services Market' (4 July 2016).

[76] Indeed, Jo Wilding's recent *Conversation* piece notes that demand for legal aid now far exceeds the capacity to supply it, with a huge collapse in the number of providers in the 18 months up to March 2023. See J Wilding, 'The Legal Aid sector is collapsing and millions more may soon be without access to justice' *The Conversation* (London, 7 June 2023). See also J Wilding, *The Legal Aid Market: Challenges for Publicly Funded Immigration and Asylum Legal Representation* (Bristol, Bristol University Press, 2021).

[77] See Amnesty International, Cuts That Hurt: The Impact of Legal Aid Cuts in England on Access to Justice (London, Amnesty, 2016).

This is supported by other research undertaken by Trinder et al in 2014, amongst others.[78] I do not dispute or seek to take away from the very real effect such changes can have on vulnerable litigants, nor do I wish to minimise the inherent difficulties of being a LiP (this is what this whole book is about). But this discourse is limited in terms of how helpful it can be for understanding LiPs. This is because in this way of thinking, LiPs become an exemplar of why one needs legal representation. And it is very difficult to separate this argument – that LiPs need legal representation – from the interest of legal professionals in maintaining dependency on legal representation.[79] This is well represented in the comments of the Law Society President, Stephanie Boyce, when commenting on challenges for LiPs in the context of the increasing use of electronic bundles:

> Often forced to represent themselves due to a lack of legal aid, litigants in person can struggle to understand court procedures and their legal entitlements. This struggle can be exacerbated by the increased digitisation of court processes, which the courts system must ensure doesn't leave people behind. Providing legal aid for early advice in family cases would help divert litigants from the court system towards mediation and the early resolution of their cases.[80]

So how does this position – that holds that LiPs are fundamentally unable to navigate legal procedure in any useful way – sit with the right of a LiP to self-represent? This right, articulated in *Bremer v South India Shipping* by Lord Diplock, provides:

> Every civilised system of government requires that the state should make available to all its citizens a means for the just and peaceful settlement of disputes between them as to their respective legal rights. The means provided are courts of justice to which every citizen has a constitutional right of access in the role of plaintiff to obtain the remedy to which he claims to be entitled in consequence of an alleged breach of his legal or equitable rights by some other citizen, the defendant.[81]

Litigants in person have a constitutional right of access to the courts to pursue claims, what Rabeea Assy calls 'a long-standing common law tradition which treats self-representation as a fundamental right'.[82]

Those who advocate for legal representation, then, do not give much consideration towards how to *be* a LiP in the first place; presumably, given the opportunity,

[78] Trinder et al (n 58); R Hunter, 'Exploring the "LASPO Gap"' (2014) 44 *Family Law* 660; F Meyler and S Woodhouse, 'Changing the Immigration Rules and Withdrawing the "Currency" of Legal Aid: The Impact of LASPO 2012 on Migrants and their Families' (2013) 35 *Journal of Social Welfare and Family Law* 55; J Mant, 'Neoliberalism, Family Law and Access to Justice' (2017) 39 *Journal of Social Welfare and Family Law* 246.

[79] This inseparability also poses a problem when it comes to assessing the efficacy *of* legal representation. Does it automatically improve outcomes? See HM Kritzer, *Legal Advocacy: Lawyers and Non Lawyers at Work* (Ann Arbor, MI, University of Michigan Press, 1998).

[80] M Fouzder, 'Bundles guidance "highlights litigant-in-person struggles"' *Law Society Gazette* (London, 22 April 2022).

[81] *Bremer v South India Shipping* [1981] AC 909, 976, per Lord Diplock.

[82] R Assy, Injustice in Person: Revisiting the Right to Self–Representation (Oxford, Oxford University Press, 2015).

legal practitioners would not want LiPs to have unlimited access without representation. In this respect such a 'right' becomes something like a category error. The most energetic proponent of this position is Rabeea Assy, who argues in *Injustice in Person* that the 'right' to self-representation needs revisiting:

> It entails overcoming the intuitive appeal of an entitlement to self-representation and the compelling force of tradition. And in the absence of previous theoretical work, possible rationales for the right must be expounded and then critically evaluated.[83]

For Assy, the concept of a right to self-representation is misplaced because LiPs are unable to do justice for themselves.[84] As such, they are better served by having mandatory representation. In Assy's argument, his primary interest is that court proceedings are in keeping with the 'overriding objective' of civil justice.[85] Such an objective is outlined explicitly in Rule 1.1 of the Civil Procedure Rules, which states, amongst other points, that this is about:

> (b) saving expense;
> (c) dealing with the case in ways which are proportionate –
>   (i) to the amount of money involved;
>   (ii) to the importance of the case;
>   (iii) to the complexity of the issues …

But this overriding objective is one in which LiPs are, as this book will show, more likely to be side-lined. The emphasis on saving money, and on prioritising cases based on their financial value or importance (*legal*, rather than any other interpretation of importance) tells us that what LiPs themselves value is of potentially less consequence to the civil justice system.[86] While this is not what the objectives in and of themselves dictate, the political context in which they operate – one in which there have been successive policy changes in favour of greater efficiency of proceedings and reduction in matters coming to court – is one in which what LiPs might find worth litigating becomes increasingly difficult to represent.

It is important to note here that while the general push towards out-of-court settlements, and the greater use of mediation, is certainly a way of reducing the caseload in the courts and avoiding unnecessary delays, it would be unfair not also to mention that for many litigants mediation can be a preferable and less expensive alternative to court-based litigation. As such, alternative forms of dispute resolution can play a valuable role in settling disagreements and resolving problems. But there remain two key concerns here. First, there is a drift towards an increasing use of mediation, particularly in an online context: for example, the

[83] ibid 2.

[84] For a good critique of Assy's work, see B Toy-Cronin, 'A Defence of the Right to Litigate in Person' (2017) 37 *Oxford Journal of Legal Studies* 238.

[85] Assy (n 82) 24.

[86] See also my short blog on this: K Leader, 'The Small Claims Pilot: Filtering out the County Court's Garbage Claims' at www.modernlawreview.co.uk/leader-small-claims-pilot/.

Ministry of Justice court modernisation programme envisions a world in which individuals would only be able to litigate as a last resort, having exhausted other options first.[87] The concern here is that any further push risks directing towards mediation cases that are simply not suitable, and this nuance may be lost in the drive to keep caseloads down.[88]

The second concern relates to the public interest in private disputes. By restricting litigants' ability to access courts, and instead pushing them towards out-of-court settlement, such disputes and their resolutions will no longer contribute to the development of precedent. Linda Mulcahy, in her article 'The Collective Interest in Private Dispute Resolution', emphasises that bargaining out of court is facilitated by and dependent on precedent.[89] The move towards narrowing, or entirely closing off, access to the courts for certain cases has, for Mulcahy, become

> [so] strong that it is time to turn to consider the equally important question of how we identify those cases that must get to trial if both the needs to individuals and the collective need of developing doctrine are to be served.[90]

And so here we face a dilemma: it is obviously in the private interests of some individuals not to litigate, but there is also a public interest dimension to consider, and balancing these two is challenging. Hazel Genn, noting the centrality of out-of-court settlement, comments that 'whether this is a matter for congratulation or concern depends to some extent on your perspective and your fundamental beliefs about the social function of civil justice and the development of common law'.[91]

In thinking specifically about LiPs, I would also argue that there is a clear conflict between the right to self-represent and the policy context that interprets and develops these objectives in the civil justice system.[92] Natalie Byrom notes:

> The cuts to legal aid have changed the manner in which services are provided to the public in a number of important ways. The reforms have reduced the absolute number of providers available; they have affected the geographical distribution of legal aid funded civil law advice across England and Wales, creating 'advice deserts'; and they

[87] Lord Justice Briggs, *Civil Courts Structure Review: Final Report* (London, Judiciary of England and Wales, 2016).

[88] For example, the online dispute court in British Colombia, the Civil Resolution Tribunal (CRT), is based on 'forced' mediation, whereby once two parties enter into discussions with a mediator; it is only that mediator who will determine whether the matter can be settled or will require adjudication. In other words, parties cannot withdraw. While the Briggs Report does not explicitly advocate for this, the CRT is an important model for the online court that is proposed. See at https://civilresolutionbc.ca.

[89] L Mulcahy, 'The Collective Interest in Private Dispute Resolution' (2012) 33 *Oxford Journal of Legal Studies* 59.

[90] ibid 61.

[91] H Genn, *Judging Civil Justice: The 2008 Hamlyn Lectures* (Cambridge, Cambridge University Press, 2009) 37.

[92] This conflict is something I explore in ch 2 when I look at how and why LiPs became LiPs and gained right of access to the higher courts.

> have altered the nature of the service provided by moving the focus away from early intervention and complex casework, onto one-off pieces of advice provided once a situation has already escalated.[93]

Byrom goes on to say that legal-aid-funded providers, including law firms, have reduced by about 50 per cent since the introduction of LASPO 2012.[94] For Byrom, these changes engender a challenge to traditional concepts of lawyering, and she argues that a new vision of lawyering 'that encompasses ideals of social justice and public service' is necessary to gain public support for the push towards providing legal aid.[95] She argues that this is necessary because, too often, debates about legal aid are framed 'in terms of its impact on the legal system and abstract legal concepts and terminology, which fails to resonate outside rarefied circles of lawyers and legal academics'.[96] I argue that the prioritising of the effect LiPs will have on the legal system over ideas of access to justice for litigants is evidenced throughout these writings. As such, this discourse can ultimately be of only limited value in understanding LiPs and what they want, even if advocated by the most sympathetic of practitioners. The answer must be more than just 'Get a lawyer.'[97]

IV. Conclusion: Moving Beyond a Legal Lens

So how does the law 'experience' the LiP? As we have seen here, literature about the LiP falls broadly into two camps: the first emphasising how much LiPs are a problem; and the second emphasising that while LiPs need help, they would still ultimately be better off with representation. But what these camps share is the limitation of seeing LiPs only from a legal perspective. We have difficulty understanding LiP experiences outside of the frames we impose on them, and it also makes it difficult (if not impossible) to consider what the law and legal process might mean to those outside of it. Let us think about this through a specific example: legal aid changes, which have led to fears of rising numbers of LiPs in the courts, something largely justified in the last 10 years. But what if we reconsider this from outside the perspective of the legal profession? As we have seen, from the perspective of many legal practitioners, there is a tendency here to think that legal aid changes mean that most individuals who would have had access to representation will now go ahead without it. But even if they are right about there being more LiPs, these LiPs probably do not look like what those

[93] N Byrom, 'Cuts and the Lawyering Identity Crisis' in A Flynn and J Hodgson (eds), *Access to Justice and Legal Aid: Comparative Perspectives on Unmet Legal Need* (London, Bloomsbury, 2017) 221, 223.

[94] ibid. See also Wilding, 'The Legal Aid sector is collapsing' (n 76).

[95] Byrom (n 93) 234.

[96] ibid.

[97] In addition, as ch 5 explores in more detail, the information and advice given to LiPs by organisations such as the Bar Council are inconsistent.

in the profession imagine. We know that the majority of LiPs are not active, vexatious claimants, but rather passive defendants. These are people who do not participate in their own defence, let alone attend their own hearings. So, the rapid growth in LiPs is likely also to encompass these passive defendants: those either unable or unwilling to participate in their own proceedings, or, indeed, to defend themselves.

Now, let us take this a step further and ask 'What if the real risk isn't rising numbers of LiPs?' Long before LASPO 2012, access to legal aid was problematic, obtaining good-quality legal representation was difficult and legal proceedings were expensive.[98] This is still the case, and LASPO 2012 has only magnified it. Lia Moses of LawWorks suggests this in her blog for the *Law Society Gazette*, asking:

> How will anyone who is not articulate, well-educated and familiar with the court system cope with the procedures in place – will they manage to pay the fees, get the forms in the proper order and get past the court office?[99]

In this context, the true worry is surely not that more people are acting as LiPs; it is that many probably are no longer coming to court at all.[100]

In summary, then, both ways in which legal professionals talk about LiPs, while very different on the surface, share a key idea: that LiPs are alien to normal legal proceedings. As Richard Moorhead notes, LiPs 'disturb the normal conventions of a courtroom': it is this departure from normality that can so easily be conflated with the LiPs themselves being 'abnormal'.[101] The result is that even those who advocate to improve conditions for LiPs tend to perpetuate this presumption. It is clear, then, that the term 'litigant in person' poses more problems than it solves. More than just a confusing concept, the term is linked to a limited understanding of self-represented parties, and it exists in a civil justice system that inadequately accommodates such individuals. So, while LiPs possess theoretical access to legal proceedings, in practice this right is largely rhetorical: LiPs do not have fair, easy or equal access to the courts.

The solution to *this* issue, I suggest, cannot just be about giving people lawyers, or working out how to prevent 'difficult' people from coming to court. Instead, we need to change the way we approach understanding those who act as LiPs, finding methods that attempt to, as sociolegal research calls for, 'reach beyond' the limitations of internal legal discourses.[102] As long as LiPs are positioned as alien to legal process they will continue to be afterthoughts, problems or objects of pity.

[98] See R Moorhead and P Pleasence (eds), *After Universalism: Re-engineering Access to Justice* (Oxford, Blackwell Publishing, 2003).

[99] L Moses, 'Helping out Litigants in Person' *Law Society Gazette* (London, 15 July 2013).

[100] Cookson (n 6) 37 suggests this, noting that individuals may be more likely to 'give up' in the context of lack of legal aid.

[101] R Moorhead, 'The Passive Arbiter: Litigants in Person and the Challenge to Neutrality' (2007) 16 *Social and Legal Studies* 405.

[102] See D Cowan, L Mulcahy and S Wheeler, 'Introduction' in *Law and Society* (London, Routledge, 2014) 1, 4.

This cannot be sufficient in a civil justice system where, as Bridgette Toy-Cronin notes, 'the contribution that the right of self-representation makes' is linked to 'the continuing legitimacy of the legal system'.[103] And this is why we need to hear their stories. In this respect, this book joins a small but growing body of literature that attempts to understand the experiences of LiPs through accessing them directly.[104] Hearing LiPs speak, *in their own words*, can help us move away from the limited 'ways of seeing' we sometimes have.

But before we get there, one more big question: How did this situation come to be? *Why* do we look down on LiPs? Have self-representing parties always been looked on as alien to legal process, or is there another story to be told? Why is there a right of self-representation in the courts when the practice of civil justice seems fundamentally to preclude LiPs? These are the questions pursued in the next chapter.

[103] Toy-Cronin (n 84) 250.

[104] See G McKeever et al, *Litigants in Person in Northern Ireland: Barriers to Legal Participation* (Ulster, Ulster University, 2018); B Toy-Cronin, 'I Ain't No Fool: Deciding to Litigate in Person in the Civil Courts' (2016) 4 *New Zealand Law Review* 723; T Tkacukova and R Lee, *A Study of Litigants in Person in Birmingham Civil Justice Centre* (Birmingham, CEPLER, 2017); J Mant, *Litigants in Person and the Family Justice System* (Oxford, Hart Publishing, 2022).

2

From Bear Gardens to the County Court: Creating the Litigant in Person

This [section of the *County Court Chronicle*] will be dedicated to the Suitor, whether by Attorney or in person. Firmly convinced that the ultimate interests of the Attorney and the Client are *the same*; that law may be too cheap as well as too dear; that bad law is worse than no law; and that there is substantial truth in the proverbial description of the man who is 'his own lawyer.

County Courts Chronicle (London, 1 June 1847) 10.

This [case] seems an exemplification of a hackneyed observation that a man who is his own lawyer has not a Solomon for his client.

County Courts Chronicle (London, 1 September 1866) 134.

Trial lasts twelve days: And Litigant Speaks for Nine of Them

Western Times (Exeter, 4 November 1927) 16.

I. Introduction

This chapter seeks to understand how we came to acquire some of the dominant beliefs and attitudes we have about LiPs.[1] As described in chapter 1, self-represented parties have been frequently described in a negative light, particularly by legal professionals, who have, both in the UK and overseas, often considered them to be vexatious, time-wasting, disturbed, incompetent or a combination of all these. This attitude has become even more noticeable in the UK since the enactment of LASPO 2012 cut legal aid for most civil claims and sparked concern over the threatened increase of LiPs in the court system. As chapter 1 demonstrated, whilst such criticism is as likely to relate to concern about the impact on the court system as it is on any perceived prejudice towards LiPs, and whilst there is no doubt that many legal professionals and scholars

[1] A version of this chapter first appeared as an article in the *Cambridge Law Journal*. See K Leader, 'From Bear Gardens to the County Court: Creating the Litigant in Person' (2020) 79 *CLJ* 260.

actively seek ways to improve LiP experiences, this negativity has potential consequences for LiPs when they try to pursue or defend claims.

But despite the persistence of these attitudes, no study has ever considered how we got here: Were people who represented themselves always considered negatively? Or is this the result of historical changes; and, if so, when and how? This is the task this chapter sets out to accomplish. As I will show, pursuing these questions is a distinct task to undertaking a history of self-representation. The term 'litigant in person' is a modern one, and taking it as synonymous with self-representation fails to reflect how important the moment of historical transformation is, from a general idea of self-representation to the creation of the LiP as a specific role. To understand *how* LiPs came to be understood as they are today demands investigation of the creation of the term itself.

This chapter, then, is a study of a particular moment when the term 'litigant in person' first appears, and the context in which this takes place.[2] I argue that this moment is a by-product of broader changes occurring in the legal profession and in legal adjudication, culminating in the sweeping Judicature Acts that created the modern superior courts. It begins with the founding of the new County Courts in 1847 and ends with the appearance of 'litigant in person' as a term in case law, and in general parlance, by the 1880s. As I will show, in a remarkably short period of time, these new County Courts, theoretically designed to provide greater access to justice for poorer litigants, become infiltrated by legal professionals, who bring in their wake a desire for greater formality of procedure and content, and this made it harder and harder for individuals to act without lawyers.[3]

Blaming 'formality' and the 'legal profession', however, for creating the LiP is an oversimplification. Instead, I will argue that what happens can best be understood as emblematic of Larson's 'professional project' in action.[4] Drawing on Larson's framework, I will show that the new County Courts become a battleground for attorneys to claim their place in a legal profession that actively discriminates between the 'higher' calling of the Bar and the 'lower' rungs of the rank-and-file practitioners.[5] This battle is a battle for *distinction* that takes place through the

[2] Whilst some references can be found to individuals conducting their own cases, these are rare, usually in criminal cases, and it is only in the County Courts where this reportage happens more regularly. One example of the former can be seen in *The Morning Post* (London, 8 April 1848) 7, where a criminal defendant 'represented herself with a good deal of skill and occasioned much amusement in the Court by the ingenious manner in which she cross examined the witnesses'.

[3] As Margot Finn argues in *The Character of Credit*, the argument that lawyers dominate the County Courts is too simplistic; rather, the new County Courts bring anxieties as to who has the right to appear, and in what circumstances. M Finn, *The Character of Credit: Personal Debt in English Culture, 1740–1914* (Cambridge, Cambridge University Press, 1993).

[4] MS Larson, *The Rise of Professionalism: A Sociological Analysis* (Berkeley, CA, University of California Press, 1977).

[5] The 'rank-and-file' practitioners are the attorneys and solicitors, with attorneys practising in courts of common law and solicitors practising in Chancery. This division ended in 1874 with the Judicature Acts, when all attorneys become solicitors. Significantly, as the *County Courts Chronicle* notes, the attorney's function in the County Court becomes more and more that of an advocate. See *County Courts Chronicle* (London, 1 October 1847) 18.

marking out of legal representatives from laypersons, the normalisation of legal expertise and the attempt to crack down on unqualified representatives.[6] It is the attempt to introduce these kinds of distinction into the County Courts that creates the LiP. What I will show, then, is that the LiP role is not simply that of self-representation; it is self-representation that occurs, and *only* occurs, in the context of the latter stages of the professional project. Perversely, this also means that the creation of the term 'litigant in person' does not indicate the facilitation of lay participation in legal forums; it instead marks the moment when laypersons are displaced. This displacement is of profound significance for the LiPs we are going to hear from in this book.

II. A Note on Sources and Scope

It is important to start this chapter by saying that this is not a history, neither of the County Courts nor of nineteenth-century changes in legal adjudication.[7] Instead, what I attempt to do is narrower: I try to understand what was happening for self-represented parties at the time the County Courts were founded and in the following decades, seeking to shed light on how the term 'litigant in person' came about and how such individuals came to be so looked down on. However, such a task does necessitate understanding of the pre-existing landscape of self-representation prior to the founding of the County Courts, knowledge of the County Courts themselves and understanding of developments in the legal profession. I therefore draw on several legal historians whose work is essential in constructing my argument: in particular, Patrick Polden's *History of the County Courts of England*, Margot C Finn's *The Character of Credit: Personal Debt in English Culture, 1740–1914*, HW Arthur's *Without the Law* and the work of Christopher Brooks, in particular *Lawyers, Litigation and English Society Since 1450*.[8] It is perhaps an irony that in order to write about people without lawyers, one must spend most of one's time talking about legal professionals. But self-representation only exists as a concept in relation to legal representation, and so they remain indelibly linked.

[6] This crackdown was unsuccessful, with 'agents' appearing well into the 1900s. See Finn (n 3) 257.

[7] The 19th century was a time of far-reaching changes: such developments touch on this research but remain tangential enough that dealing with them directly would take this research too far from the key questions. See RW Andrews, *The Supreme Court of Judicature Acts, and the Appellate Jurisdiction Act 1876: With Rules of Court and Forms to May, 1880. Annotated So As to Form a Manual of Practice. Adapted Chiefly to the Chancery and Common Law Divisions* (London, Bibiobazaar, 2015 [1880]). See also M Lobban, 'Preparing for Fusion: Reforming the 19th Century Court of Chancery, II' (2004) 22 *Law and History Review* 565.

[8] P Polden, *A History of the County Courts: 1846–1971* (Cambridge, Cambridge University Press, 1999); HW Arthurs, *Without the Law: Administrative Justice and Legal Pluralism in 19th Century England* (New York, Buffalo, 1985); P Brand, *The Origins of the English Legal Profession* (Oxford, Blackwell Publishing, 1992); C Brooks, *Lawyers, Litigation and English Society Since 1450* (London, The Hambledon Press, 1998); C Brooks and M Lobban (eds), *Communities and Courts in Britain: 1150–1900* (London, The Hambledon Press, 1997).

In addition to the legal historical literature that provides a background to this analysis, this chapter draws on two primary sources for information about the County Courts. First, the House of Commons (HC) and House of Lords (HL) debates that took place around the establishment of these courts, and which occurred over a nearly 30-year period from 1821 until 1849. My research into the HC and HL debates was based on the online searching of Hansard database, using 'County Courts' as the key search term.[9] I read any debate explicitly mentioning the County Courts as a means of understanding the grounds on which the legislation establishing the new courts was introduced.

Second, and most importantly, this chapter draws on the *County Court Chronicle*, a publication that was founded with the introduction of the new County Courts in 1847 and which continued until 1920.[10] The *County Court Chronicle* provides court reports, editorials, discussions of relevant legislative and procedural reforms, and letters to the editor from both litigants and lawyers: as such, it offers an unmatched insight into debates taking place around the time. The alteration in the *Chronicle's* style and focus is a useful method of charting the shifts in process relating to the LiP that I seek to identify in this book. As I will show, within a short space of time, the *Chronicle* goes from being a journalistic, almost gossipy, account of cases, many of which have unrepresented parties, to becoming a distinctly different publication in keeping with the development of the professional project.

It is important to note here, though, that although the *County Court Chronicle* is an invaluable resource, I am aware that there is a danger in relying too heavily on it for evidence of what happened in the County Courts.[11] Even in the first year of its publication, where the number of cases reported was significantly more than the number reported 10 or 20 years later, this was only ever a fragment of the proceedings actually taking place. What we *can* do is consider the reporting in the *Chronicle* as indicative of what was important to the authors (legal professionals) and their readership (largely legal professionals).[12] The diminishment of cases reported involving self-represented parties in later editions of the *Chronicle*

[9] Other search terms included 'small debts' and 'small debts act', as this was the working title for some of the earlier proposals that preceded the County Court Act.

[10] The *County Court Chronicle* was absorbed into the *Law Times* in 1920 and ceased to be a separate publication before disappearing altogether.

[11] My exclusive focus on the *County Courts Chronicle* is largely a matter of necessity; it is the only publication reporting regularly on the County Courts. For more information on the development of press on legal proceedings, see MP Jones, *Justice and Journalism: A Study of the Influence of Newspaper Reporting upon the Administration of Justice by Magistrates* (Chichester, Barry Rose, 1974) 38.

[12] While I have been unable to find any explicit circulation figures, the publishers of the *County Courts Chronicle* were also those involved in the publication of legal circulars, most notably the *Law Times*, which began in 1843 and ran until 1965, billing itself as a publication for 'law and lawyers'. Its sister publications included *The Jurist, Solicitor's Journal* and *Legal Journal.* We can therefore speculate that the *County Courts Chronicle* was for a select, mainly legal professional, readership. A *Chronicle* entry described it as 'well known', as the 'organ of the legal profession'. *County Courts Chronicle* (London, 1 March 1858). See also E Sunderland, 'The English struggle for procedural reform' (1926) 39 *Harvard Law Review* 734.

does not indicate that they disappear (we know that they do not), but it does tell us that they are marginalised from what is perceived to be the 'real work' of the courts, or at the very least they are marginalised from the dominant interest of that publication: that of legal professionals arguing matters of legal interest. It is this marginalisation that I deem to be critical to how the concept of the LiP developed.

III. The Professional Project

This chapter thinks about Larson's professional project to help illuminate *retrospective* developments, but it does not suggest there is a simple, structuralist account of such complex changes.[13] Ultimately, long-term alterations in practice come down to a complex web of individual behaviours shaped by social belief and education, such as is illuminated by the scholarship and contemporary accounts of commentators, legal historians and those who study the legal profession. However, what makes Larson's work of particular value is her attention to how the dual goals of the professional project – consisting of both monopolisation of the market and the attainment of social status – develop. Larson argues that critical to the development of a profession is attention to standardisation of practice, the development of a 'cognitive commonality' and the move to eliminating any competition from unregulated actors. All of these tendencies are orientated towards the ultimate goal, which is the social distancing of these professionals from non-professionals, and the consequent status that arises from this distinction.[14]

However, it is important to nuance Larson's framework with close attention to the specificities of nineteenth-century legal practitioners. For this purpose, the work of Christopher Brooks is essential. As Brooks persuasively argues, rather than seeing the nineteenth century as a time of the 'rise of professions', the specific case of the law might better be described as a *re*professionalisation that takes place during the nineteenth century after a significant period of decline in the seventeenth and eighteenth centuries. As Brooks notes, this earlier period was marked by a significant decline in practitioners, as well as a falling off of standardisation of methods of admission to the profession. Brooks argues that it is therefore not clear that lawyers map on to what 'might be called a classical agenda of "professionalisation"'.[15] For Brooks, the risk of applying contemporary theories of professionalisation, such as Larson's model, is that of anachronism. Instead he suggests that

> rejecting professionalisation as a characterisation of the way the present differs from the past opens the door to a consideration of lawyers for what they were: a diverse group of people who were at the centre of the creation and exchange of one of the major

[13] Larson (n 4).
[14] ibid 77.
[15] Brooks (n 8) 186.

> social discourses of the day: the set of norms, practise and ideologies known collectively as 'the law'.[16]

I would argue, however, that it is possible to take into account Brooks' caution without having to dismiss Larson. It is clearly essential to be careful about any overarching or simplistic claims that obscure the diversity of those practising within the profession; however, this does not stop a framework of professionalism from being useful for charting developments that affect self-represented parties without falling into anachronism. As such, I will draw on Brooks' and other historians' research on the legal profession throughout this work to qualify Larson's thesis.

IV. Before 1847: Self-Representation in Civil Proceedings

The presence of self-represented parties in civil proceedings is a longstanding feature of English legal history.[17] As Paul Brand notes, 'England before the middle of the twelfth century was a country without professional lawyers largely because there was little for them to be expert about'.[18] Prior to the emergence of the legal profession, litigants brought their suits in person. The introduction of specialised King's Justices and tribunals created the initial need for specialists. From the thirteenth century onwards, the courts used a writ system that required legal experts to advise litigants which of the recognised causes for action inhered in their particular case; whilst the details were recorded orally from the litigant, they were then written down by the clerks of chancery.[19] There were also professional pleaders who presented cases in court.[20] The superior courts were therefore dominated by legal representatives from a very early point, as they relied on expertise in substantive issues and pleading.[21] Once representatives were involved, though, this raised the costs of appearance, thus excluding many individuals who could not afford to hire representatives.[22] It was simply not a practical option to pursue matters in these courts unless one had money to spend, given that one might potentially lose. It is therefore misleading to suggest

[16] ibid.

[17] For the parallel story of criminal proceedings, see J Langbein, *Origins of Adversarial Criminal Trial* (Oxford, Oxford University Press, 2003).

[18] Brand (n 8) 5.

[19] ibid 34.

[20] By the time we reach the establishment of superior courts under Henry II, we have courts where Brand notes almost all litigants were 'outsiders': ibid 69.

[21] P Tucker, 'London's Courts of Law in the Fifteenth Century: The Litigant's Perspective' in Brooks and Lobban (eds) (n 8) 29.

[22] See M Hastings, *The Court of Common Pleas in the 15th Century* (Ithaca, NY, Cornell University Press, 1947) 169.

that legal representation ends *any* individual's ability to self-represent. Even before lawyers, this ability was already largely limited to those with resources.[23]

It is apparent, then, that the courts at Westminster were inaccessible to laypersons from an early stage. But these were not the only courts in pre-nineteenth-century England. Self-representation continued to flourish in other courts and tribunals, such as the Anglo-Saxon derived hundred courts and the manorial courts, alongside a host of specialised tribunals that existed throughout England and Wales well into the nineteenth century.[24] Several factors help explain why self-representation continued in these courts: first, many of these courts and tribunals remained primarily oral, with individuals able to attend and make their complaint on the day. This meant that disputes were resolved quickly, and also meant that, with no elaborate writ system, literacy was not necessary.[25] Second, there was no need for legal expertise, as adjudication was not necessarily bound by precedent and there were no superior courts to which these courts had to answer.[26] Finally, these courts were held locally, making them not only more physically accessible for those who could not travel to London, but also tribunals that could dispense a kind of communal justice that the Westminster courts could not.[27]

This is obviously a simplified overview of diverse and complex tribunals. But I provide this narrative to draw out two important points. First, it is inaccurate to claim that self-representation becomes impossible only in the nineteenth century. Self-representation always required facilitation by certain factors to be effective: proceedings that are oral, and forms of adjudication that do not rely on knowledge of legal doctrine. It is when litigants lose access to these kinds of proceedings that self-representation becomes more difficult. Second, understanding that England was a landscape of multiple courts and tribunals in the mid-nineteenth century helps us to understand the impact of the County Court Act 1846. This is because this statute does not simply create a new court for litigants, it replaces another: the Courts of Request.

V. The County Courts and the Courts of Request

The County Courts Act 1846 came into force in 1847. The Bill, which was debated, drafted and redrafted over a nearly 30-year period,[28] did not create County Courts,

[23] Brand (n 8) 9. It is important to note, however, Brooks' research, demonstrating that a wider section of the population accessed early modern courts than has been assumed to be the case. See Brooks (n 8) 15–16.

[24] For an overview of this multi-court landscape, see Arthurs (n 8).

[25] Some tribunals required an initial written plaint, but the clerks at the courts themselves could draft this on the oral application of the plaintiff.

[26] This is not the case for the Eyres, which did employ common law and travelling King's Justices established from 1176 without legislative authority.

[27] For a fuller account of communal justice and local courts, see JH Baker, 'The Changing Concept of a Court' in JH Baker, *The Legal Profession and the Common Law: Historical Essays* (London, The Hambledon Press, 1986).

[28] Polden (n 8).

which in fact already existed, but was intended to reform them in order to provide an accessible and inexpensive forum for pursuing small debts.[29] The superior courts were accessible only by the wealthy, required legal representation and were criticised for their 'dilatory' proceedings. Joseph Parkes, writing about his own experience of the Warwick Assizes of 1827, says:

> I brought an action for £25. It was defended; six witnesses, besides the respective attorneys and parties, attended five days: I obtained a verdict: my costs to the defendant were £66, and probably his own costs due to his attorney would be an additional sum of £50; thus the original debt in dispute was more than quadrupled.[30]

In addition, by the 1300s, the superior courts were applying a rule that they would not give judgment for damages under 40 shillings, and this amount remained in place until the 1800s.[31] Although the relative value had decreased markedly, meaning that the sum of 40 shillings was less than 500 years previously, it still amounted to more than a trivial sum in the nineteenth century. The fact that a suit's importance was formally determined by how much was at stake financially, barring it from the superior courts, was criticised by Jeremy Bentham, amongst others:

> What to one man may be trivial, to another may be of high importance … In pecuniary cases, the smaller the sum in dispute the less reserve is used in branding the conduct of parties with the charge of litigation, of which, in such cases, the reproach is apt to fall principally, if not exclusively, to the plaintiff's share.[32]

As Bentham and other contemporary commentators, including Sir Robert Peel, Viscount Althorp and Lord Falconer, argued, the arbitrary corollary between financial value and merit misrepresented what the value of the suit might be for the individual bringing it.[33]

Any suits of lesser value therefore had to be pursued in the lower courts. And the existing County Courts were considered by many to be as bad as the superior courts. These courts shared the charges of delay and expense levelled at the superior courts, but were also regularly accused of corruption and criticised for their infrequency.[34] John Smith, in an early HC debate on County Court reform,

> [p]resented a petition from the inhabitants of Brighton, complaining of the serious evils which arose from the abuses of the practice of the County Courts … [A]mong others

[29] As I go on to outline, the new County Courts both replace the old County Courts and close down the Courts of Requests. See HC Deb 23 February 1824, vol 10, cols 303–04. See also Finn (n 3) 236–77.

[30] J Parkes, *The State of the Court of Requests and the Public Office of Birmingham, with Considerations on the Increase and Prosecution of Crime in the County of Warwick, Etc* (Birmingham, Beilby, Knott and Beilby, 1828) 5.

[31] The Statute of Gloucester 1176 stated that writs for goods had to have a minimum value of 40 shillings.

[32] J Bentham, *A Protest Against Law Taxes* (London, J Debrett, 1795) 34–36.

[33] See R Peel, HC Deb 20 June 1827, vol 17, cols 1350–61. See also Brougham, HC Deb 29 April 1830, vol 24, cols 243–89.

[34] Arthurs (n 8) 16.

> he mentioned the case of a poor woman, who was sued for a debt of 14s, and an execution being taken out against her for that sum, and for 15s costs upon it, her goods were seized for a sum considerably exceeding the amount of both debt and costs; her bed, her pillows, and several other articles of furniture were taken from her … nothing was returned.[35]

Politicians and jurists, then, proposed the County Court legislation ostensibly as a means of extending justice to poorer litigants, and as an explicit reaction to the inaccessibility of the current courts.[36] However, although there were altruistic motives involved, the legislation was less about giving access to justice for poorer litigants than about allowing tradesmen to pursue poorer individuals for debts.[37] Most importantly, the implication of comments made by figures such as Lord Falconer is that the Act was needed to provide courts where there were no courts before, or only the bad old County Courts.[38] But this assumption ignores the Courts of Request.

Courts of Request were courts where cases were decided locally according to 'equity and good conscience'. As Shaunnagh Dorset points out, this means that such courts were

> neither a court of common law nor equity and decisions were to be made according to the more discretionary norms of 'real justice and good conscience' … [S]uch courts were designed to allow matters to be determined in a manner that was shorn of the need for technicalities, difficult pleading or even lawyers, and they were often run by laypersons.[39]

As Margot Finn argues, Courts of Request practice was one of 'equitable reasoning', which 'referred less to the formal practices of the central court of Chancery, than to tempering the strict letter of the law by taking account of particularistic, mitigating personal circumstances'.[40] Each Court of Request was a separate entity created by local municipal statute.[41] The cases in question in these courts were usually small and the procedures were relatively simple, and parties could testify in person.[42] The Courts of Requests were also popular. By 1847, these courts existed in over 400 locations and dealt with several hundred thousand suits annually, with the 'defendants derived overwhelmingly from the lower

[35] J Smith, HC Deb 09 April 1827, vol 17, cols 297–99.

[36] ibid.

[37] See P Johnson, 'Creditors, Debtors and the Law in Victorian England' (1996) LSE Economic History Working Papers 31/96, 1.

[38] Indeed, this is precisely the case made in one of the earliest pamphlets directly discussing 'accessibility of justice', published in 1830. See Editorial, 'Mr Brougham and Local Judicatories,' *Westminster Review* 13 (1830).

[39] See S Dorset, 'Destitute of the Knowledge of God: Maori Testimony before the New Zealand Courts in the Early Crown Colony Period' in D Kirkby (ed), *Past Law, Present Histories* (Canberra, ANU E-Press, 2012) 39, 46–47.

[40] Finn (n 3) 205.

[41] Polden (n 8) 47.

[42] ibid. See also Arthurs (n 8) 26. Testifying in person is distinct from self-representation, referring to a party in the case giving a sworn account of what happened to a court.

and working classes'.[43] This was where the majority of small debts claims were made, alongside a host of other kinds of minor disputes. As HW Arthurs puts it, '[i]t is hardly an overstatement to say that, for most Englishmen of the period, the local Court of Request dispensed the only form of civil justice they would ever know'.[44] Far from there being no forum for litigants pursuing small claims, there were courts already operating that were successful.[45]

So why do the drafters of the County Court Act argue that the new County Court was needed? One explanation is that the Courts of Request were no place for those who considered themselves members of the legal profession.[46] As a *Chronicle* correspondent would note later, 'Courts of request were bear gardens in noise and confusion, and their character was at the lowest ebb.'[47] While there is some evidence of attorneys involved in the Courts of Request, such individuals were looked down on as debasing the reputation of the profession.[48] Courts of Request do occasionally appear in the HC debates about the new County Courts, but they are not depicted in a flattering light. Lord Brougham expresses a typical attitude here:

> It happens that tradesmen, who know nothing of law, and who may not have much occupation in their own business, preside in these Courts of Request, and administer justice as well as might be expected. I say it is better to have these courts and these judges than to have none.[49]

So, while the Courts of Request were considered to serve a purpose while there was no better alternative, they were generally considered beneath the dignity of the profession.[50]

But another, more persuasive explanation for why the Courts of Request were replaced can be found through examining the criticism in closer detail. Such criticism demonstrates that for many in the legal profession, the Courts of Request were not just undignified, they were not *courts* at all. The language of the criticism evidences this: these courts were, as noted previously, described as 'bear gardens'.[51] Other commentators refer to them as

[43] Finn (n 3) 18.

[44] ibid 26.

[45] See Polden (n 8) 11.

[46] A barnstorming address by the Lord Chancellor in 1830 outlines the reasons to 'absorb' the courts of conscience or requests and create the new County Courts. It can be found in HL Deb 2 December 1830, vol 1, cols 707–40.

[47] *County Courts Chronicle* (London, 1 July 1847) 34.

[48] Finn argues there is 'active hostility' to the profession in these Courts of Requests, with Bath banning legal professionals from acting as judges and fining attorneys £20 for appearing in court, and this practice and attitude being 'commonplace': Finn (n 3) 205. See also Brooks (n 8) 42.

[49] Lord Brougham, HC Deb 29 April 1830, vol 24, cols 243–89. See also Caldwell, quoted in Finn (n 3) 221.

[50] *The Legal Observer and Journal of Jurisprudence* notes 'It is a striking and important fact that public opinion has always been against such courts as are now contemplated. The decent part of the community feel it discreditable to resort to them, and even the very rabble despise them.' (1830) 1 *The Legal Observer and Journal of Jurisprudence* 104.

[51] *County Courts Chronicle* (London, 1 July 1847) 34.

'but tribunals'.[52] Such language is more than a character assessment: it is a policing of boundaries, symptomatic of what John Griffiths identified as 'legal centralism', defined as the idea that 'law is and should be the law of the state, uniform for all persons, exclusive of all other law, and administered by a single set of state institutions'.[53] Courts and tribunals operating outside of the auspices of this central administration were therefore not real courts. But legal centralism is a claim, not a fact. As Marc Galanter comments in his article on indigenous law and legal pluralism, 'Just as health is not found primarily in hospitals or knowledge in schools, so justice is not primarily to be found in official justice-dispensing institutions.'[54]

Following Griffiths and Galanter, the County Courts Act 1846 can be read as an ideological claim to a specific kind of justice: a justice that can only be found via the legal profession. The statute's preamble explicitly stated that 'it is expedient that the Provisions of such Acts should be amended, and that One Rule and Manner of proceeding for the Recovery of Small Debts and Demands should prevail throughout *England*'.[55] As such, the County Courts Act 1846 effected more than simple reform: it was part of a wider thrust of legal centralisation taking place throughout the nineteenth century, dismantling unregulated courts and transforming them into new areas of practice for the profession.[56]

The County Courts Act 1846, then, was drafted to provide *proper* courts for poorer litigants. These new courts would be overseen, and ideally frequented, by legal professionals.[57] As Patrick Polden states, 'from the point of view of the profession … it was imperative that the county courts should be established on a basis that would give lawyers access to a lucrative new area of practice'.[58] Here we see the mix of altruism and self-interest that largely characterises these developments. So while it would be overstating it to say that the new County Court was established purely in the pursuit of a professional monopoly, it would be naive to believe that this was not also a factor in its development.[59] In keeping with Bourdieu's sociological theory, instead, we can see these two motives are entirely blended: it was not the case that the legal profession wanted a monopoly of the new courts purely out of self-interest;[60] instead, lawyers genuinely believed

[52] ibid.

[53] J Griffiths, 'What is Legal Pluralism?' (1986) 18 *The Journal of Legal Pluralism and Unofficial Law* 3.

[54] M Galanter, 'Justice in Many Rooms: Courts, Private Ordering and Indigenous Law' (1981) 13 *Journal of Legal Pluralism and Unofficial Law* 10.

[55] Preamble, County Courts Act 1846.

[56] HW Arthurs, 'Without the Law: Courts of Local and Special Jurisdiction in Nineteenth Century England' (1984) 3 *Journal of Legal History* 143, 144.

[57] Larson (n 4) 9–10.

[58] Polden (n 8) 43.

[59] ibid.

[60] Christopher Brooks notes 'there was a conflict between the professional desire to maintain a monopoly over specialised fields of knowledge and the belief that these were too important to society at large for them to be withheld': Brooks (n 8) 234.

that their presence would serve the ends of justice.[61] This attitude is exemplified in this *County Court Chronicle* editorial in the year the Bill passed:

> There is undoubtedly an inclination at present to stand aloof from the County Courts – to look upon the practices as *low*, and to leave it to the lowest grade of practitioners … But this is a grievous mistake, and if persisted in will be seriously injurious both to the Courts and to the Profession.[62]

The implicit argument here is that the presence of legal professionals is necessary in these new courts, because their presence will *transform* the proceedings from 'bear gardens' into real courts.

VI. An Occupational Hierarchy

At this point it is far too simplistic to keep referring to the 'legal profession' as a monolithic group, particularly if we want to understand what happens in the County Courts and how it affects self-represented parties. This is because the legal profession, like any other profession, has its own occupational hierarchy. More than that, the status of the law as one of the 'older professions' means that its professional structures were developed earlier than those of many other professions.[63] While it is important not to get lost in these histories, it is essential to note the gap between members of the profession who practised at the Bar and those who occupied a lower status in the profession: the rank-and-file attorneys and solicitors. While such divisions persist in different forms today, historically, these divisions cut deeper. They were indicative of a distinct class difference: those admitted to the Bar came from loftier backgrounds, compared with attorneys and solicitors who were from humbler origins.[64] In the pre-nineteenth century, this division denoted the difference between practitioners at the Bar, who were considered 'gentleman', and those who were seen *by* the Bar as merely working for money.[65]

This of course was not the case for attorneys, who lacked these social privileges and who were dependent on a steady income to survive. But the late eighteenth and early nineteenth centuries constituted a time of radical changes: new markets opened

[61] P Bourdieu, 'The Force of Law: Towards a Sociology of the Juridical Field' (1987) 38 *Hastings Law Journal* 814, 819.

[62] *County Courts Chronicle* (London, 1 July 1847) 33; see also ibid 35 on legal professionals giving 'character' to a court.

[63] Law is considered one of the 'old professions', along with medicine and the Church.

[64] This is arguably still the case for the Bar, whose members are disproportionately drawn from Oxbridge and public schools. See M Blackwell, '"Old Boys Networks", Family Connections and the Legal Profession' (2012) 3 *Public Law* 426.

[65] D Duman, 'The Creation and Diffusion of a Professional Ideology in Nineteenth Century England' (1979) 27 *The Sociological Review* 115. See also D Duman, 'Pathway to Professionalism: The English Bar in the Eighteenth and Nineteenth Centuries' (1980) 13 *Journal of Social History* 622.

up in new urban centres, and the class structure of the whole country changed too, from one structured by landowners and peasants, to one centred around the market.[66] The consequences for the legal profession of these changes were significant. While, up to this point, the Bar had thrived on a pre-nineteenth-century guild-like exclusivity, by this time, as TH Marshall notes:

> The professional had to change his ground. He had to admit that his occupation was laborious, like the tradesman's – and even to glory in the fact – but to assert that it was labour of a superior kind. The idea of service became more important than the idea of freedom.[67]

In the legal profession, this changing of ground happened at both the higher and the lower ends: the Bar re-orientated itself, subscribing to a model of service. But large sections of the 'lower-rungs', increasingly made up of the new, socially-mobile middle class, were also eager to improve their own prospects. This nevertheless did not preclude a continuation of emphasising the division between barrister and attorneys. As Brooks notes:

> Drawing heavily on classical antecedents and humanist approaches to jurisprudence, the Inns of Court and the Bar claimed that theirs was a scientific subject which involved 'liberal' learning. By contrast, the attorneys were often described as merely 'mechanical' practitioners of a distinctly lower social and political status.[68]

An illustration of the Bar's sense of being superior, both in education and in class, is evidenced in the *County Court Chronicle* in 1848, where the speaker – a barrister – emphasises the 'superior' class of practitioners at the Bar: 'the Bar look upon the judges as one of themselves, and only of equal rank and status in society. But the attorneys are of a class below the Court in professional rank, and have not the same status in the world'.[69]

The division between the upper and lower rungs of the legal profession was therefore not simply a social one but was actively policed. Attorneys were discouraged from joining the Inns of Court and could join the Bar only if they 'abandoned their practice in the lower branch for at least two years before being called'.[70] In short, at the time of the founding of the County Courts, many areas of practice in the superior courts were inaccessible to the lower rungs of the profession because they did not have rights of audience, with the Bar enjoying a total monopoly on superior court advocacy.

[66] Marx and Engels identified this as central to the development of the 'cash nexus'. See K Marx and F Engels, *The Communist Manifesto* (London and New York, Simon & Schuster, 2013) 61.

[67] TH Marshall, 'The Recent History of Professionalism in Relation to Social Structures and Social Policy' (1939) 5 *The Canadian Journal of Economics and Political Science* 325.

[68] Brooks (n 8)150.

[69] *County Courts Chronicle* (London, 1 March 1848) 193. Attempts to restrict access to advocates in favour of the Bar were met with anger and virulent debate: see also (1852) 19 *Law Times* 117.

[70] Larson (n 4), 11.

In this context, then, the new County Court became critically important because it offered a new site of practice to attorneys and, through them, a means to establish themselves and become recognised advocates.[71] Such a move could both distinguish them from lay practitioners and allow them to access areas of practice that were previously the exclusive reserve of barristers.[72] This echoes Larson's argument of the 'double' nature of the professional project that 'intertwines market and status orientations, and both tend towards monopoly – monopoly of opportunities for income in a market of service, on the one hand, and monopoly of status in an emerging occupational hierarchy, on the other'.[73] The new County Courts were therefore not only a new forum for poorer litigants to pursue debt claims or a new area for legal professionals to expand into. They were also an opportunity for attorneys to stake a claim to be taken seriously as advocates. And it is when attorneys begin staking their claim that the LiP begins to emerge.

VII. The Early Years of the County Court

In June 1847, the first edition of the *County Court Chronicle* was published, advertising itself on its masthead as a monthly publication by the editor of and contributors to the *Law Times*. At this point, the courts themselves had been in operation for less than two months. The front cover of the *Chronicle* is dedicated to notices of the next County Court sessions on each circuit, followed by seven pages of law reports from across the country. The bulk of the rest of the publication is devoted to specific subsections on particular roles. The mission statement the *Chronicle* outlines for itself is 'to provide for all who are engaged in the County Courts, whether as Judges, Clerks, Bailiffs, Practitioners or Suitors, a medium for mutual information and intercommunication on the matters relating to the administration of justice by a tribunal which is of incalculable importance'.[74]

The tone of the first edition is journalistic and experimental. The *Chronicle* itself acknowledges the provisionality of its current layout and arrangements, and the court reports themselves frequently give descriptive accounts of the circumstances of the courts in addition to specific cases. For example, 'Narbeth, May 20. There were thirty-six cases entered. The courtroom, which is much too small, was crowded to excess with upwards of 100 persons being obliged to wait in the street outside.'[75] In the reports themselves, self-representation is clearly common, with

[71] As Paul Johnson notes, although there was never an acknowledged 'County Court Bar', it was attorneys (and later, solicitors) who gained a near monopoly on representation in the new County Courts: Johnson (n 37).

[72] For more discussion of the relevant merits of attorneys versus barristers, see also *County Courts Chronicle* (London, 7 January 1850) 14; (London, 1 March 1870) 63; (London, 2 March 1868) 81–82; (London, 1 February 1868) 53; (1852) 16 *The Jurist* 205.

[73] Larson (n 4) 79.

[74] *County Court Chronicle* (London, 1 June 1847) 11.

[75] ibid 3.

up to half the cases in the first half dozen issues involving at least one individual appearing in person, if not on both sides. It is difficult to make any estimates of the proportion of self-representation in general, because the reports cover only a fraction of the cases that were heard, but it is reasonable to assume that an even higher proportion than that which appears in the law reports self-represented in actuality.[76] This is because there is an explicit agenda on the part of the *Chronicle* to report cases of *legal* interest. For example, in Berwick, on 29 May 1847, 'At the first Court there were twenty-five cases entered, while at the last there were upwards of sixty. The only case interesting to that of the Profession was …' followed by an account of a dispute between an agent and a represented defendant.[77]

For a case to be of legal interest, the concept must be understood in legal terminology: this is more likely to arise in cases with represented parties. Consequently, matters of unrepresented parties are more likely to go unreported. However, although the *Chronicle* is staffed by members of the profession, with their concomitant clear interest in drawing out relevant legal issues, the publication commits itself to the interests of self-represented parties as well as that of the profession. The *County Court Chronicle* dedicates a section to the 'Suitor': in other words, to the litigant, who was more likely than not to be self-representing. This section is filled with information that is intended to assist such individuals. As the editor explicitly states in the epigraph opening this chapter, a Suitor in person and an attorney representing a client are of equal dignity and status.[78] At this point, then, we may safely observe that self-representation is seen by the authors of the publication as relatively normal.[79]

So, although I have made much of the radical transformation resulting from the County Courts Act 1846, it began as an attempt to combine the introduction of more professional practices without completely dismantling what came before, thus retaining enough of the old Courts of Request to ensure the new court's popularity. This hybridity may be seen in several ways. First, and crucially, the County Courts Act 1946 clearly outlines the right of trained attorneys to represent litigants and restricts the ability of other third parties to act as representatives:[80]

> One of the most serious evils to which the suitors resorting to inferior tribunals have been exposed – that of being duped into the employment of sham practitioners – has

[76] An 1858 commentator notes that 'for the most part the business of the court is either conducted without the assistance of professional men' or by unlicensed attorneys. See *County Courts Chronicle* (London, 1 May 1858) 131; (London, 1 February 1853) 25; (London, 1 February 1852) 26; (London, 9 August 1850) 513; (London, 1 March 1859).

[77] *County Courts Chronicle* (London, 1 June 1847) 4. This is echoed by the account from the 27 April session at Whitby in *County Court Chronicle* (London, 1 June 1847) 6.

[78] *County Courts Chronicle* (London, 1 June 1847) 10.

[79] From the beginning of the *County Courts Chronicle*, the normality of being unrepresented was linked to the perceived simplicity of the case. See in particular *County Courts Chronicle* (London, 2 July 1855) 131 and *County Courts Chronicle* (London, 1 February 1853) 25. For more evidence on the normality of individuals representing themselves, see *County Courts Chronicle* (London, 2 July 1860) 15–16.

[80] This includes those who were not legal professionals but who still acted for others, including family members or work colleagues, in a paid or unpaid capacity. The early days of the County Court show

> already received a very decided check from the Judges presiding at Southwark and in Bloomsbury.[81]

Indeed, who had the right to appear, for whom and in which circumstances are critical issues.[82] The crackdown on unregulated individuals is one that Larson argues is characteristic of the professional project, and it receives regular and consistent coverage in the *Chronicle* over the years.[83] At the same time, in the early days of the County Court, a fees cap was in place, stopping legal representatives from claiming costs from the court in any proceedings worth less than £5.[84] This meant that the County Courts were working towards greater regulation of the profession by weeding out third parties, but also restricting access to legal representation in practice, as the majority of disputes fell below this threshold.[85] This was in keeping with the intention stated by the initial proposers of the new County Courts that they would be as accessible and simple as possible.[86]

There is also a clear attempt to link the County Courts to the superior courts in an effort to legitimate them: the *Chronicle* advises that the judges keep an eye to the 'dignity', 'decorum' and 'tone' of the superior courts. The following extract is typical of these kinds of editorials:

> The new courts, for all practical purpose, dispense very nearly the same law as the superior courts, and have jurisdiction over almost as many subjects. True, the amount is limited; but that does not affect the real importance of the Courts; for the same legal questions, the same philosophy of evidence, the same care in the judgment, the same skill in the advocacy are required, whether the sum in dispute be 20*l* or 50*l*.[87]

some instances of family members being allowed to act as proxy, and others where they were not. This inconsistency is rectified through the increased crackdown on any unrepresented parties, meaning family members and agents alike were prevented from representing a plaintiff or defendant. There is an interesting link to be made here between the desire of the legal profession to stamp out non-legal representation and the later relationship between the courts and McKenzie Friends.

[81] *County Courts Chronicle* (London, 1 July 1847) 28.

[82] For more on the fascinating question on who has the right to appear, and the role of women as agents, see Finn (n 3) 255–57.

[83] See, eg, *County Courts Chronicle* (London, 2 August 1847); (London, 1 April 1848) 9-15; (London, 1 June 1848); (London, 1 January 1849); (London, 1 May 1849) 119; (London, 1 December 1856); (London, 2 February 1857); (London, 1 July 1858) 161; (London, 1 September 1859); (London, 1 April 1862) 92; (London, 1 July 1862); (London, 1 June 1865); (London, 1 January 1869) 313; (London, 1 January 1869) 2; London (1 May 1863).

[84] County Courts Act 1846, s 91.

[85] There are no court statistics available from the early days of the County Court; however, the *County Courts Chronicle* publishes court statistics for 1867, which notes that of 872,437 plaints issued, 864,193 were issued for sums under £20. Whilst this is more than the £5 limit described above, it is still evidence that the vast majority of cases dealt with in the County Court 20 years into its existence still overwhelmingly involved very small debts. See *County Courts Chronicle* (London, 1 January 1868). Another bulletin on court statistics comes in the following year: see *County Courts Chronicle* (London, 1 November 1868) 541–42.

[86] See R Peel, HC Deb 20 June 1827, vol 17, cols 1350–61.

[87] *County Courts Chronicle* (London, 1 July 1847) 34–35. See also *County Courts Chronicle* (London, 2 December 1867) 282; (London, 1 May 1858) 112; (London, 1 August 1868) 187.

This is reflective of the concerted desire to get these County Courts more in line with the 'dignity' of superior proceedings, thus making them an appropriate forum for respectable professionals. But on the other hand, there was still no appeal avenue *to* the superior courts in the vast majority of cases, as the Newcastle County Court judge points out, 'I am not bound by the specific rules of practice of the superior courts, nor by those of the County Court'.[88]

The attempt to achieve this new hybrid court, where professional standards could be introduced while informality and simplicity could be retained, quickly runs into difficulties. We can see this in the cases reported in the *Chronicle* in the 1840s. For example, in *Phillips v Edwards*, the plaintiff in person fails to make out his case and applies for an adjournment: this is granted, but only on condition that he pays the defendant's costs for attendance that day.[89] But in Newcastle, an illiterate man who fails to bring his daughter to assist him in his plaint is also allowed to adjourn without paying defendant costs.[90] In Warwickshire, the judge states that he will not allow anyone to speak for the plaintiff except a member of the plaintiff's family, but in *Phillips v Edwards*, the brother of the party asking for adjournment is not allowed as the judge refuses to recognise him.[91] Similarly, in *Lloyd v Jones*, the judge will not recognise the plaintiff's wife.[92] Inconsistencies between judges emerge very early, indicative of the separate municipal existence of the previous Courts of Request.[93]

This also means the question of who should have *legal* representation and in what circumstances, also varies. Many judges expressly argue that they want to encourage the presence of attorneys in the new County Courts.[94] But other judges argue that legal representation is unnecessary, stressing that lawyers are a 'luxury, not a necessity'.[95] In *Jennings v Shepherd*, 'His Honour said he should be glad to allow costs where there was any necessity for an attorney's attendance; but in ordinary cases he should not, nor would he lay down any rule, but judge each case *per se*'.[96]

[88] *County Courts Chronicle* (London, 1 June 1847) 1. At the time the judge states this (1847), there are no formal practice rules for County Courts, nor do County Court decisions bind other County Courts. Consequently, the judge is free to make a determination that is not based on any other court's judgment. According to the County Courts Act 1846, s XC, only sums over the value of £5 could be taken to an appeal court, and only at the discretion of the judge.

[89] *County Courts Chronicle* (London, 1 June 1847) 1.

[90] ibid, 1.

[91] ibid 2.

[92] ibid 2.

[93] These inconsistencies are particularly marked as regards the question of who has the right to appear in court. There is, as previously noted, a clear desire to crack down on the uncredentialed 'sham lawyers'. But at the same time, sympathetic commentators note that the majority of those who wish to pursue a claim are tradespersons who have multiple business responsibilities, which may mean that appearing in person is difficult, but who are seeking relief for such a small amount that employing a legal representative would not be a cost-effective decision. See *County Courts Chronicle* (London, 1 April 1852) 45.

[94] This is echoed by the judge in *Martin v Marshall* (London, 1 August 1847).

[95] *County Courts Chronicle* (London, 1 July 1847) 5.

[96] ibid.

This lack of consistency is also apparent in the court environment itself, which greatly exercises the *Chronicle* from the beginning. Consider, for example, this memorable account of Brentford County Court in 1847:

> The Court is held at a public-house, in a room capable of accommodating a hundred or a hundred and fifty persons; the judge, clerk, high bailiff, &c being all seated together at a common tavern table, none of them being distinguished by any badge of office … there must have been not less than five hundred people present, at the lowest calculation. These were distributed in the court (as many as it would most inconveniently hold), and the rest all over the house nearly, the greater part being on the staircase, and a great many, both there and in the court, intoxicated and withall noisy. The disgraceful confusion which these state of things produced is perfectly indescribable; not to be witnessed, I hope and believe, in any other court of law in the kingdom.[97]

The choice of venue, a public house, draws attention to the lack of dedicated court buildings at this point in time.[98] The writer goes on to note:

> It was the whole work, and hard work, too, of the poor wicket keeper or sub bailiff to prevent regular pitched battles, to say nothing of 'words of violence' to check which his continued entreaty was — 'Silence, ladies! silence! You really must be quiet, ladies; and go out if you want to talk'. But little the 'ladies' reckoned, or the gentlemen either, for they still cut their jokes and vented their wrath, as the humour was upon them, in the most boisterous manner.[99]

The gloriously mixed metaphors employed by the distressed attorney above emphasise that what he sees is not what he recognises as proper court practice. This is due to the absence of uniformity and distinction, which leads to a lack of respect by the audience and other participants (who, outrageously, felt that they had the right to speak: even *women*!).

But while these accounts are an entertaining demonstration of the lack of standardisation of practice in these new courts, what they also reveal is the social anxiety felt by these attorneys. Larson notes that '[w]ithout … visible signs, respectable common practitioners found themselves helpless against the competition of the unscrupulous and the inept, who proliferated in unregulated markets'.[100] I argue, following Larson, that it is the battle for 'visible signs' that the *Chronicle* wages in the early years of the County Court.[101]

And this explains why attorneys are so upset by proceedings such as those taking place at Brentford. It also explains why time is spent in the *Chronicle* discussing the regulation of dress. One upset writer complains in August 1847 of a professional wearing a 'ginger-beer blouse', commenting that it was 'wholly out

[97] *County Courts Chronicle* (London, 1 September 1847) 77.
[98] See C Graham, *Ordering Law: The Architectural and Social History of the English Law Court to 1914* (London, Routledge, 2003).
[99] *County Courts Chronicle* (London, 1 September 1847) 77.
[100] Larson (n 4)12.
[101] Polden (n 8) 43.

of place and, under the circumstances, disgraceful'.[102] While this might come across at first glance as snobbish, it emphasises the importance of distinction in legitimating courts and the practitioners operating within them. Attorneys are trying to work out *what a proper court is* in the shadow of the nineteenth-century superior courts. It is the growth of these markers of distinction that starts to undermine self-representation, as we begin to see from the 1850s onwards.

VIII. The Disappearance of the Self-Represented Party

> To the Editor of the COUNTY COURTS CHRONICLE
>
> Sir—I have before now expressed my opinion at some length on the CCs. Perhaps you will allow me however to summarise my reasons for thinking any further extension of jurisdiction in these courts most undesirable. 1. The fact of the many *small* yet *defended* and virulently contested cases between an uneducated plaintiff and an obstinate defendant. Everyone who has practised in the rural districts knows the result: Dreadful waste of time, impeded business, and ruffling of judicial equanimity.[103]

The 1850s, 1860s and 1870s in the County Courts was a time of increasing standardisation of practice and creeping formality that manifest in several different areas. By this period, there are codes of rules, all judges have seven years' experience at the Bar and there are qualified registrars.[104] Successive alterations to the statute also raise the ceiling on the amount that can be disputed.[105] The fees cap for attorneys is also continuously raised.[106] This move was undoubtedly partially in response to the *Chronicle*'s repeated advocacy. Both changes mean that by the 1860s and 1870s, financial recompense was reasonable enough not to exclude attorneys from the County Courts, and more begin appearing. At the same time, regulations are tightened to ensure that only credentialed individuals can act as representatives, with an emphasis on weeding out 'sham attorneys'.[107]

On top of these developments, calls for a greater connection to superior courts result in the eventual fusing of the County Courts to the appeal circuit in

[102] *County Courts Chronicle* (London, 2 August 1847) 59. Other references to judicial costume, dress and dignity appear in *County Courts Chronicle* (London, 1 August 1868) 187; (London, 2 December 1867) 282.

[103] *County Courts Chronicle* (London, 1 December 1870) 285.

[104] Johnson (n 37) 11.

[105] This begins at amounts below £20 (or higher amounts if the parties agree that the amount awarded will not exceed £20) in 1847. It is then raised to £50 in 1850 and £100 in 1903.

[106] Section 91 of the original Act determined the ceiling of pay awardable to an attorney in the County Courts. By 1850 a separate section of the Act (s 6) dealt specifically with fees to be paid to attorneys and barristers, stating that fees should not exceed £2 10 shillings and that court costs were to be allocated at the discretion of the judge. This was revisited in 1852, 1856, and 1875, with continual incremental increases in fees before the 1882 reform, essentially moving the question of fees into the court costs, thus facilitating an expansion of professional presence.

[107] Larson (n 4) 14.

the 1870s.[108] This was part of wider, sweeping changes to the courts through the Judicature Acts of the 1870s.[109] This fusion does not result in universal acclaim. As one *Chronicle* correspondent expresses it, such fusion would be 'subjecting a sphere to the rule of the square'.[110] As he goes on, 'we have often to protest against the public's allowing itself to be guided upon questions of law reform by the profession, whose habits or interests are bound up with the abuses'.[111] However, this development also reflects the County Court's success. By the 1870s, it was adjudicating on almost all civil matters, having been granted jurisdiction on bankruptcy and admiralty matters. Common practitioners now had access to areas of practice that had once been completely out of their reach.[112]

These changes are reflected in the *Chronicle*, which by the mid-1850s was a noticeably different publication. By late 1849, the *Chronicle* was reporting relevant superior court decisions.[113] While it is only logical that superior court decisions should be reported once there are precedents that bind the court, the decision to include superior court decisions *before* there are official appeal courts underlines the *Chronicle*'s strong desire to emphasise that the County Courts are of equal respectability and scrupulousness to the superior courts. These changes also meant that the County Court reports were given much less prominence than originally, with the bulk of reporting now being of superior court decisions.

By June 1849, there were 18 pages of superior court decisions before the County Court decisions (covering less than six pages). Ten years later, in June 1859, the *Chronicle* contained only three pages of County Court reports out of 16 pages in total. By June 1869, County Courts accounts are no longer listed: the report section is dedicated to superior courts only, and the reports are grouped together by subject matter (contract, equity and so on).[114] There are four County Court reports, each of which covers a single case, represented on both sides, with extended discussion on a point of law for between half a page to two pages. This format continued throughout the 1880s, with it being difficult to find any County Court reports in the publication, let alone a self-represented party.[115] By 1889, the *Chronicle* was described as 'a report of cases required in the County Court and argued and determined in the Superior Courts'.[116]

[108] *County Courts Chronicle* (London, 6 May 1850) 138.
[109] *County Courts Chronicle* (London, 1 July 1875) 163.
[110] *County Courts Chronicle* (London, 6 May 1850) 138.
[111] ibid 138.
[112] An account of a Junior Bar meeting in the *County Courts Chronicle* describes this accumulation of jurisdiction as resulting in attorneys effectively 'stealing' their work and suggesting they are owed compensation. See *County Courts Chronicle* (London, 1 February 1868) 53.
[113] *County Courts Chronicle* (London, 1 December 1849) 328.
[114] This formula continues into the 1870s onwards, giving, for example, a table of contents in which the subheading under 'contract' might be 'Liverpool county court; a novel question of ownership liability': *County Courts Chronicle* (London, 1 October 1870) 237.
[115] Again, it is important to reiterate that the majority of cases in the County Court were still small debts, and probably still unrepresented – but in the absence of clear statistics on representation, this remains speculative.
[116] *County Courts Chronicle* (London, 1 July 1889).

Throughout this period, we also see repeated advocacy by the *Chronicle* to formalise procedure even further. The following extract comes from the *Chronicle* in 1870:

> I ask why should not a defendant be obliged to set out in writing a statement of his defence, and deliver it to the plaintiff or his attorney within a limited time before the hearing, and that in default the plaintiff be at liberty to sign judgement if the cause exceed a certain criteria?[117]

The idea that defendants should submit written outlines of their defence was not new; in fact the initial proposal came in 1849, two years into the new County Courts.[118] But what it *does* point to is the degree to which the presence of legal professionals in the court is normalising the need for legal skills. The argument outlined above is an argument recognisable today: that it is a simple matter to submit a written statement in plain English. But as we already know, such a requirement is far from a simple task for a self-represented litigant.[119]

And here we see the slippery slope: as more attorneys frequent the County Court, legal skills become seen as essential. As a concerned letter writer notes in 1868, 'now we fear very much that the extended jurisdiction has been given to the CC without sufficiently providing facilities for the useful exercise of it. Procedure has not been adapted to the needs of the suitors'.[120] This shift happens without, necessarily, recognition of how these changes might exclude self-represented parties from being able to act effectively.[121]

IX. A Change in Attitude

The changes taking place in the County Courts resulted in a sea-change in attitude towards self-representation in the *Chronicle* too. In 1852, the *Chronicle* emphasised that 'every man has a common law right to appear and conduct his own case in

[117] *County Courts Chronicle* (London, 1 December 1870) 270; see also *County Courts Chronicle* (London, 1 November 1870) 247.

[118] *County Courts Chronicle* (London, 1 February 1849).

[119] It is also during this time that the stamp duty on newspapers was abolished, leading to more press reporting on matters of interest in the courts, including, occasionally, that of self-represented parties. For example, the *London Observer* (12 November 1860) reports on *Sneddon v Sneddon*, noting 'In the probate and divorce court, a judgment was given … favourable to the lady who, with so much ability and self-possession, has conducted her own case before the court after her counsel declined to proceed': ibid 6. The tone of admiration here indicates that those who represent themselves can be viewed in a heroic light – in this case, because the lady had no choice but to represent herself when her counsel would not. The self-represented litigant winning (even if only partly) against the odds is a recurring theme, reminiscent of more modern examples, such as the McLibel case (see *McDonald's Corporation v Steel & Morris* [1997] EWHC QB 36).

[120] *County Courts Chronicle* (London, 1 February 1868).

[121] This is not always the case. In 1849, the *Chronicle* praises the County Court's ongoing use of 'plain English' instead of formal pleading: *County Courts Chronicle* (London, 1 February 1849) 44.

any Court in the kingdom'.[122] But 'The Suitor' section has disappeared by August 1849, indicating a presumption of the normality of legal representation even at this early point. From 1852–62, the section reporting County Court decisions was renamed 'County Court Curiosities'. This section covered 'amusing' incidents, frequently ones that occurred at the expense of self-represented litigants.[123] A good example of the tone of this section was reported in the memorable case of 'Who "robbed" the dead pig? *Damage to a pig*, 6'.[124] In this case, the parties were both self-represented and the dispute was over whether or not the defendant disembowelled ('robbed') a pig to the value of 6 shillings of innards against the instructions of the plaintiff. Citing the exchanges verbatim, the report becomes a kind of mini-play, complete with laughter from the court and dramatic escalation, culminating in the plaintiff's flopping the pig corpse on to the courtroom table: '(continued laughter, while plaintiff tumbled the two lumps of pork about the court-table with extraordinary agility, to the great amusement of the spectators)'.[125]

Most significantly, in September 1866, the *Chronicle*, reporting an incident involving a self-represented party, commented '[t]his seems an exemplification of a hackneyed observation that a man who is his own lawyer has not a Solomon for his client'.[126] By this time, then, we have a reversal of the original 1849 stance of the *Chronicle* seen in the opening epigraph of this chapter. As we saw then, there was a commitment to the role of self-representation in the County Courts and an implicit presumption of its normality. But less than 20 years later, the idea that an individual would go to the County Court without a lawyer is seen as indicative of a lack of judgement.

This belief in self-represented parties' lack of judgement is made explicit by one *Chronicle* writer in 1859 advocating the abolition of trial by jury.[127] The author outlines exactly what legal training provides:

> The faculty of hearing without being deluded by sophistry and eloquence ... The Greeks fabled that the Goddess of Wisdom sprang fully armed and grown from the head of Zeus. The English seriously believe that judicial wisdom springs forth mature from every tradesman's head. This is a fit article of faith for a nation of shopkeepers.[128]

[122] *County Courts Chronicle* (London, 1 June 1847) 10.
[123] *County Courts Chronicle* (London, 1 February 1860) 14.
[124] ibid, 12–13.
[125] ibid. The reportage of humorous cases, whether involving self-represented parties or not, is common in the wider press mentions of the County Courts at the time. Where cases are reported, they tend to be those that may be of wider interest – sometimes for legal reasons, but often because they are unusual. For example, multiple papers, including *The Guardian* and *The Patriot*, reported on the case of Mr Samuel Marsden, whose cat had been shot by a gamekeeper. *The Patriot* notes the 'considerable amusement' of the court as the defence sought to establish that cats were 'ordo fere naturae, and therefore worse than worthless'. See *The Guardian* (London, 2 January 1850) 9 and *The Patriot* (London, 3 January 1850) 2.
[126] *County Courts Chronicle* (London, 1 September 1866) 134.
[127] *County Courts Chronicle* (London, 1 August 1859) 108.
[128] ibid; *County Courts Chronicle* (London, 1 June 1859) 66.

This argument – that those who were not lawyers lacked the ability to effectively pursue or defend a claim – was common in the *Chronicle* from the 1850s onwards.[129] The irony here is that while the argument for the necessity of legal skills was initially targeted at weeding out 'sham' attorneys, it eventually undermined self-represented parties too. Once the proposition that only properly educated, credentialed and regulated professionals could provide representation, the discourse quickly widened to suggest that only such qualified individuals had any business at all being in court.

These changes did not, however, stop individuals from self-representing. As Paul Johnson points out. '[t]here was no obvious sign of this growing legal formalism crowding out the layman's direct access to the due process of law'.[130] But the self-represented party tended to be either ignored, or mocked and derided, by the 1870s.[131] At this point, this was arguably because self-represented parties ceased to be valued informants. Because they lacked the specialism to understand the nature of their dispute in legal terms, the information they contributed became irrelevant and counterproductive. Thus, two factors existed that persist today: a derogatory attitude towards self-represented parties, and a tendency to render such parties invisible in official legal accounts.

X. Whoops! We Let the Litigants In

Amusing incident at the law courts

In a Divisional Court of Queen's Bench on Wednesday, Miss Carroll, a lady well known in the courts as a litigant, appeared in person before Mr Justice Denman and Mr Justice Vaughan Williams. She said she had an 'ex parte' application to make

—*Mr Justice Denman*: What is your name?

—*The Applicant*: Octavia Carroll; otherwise, 'the lady without a name'. (Laughter.) My application is this:—I have obtained two orders to enable me to call witnesses, but the committee of the Incorporated Law Society keep the orders and will not give them up to me.

—*Mr Justice Denman*: But we can't do anything unless we have the order before us. We have nothing to go upon.

—*The Applicant*: My Lord, give unto Caesar that which is Caesar's. (Laughter.)

—*Mr Justice Denman*: There is nothing before us.

—*The Applicant*: My Lord, England expects that every man this day will do his duty. (Laughter.)

[129] *County Courts Chronicle* (London, 1 June 1847) 5; *County Courts Chronicle* (London, 1 January 1861) 25–26; *County Courts Chronicle* (London, 1 December 1870) 285.

[130] Johnson (n 37) 17.

[131] For example, the self-represented party is an 'eccentric and talkative little man' (*County Courts Chronicle* (London, 1 October 1870) 14). See also *County Courts Chronicle* (London, 1 January 1861) 25–26; *Grantham Journal* (Grantham, 15 August 1891) 7.

—*Mr Justice Denman*: I can't help that. (Laughter.) We have no duty to do now. Sit down.

—Miss Carroll then made a profound bow and left the court.[132]

The above sketching out of the development of the County Court seeks to demonstrate the degree to which self-representation becomes derided in tandem with broader developments in the nineteenth-century professional project. But what does this mean for the creation of the term 'litigant in person'? The term itself never appears in the *County Court Chronicle.*[133] But it does begin to make an appearance in other publications in the 1880s. By that time, it almost invariably refers to the pathological or vexatious litigant:

> Mrs Thompson, the well-known litigant in person at the London Law Courts, was charged at Marlborough Street Police Court with being drunk in Piccadilly. The defendant emphatically denied the offence, but the constable's view as to her condition was confirmed by medical evidence and a small fine was imposed by Mr Hannay.[134]

In 1884, the *London Evening Standard* is talking of woman who is 'well-known' as a 'lady litigant in person'.[135] In 1890, *The Morpeth Herald* too refers to a lady 'litigant in person'.[136] While the proceedings relating to Mrs Thompson, referred to above, are clearly criminal, it suggests the kind of individual that was indicative of those who self-represented. Mrs Thompson, serially litigious and incompetent, is already recognisable as the stereotypical LiP we see today.[137] By the time the term appears, it is also clear that successful LiPs are exceptional.[138]

But what exactly does the term 'litigant in person' mean? Its first appearance in case law, in 1896, occurs in the observation that, 'in case law, every litigant in person has an absolute right of audience'.[139] But what this chapter has

[132] *Grantham Journal* (Grantham, Saturday 15 August 1891) 7.
[133] *County Courts Chronicle* (London, 1 September 1866) 194.
[134] *Falkirk Herald* (Grangemouth, 20 October 1897).
[135] *The Standard (London Evening)* (London, 5 November 1884) 3.
[136] *Morpeth Herald* (Morpeth, 21 June 1890).
[137] *Yorkshire Evening Post* (Leeds, 27 September 1922) 5.
[138] See *Pall Mall Gazette* (London, 18 January 1894); The Star (Guernsey, 6 May 1890); *Dundee Evening Telegraph* (Dundee, 30 July 1913). An interesting case in point of the growth of high-profile LiPs is that of Georgina Weldon, whose story could fill a whole book, let alone a footnote. Mrs Weldon, whose husband tried to have her committed to an institution, successfully brought civil suits against all those who had assisted in the attempt: she was known for conducting multiple lawsuits at the same time, and for always representing herself. As a high-profile personality and a prominent spiritualist, her cases were reported with relish by numerous publications: see, eg, *London Magnet* (London, 6 April 1885); *Lloyds Weekly London Newspaper* (London, 16 March 1884); *The Guardian* (Manchester, 30 July 1884). The tone adopted when she was discussed is typical; much was made of her spiritualism, with the newspapers noting that she believed her dog 'had the spirit of a man'. When the courts suggested that hearing voices was a sign of madness, she noted 'Joan of Arc heard voices: was she crazy? You see, I do not believe in mad doctors, but I do believe in spirits.' See *Lloyds Weekly London Newspaper* (London, 16 March 1884) 7.
[139] *The Queen v Justices of London* [1896] 1 QB 659, 662. This case is significant in underlining LiPs' rights of access to the higher courts; earlier newspapers reported cases where LiPs were denied a hearing. See, eg, *Edinburgh Evening News* (Edinburgh, 10 August 1892). While this is a Scottish case, it is notable that the LiP prevented from being heard protests that there is no evidence of such a rule banning self-represented litigants.

sought to demonstrate is that a 'litigant in person' is much more than this. It is a concept that only makes sense when legal representation is the norm. More than this, the term only exists in the context where self-represented parties have lost their less formal forums. The term 'litigant in person' references the context of a formalised legal process indicative of the latter stages of the professional project: where unregulated practitioners have been largely stamped out, and where strict attention is paid to the distinction between legal practitioners and laypersons. The appearance of the term, then, does not signify LiPs' incorporation into legal process; instead, it marks their *distance* from what is legally appropriate. Litigants in person are created in the moment when they are no longer competent: they are established as a phenomenon by virtue of their failure to mimic legal professionals. The LiPs' incompetence, then, is not a failure of their role, it *is* their role. Their inability to perform successfully (although there are exceptions, these are only considered as exceptions) reinforces the need for legal professionals.[140]

Tellingly, while self-represented parties were mocked in the *Chronicle*, criticism of LiPs was overwhelmingly found in the higher courts (perhaps telling us why the term never appeared in the *Chronicles*).[141] For example, in 1892, the *Gloucester Herald* ran an interview with a County Court judge. The judge noted the difficulties caused by LiPs in the superior courts as compared with the relatively trouble-free experience of them in the lower courts, where, as we have seen, they were complained about by legal professionals but persisted, largely unnoticed. And this leads to the most compelling reason *why* LiPs are talked about the way they are: it is because the fusing of the County Courts to the appeal circuit gave self-representing parties access to the superior courts. This means that parts of the legal profession that had no association with the County Courts – specifically the Bar and the superior court judiciary – met self-represented litigants for what was likely to be the first time in their professional lives. It is the collision between the unrepresented parties who had been operating in parallel court processes, *separately* from those working in the superior courts, that creates the LiP. This is why the term does not appear in the *County Court Chronicle* but emerges at the time of fusion with the appellate courts. The decision to integrate the County Courts with the superior courts seems to have been taken *without realising* that not only would standardised practice filter downwards, but also that self-represented parties would filter upwards: and by the time they got there, they were LiPs.[142]

[140] See Letter from 'Parochial Critics' in *County Courts Chronicle* (London, 1 November 1870) 262.

[141] *Aberdeen Evening Express* (Aberdeen, 9 August 1892).

[142] Another good example of the growth of high-profile, litigious LiPs is that of Alexander Chaffers, a former solicitor, who mounted multiple claims in multiple courts that eventually led to his being the first individual branded a vexatious litigant and prevented from pursuing further litigation. His litigation spree began in the 1870s and continued for decades, including at one point suing the Archbishop of Canterbury in the County Courts. His claims, which became increasingly outlandish, set the template for much of what we perceive to be emblematic of the stereotype of a LiP. For an excellent and detailed account of Chaffers' life and suits, see M Taggart, 'Alexander Chaffers and the Genesis of the Vexatious Actions Act 1896' (2004) 63 *CLJ* 656.

XI. Conclusion

In this chapter I have argued that the LiP and attitudes towards the LiP are inseparable: the LiP is a role of failure, created as a by-product of the professional project in action, seen through developments in the new County Courts, which include increasing standardisation and distinction. Critical to this development is the fusing of the County Courts to the superior courts: once LiPs gained access to the superior courts, the 'gap' between their skills, behaviour and knowledge and those in the higher court proceedings marked them out as far from what can be considered appropriate or productive. But while this explains *why* there is such a negative attitude towards LiPs – they are productively anomalous, their presence emphasises the competence of the profession – this has never prevented individuals from self-representing. Litigants in person are still there, even if they are not written about. The very irritation they cause to many legal professionals informs us of their continued presence. The problem, of course, is that when legal records only publish matters of 'legal interest', most actions involving LiPs go unnoticed, which is why we do not find it easy to find material about them and it is why we have so much trouble understanding their perspectives.

But what this chapter has also tried to show is that as long as LiPs operate in an environment constituted by a professionalism that functions through exclusion of non-credentialed parties, it is difficult to envision them as being perceived positively. So whilst LiP behaviour may vary from individual to individual, the wider negative perceptions may have much less to do with anything specific LiPs *do*, and far more to do with the structural development of a profession that, in its success in extending its ambit to the lower courts, has largely displaced the self-represented party. In chapter 3, we turn to the voices of the LiPs: their experiences in legal processes underscore the challenges faced with existing only in the context of the latter stages of the professional project.

3

Who are Litigants in Person?

I. Introduction

So, who are LiPs? This is a simple question to pose, but a hard one to answer. So much of the time, LiPs remain unknowable in the civil justice system: in Moorhead and Sefton's 2005 study, for example, they had to infer that individuals were LiPs because of the absence of a representative's name. Litigants in person therefore exist in the spaces and recesses of legal professionals. And that leads us to another question: can those who are *not* legal professionals constitute a meaningful group in and of themselves? As the previous chapters outlined, we speak of LiPs in a way that suggests more stability than exists. As this chapter will show, the stories told here are not generalisable as to demographic, legal issue or personality type, childhood experience, level of education or income. There is a variety of attitudes towards legal institutions, a variety of experience of such legal institutions and a variety of beliefs about authority.[1] As John Baldwin noted, 'the average litigant or the typical court user does not exist, and any attempt to generalise about them is hazardous and probably in most circumstances misleading'.[2] So, with this warning in mind, what this chapter does instead is to think about who the people I interviewed are, before and beyond being labelled as LiPs.

I start by exploring material that addresses LiPs' lives up to the first point of contact with legal proceedings, looking at interviewees' childhoods, including formative experiences such as bullying and interactions with authority figures. I then canvass what contact interviewees had with the legal profession prior to becoming involved in any legal proceedings. These questions allow a range of experiences and attitudes to emerge, from those who have idealised beliefs about authority, to those who have explicitly negative experiences, for example being racially profiled by police. Even within this relatively small sample, though, what section II suggests is that we are on shaky ground if we assume LiPs as more likely to be anti-authority, conspiracy-minded or distrustful people: they simply do not cohere as a meaningful category beyond being assigned the label of LiP.[3]

[1] This is in keeping with Hazel Genn's findings. See H Genn, *Paths to Justice* (Oxford, Hart Publishing, 1999).

[2] J Baldwin, 'Litigants' Experience of Adjudication in the County Courts (1999) 18 *Civil Justice Quarterly* 12, 20.

[3] These questions, as outlined in the introduction, are intended to explore some of the pre-existing suppositions in the literature about LiPs that tends to assume such individuals are a 'type'.

So, what *can* we learn from these disparate stories? First, we can start to understand these individuals as people; bringing them back as fully formed characters, not individuals caught (or not caught, as the case may be) in statistical data. The importance of this, in a system that is largely incapable of doing this, cannot be overstated. Second, we can start to think about how these individuals become LiPs. Here, I suggest a commonality does emerge. Most of the interviewees in this sample had negative experiences with legal professionals they had instructed. They did not choose to go it alone but ended up losing their trust in their representative's ability to assist them. This seems to be a key factor in creating LiPs, at least in this small sample.[4] So, what this chapter ultimately suggests connects to a central claim of this book: to understand more about *how* and *why* these individuals come to be LiPs, the answer does not lie in their personalities or life experiences alone; instead we need to think in more detail about their relationship and contact with legal professionals.

II. Early Lives

Marie, the youngest participant in this study, was in her mid-20s at the time of interview. Born in the North, she had a violent, aggressive father and a mother 'who didn't know how to look after us properly'. She tells me 'One of my earliest memories is my dad would shout for some reason, he'd try grabbing hold of me, I'd run to the dog's bed and he went to try and drag me out of the dog's bed and the dog bit him [laugh].' Taken into care at the age of 6 with her sibling, she would later find out that her mother had also been in care as a child:

> I found out that's because she'd been placed in homes … from the age of two so you never had that care herself, so she was never able to show us any emotions or love or connections with us 'cause she was, that's the way she were brought up.

Moved around multiple care homes, Marie tells me:

> I actually walked into school, I think I was only like six or seven, and I actually turned round and told the kids I was an alien and I think that in itself sums up how a child feels when they're taken into care and everything's changing and there's no consistency and there's nothing there to actually say to the child that they're normal.

For Marie, the constant moving around from foster home to foster home had a profound impact on her ability to trust people:

> It set up basically the mechanisms I've got today. I do, I find it hard to like relate to people, I find it very hard to trust people, I find it very hard to make friends and maintain friendships because at that point in time because the moving, movements, being

[4] This echoes the findings in McKeever et al's exploration of LiPs in Northern Ireland, which also identifies this as one factor motivating individuals to become LiPs. See G McKeever et al, *Litigants in Person in Northern Ireland: Barriers to Participation* (Ulster, Ulster University, 2018).

> in care. It was just where you'd, you just, basically you just grind to a halt and any emotions, any attachments because everyone's been broken since you've got attached, you just learn to not get attached.

Bullied at school, Marie aspired to be a vet but left school at 16, became pregnant at 19 and was 20 when her son was taken into care by social services. She describes the anxiety she had around having and keeping her son:

> It was more, I was petrified of losing my son, being bombarded with assessments and this, that and the other you know what I mean it was, again it wasn't normal. I felt, I felt I was being targeted because I had been in care. I felt I was basically guaranteed to lose my child. It prevented me from bonding with my son when I first had him and it was very, very difficult to cope with not only being a new parent, but being a new parent with social services involved is, it puts so much pressure on parents. It puts so much distress.

In her own words, when her son was taken into care, 'My life stopped at that point.' Since then, Marie has been involved in litigation in one way or another to try to be reunited with her child.[5]

Clive, on the other hand, was born in 1932 and grew up outside London, until war broke out and he moved with his father, who had a reserved occupation, to Liverpool. Clive remembers bombing raids over Liverpool and parading in gas masks as a child.[6] After the war, the family moved south again to a large, detached house, and Clive attended grammar school. Describing his family as 'lower middle class', Clive was one of seven children. Keen on the boy scouts and sports, Clive does not recall being bullied, any violence at home or any issues at school:

> There must have been cases and there was corporal punishment at school you know you had to drop your trousers and you got three of the best with the cane but I don't think I ever had that, I wouldn't have been worried if I had you know it was almost a badge of honour if Flash had given you three of the best, you know that, it was a little bit, it was sort of shades of a public school in that sense.

Going into the RAF, Clive then started a series of businesses. Put into administration in the early 1980s, much of his subsequent litigation relates to pursuing claims against banks and mortgage providers relating to the bankruptcy of his business and repossession of his home, which, as he puts it, 'in broad brush is why I come to be living here in a rented house'.

Unlike Clive, Anna was born after the war, but she also remembers a childhood strongly influenced by it. Describing her childhood as mainly 'sad memories', she recalls 'being locked in the cellar' by her Polish mother, who 'had such horrific experiences during the war that it badly affected her, and although she wanted

[5] We shall hear more about Marie's story in ch 5.

[6] Martin also has memories of the Second World War, recounting the story of a German plane that was caught in searchlights and shot down, and hearing air raid sirens. Martin's litigation is similar to Clive's, beginning with a failed business, a disputed bankruptcy and consequent disputes arising from banks' attempts to repossess their properties.

the best for us, she believed that excessive discipline was the way forward'. She continues 'I've got very strong memories of my mother being very upset over what the Jews did to her, her family and her friends during the war.'[7] Her father died in an accident while she was still living at home, and she began helping her mother with the family business until it was sold. Anna attended religious schools as her mother was a devout Catholic, and recalls the strict environment there:

> They were strict disciplinarians, I can remember the convent that I was at between 11 and 16, we'd have this assembly every morning in this great big hall and we'd stand in these lines, and quite often the headteacher would stand up there and say that somebody had done something wrong. Yes, like – I don't know – flooded the toilets or whatever, and I would always stand there and think, *she probably thinks it's me*. I would stand there and go bright red and yet it wasn't me but that's the way I would think.

When I asked her why she had that reaction, she said 'I ended up, I mean I had very low self-esteem, so by the time I had left home I had very low self-esteem'. Anna was raped sometime after leaving home and going to university, which she says worsened her self-esteem. She never reported the rape. Anna became suicidal in her early 20s. She managed to finish her degree after time spent in a mental health facility, and she became a teacher. She describes herself as determined to ensure her children were more confident and self-assured than she was. She explains:

> So, you know, that [lack of self-esteem] was a big problem. So, the one thing I was very focused on with both my children was that they were going to be, have good self-esteem, assertive skills, be able to run their own business, stand on their own two feet. They weren't going to go through what I went through, and that's the way they've turned out.

For Anna, defending herself in legal proceedings has been part of her ability to 'stand on her own feet'.[8] Anna's protracted litigation in various courts and tribunals includes bankruptcy proceedings, medical negligence claims, employment tribunal cases and others, and her account of this is marked by antisemitic and Freemason conspiracy theories about the courts, lawyers and banks.[9]

[7] Anna's antisemitism was a marked feature of her interview, although she claims she did not share her mother's views until later in life. Antisemitism was a feature of a number of these interviews: this is dealt with explicitly in ch 6. A small note here to say that oral histories are predicated on interviewees' being allowed to tell their story without interruption: the above is a good example of the ethical conundrums this poses, which I think needs further reflection. In all these cases, I did not tell the interviewees I was Jewish.

[8] In this respect, we might see the substance of her litigation as not directly connected to her childhood experience like Marie's, but her attitude to litigation as a means of independence or self-defence seems informed by it.

[9] Russell has a similar litigation profile: also antisemitic and talking of Masonic conspiracy, Russell has been involved in multiple proceedings relating to bankruptcy, repossession proceedings and employment tribunals. There is a clear link between conspiracist antisemitic beliefs and those who are pursuing litigation against banks and other financial institutions (although the exception to this is Martin, who has a similar litigation profile but is Jewish and who does not entertain conspiracy theories.).

Unlike Anna, Tim has only ever been involved in one legal proceeding. Jewish and a Freemason, Tim grew up in a middle-class neighbourhood and was in his early 30s at the time of interview. He talks about being an only child: 'obviously the love and devotion that you get from your parents having spoken to other friends of mine who are only children, you know rather than it being spread out over various people it ends up being focused in one respect'. Tim describes a liberal, artistic environment growing up, where his parents read *The Guardian*. He attended an Orthodox synagogue and a Jewish school, although he says he did not feel particularly religious. He recalls an experience of antisemitism in his teens:

> I was on my way back from school probably sixth form, I was on the bus, coming through Edgware and it must have been either Rosh Hashanah or Yom Kippur, one of the festivals or just beforehand because everyone was out sort of buying all their bits and pieces. I was having this wonderful chat with this guy, old boy sat next to me and we were sort of talking away and all of a sudden he just came up with this line, 'Oh these bloody Jews they're taking up all our spaces', and for whatever reason I never really felt this before, I felt the need, I didn't say anything I just put my hand in my pocket, took out my kippah and put it on my head. He looked at me and he got off at the next top and carried on walking the same way as the bus, so I'm guessing he didn't feel comfortable for whatever reason, and at that point I was like okay, there's a sense of Jewish pride there somewhere.

Achieving at school, Tim went on to a prestigious university and got a law degree, although he does not now practise as a lawyer. Tim ended up as a LiP in the small claims court, trying to recoup losses incurred when he pulled out of a house purchase because he argued that the seller had failed to disclose information. He was unsuccessful.

Charles, in his 40s at time of interview, had a far stricter upbringing. He recalls being told very early in life by his grandmother (who raised him in Jamaica, prior to his joining his parents in the UK) not to trust people and to be careful with whom he became friends:

> Because I was always sort of told that you can't really trust, you've got to be mindful of other people and if you have too many people around you, you can't really control what happens, sorry you can't trust everybody so it's better to just have one or two friends. We were just told not to have too many friends because there are people in Jamaica who could be quite jealous and envious of you and sometimes you'd never know what they would do, it was always that suspicion that if they didn't like you they could poison you. [Laughs.] That's just the way we were brought up.

He recalls extensive racial abuse in his childhood, noting that in his case this was a serious issue at school, and he remembers his teachers' failure to do anything about it, as well as perpetuating discriminatory attitudes towards him:

> I say, school wasn't a very good experience for me because my brother who was a couple of years older, he went to another school … [A]t the time there was only a handful of Black people there, because there wasn't really that many Blacks in this country. There was about maybe two or three Blacks and maybe one or two Indians. And the racial abuse, it was just rife. You know it was really, really terrible.

He felt that most teachers 'wrote you off' and expected less from him, putting him in inappropriately lower sets:

> [A]cademically I was actually quite good, my maths and English were quite good because we had to learn tables and that sort of stuff but unfortunately when I came here all that suffered because they assumed that because you're a West Indian you can't speak English and that sort of stuff and put you into a remedial stream and while I could join up and all that sort of stuff in Jamaica, I had to start all over again.

This led to his being 'fairly quiet and reserved' and 'sort of protective of myself'. Charles experienced violence at home when he came to the UK. Leaving home as soon as he could (he won a scholarship to college), he recounts:

> It was because of the beatings. I didn't think, I thought they were unjustified. I think you can scold a child if they do something wrong … but what I say is you could say it's justified, not that you should, but I could say it's justified if we were doing something wrong but when you're not actually doing anything wrong … She [Charles's mother] was always the instigator and she asked him [Charles's father] to beat us. That's when the strap would come out and sometimes we would go out when we were young teenagers we would go out and come in a bit late and somebody who hadn't gone out would open the window for us and we would sneak in and Dad would get the strap and beat us and that's how it went. I think I got beaten a couple of times and thought no, this isn't going to happen again and eventually left.

Charles has been involved in multiple litigations spanning decades, relating to disputes over a shared business, a claim against his former solicitor, custody proceedings and an employment tribunal case.[10]

In contrast to Charles's experiences of violence and uncertainty, Oliver describes his childhood as 'spoiled'. One of the older interviewees, he was in his mid-70s at time of interview and was born towards the end of the Second World War:

> Silver spoon in my mouth. Nothing, if mother decided if I needed to learn to ballroom dance, mother made sure that I had dancing shoes, you know, those shiny things. What was I then, thirteen, fourteen years old. Nothing was too much.

Oliver, from a wealthy, upper middle-class family, remembers his father's being extremely busy, and so describes how their gardener took on a 'proxy father' role towards him before he was sent to boarding school, as were all of his siblings. He was aware of his privilege at a relatively young age:

> [W]hen I got up to about fourteen or fifteen at school, I then began to realise that I was one of the privileged. And that some of the boys that were sent from Africa and various countries to be at this school, there was no money left for them to do anything other than the basic education. Like I had extra music lessons to try and learn to play the piano. I had extra French lessons and physics lessons to get into university and without those I would not have got in.

[10] Charles's story will be discussed in more detail in section V.

Oliver's litigation results from a dispute with the police, who he alleges assaulted him. Oliver believes that because he pursued litigation against them, the police have subsequently gone out of their way to actively harass and undermine him, including repeatedly arresting him and pursuing what he perceives to be a vindictive campaign against him. Oliver's litigation has been going on now for over 30 years.

So, what do we do with this snapshot? As the above shows, the individuals in this sample range in ages, education, income, socio-economic circumstances, religion, political attitude and more. Other interviewees not detailed here report childhoods where some were fulfilled, some were abandoned, some were separated from their parents and others unhappily coexisted with their parents. Some experienced security and some experienced abuse. In this respect, this echoes what Hazel Genn made explicit in *Judging Civil Justice*:

> [O]ne of the problems in understanding civil justice is its complexity in terms of range of subject matter and configurations of parties and that this diversity inhibits conceptualization and theoretical development – so many different types of parties, so many different types of dispute.[11]

Perhaps, then, these accounts serve to remind us that just as wide a sample exists amongst all those who act as LiPs in our complex civil justice system, and just as many stories could be told.

III. Contact with Authorities

So there is perhaps little we can obviously take from accounts of early childhood here, beyond a confirmation of their diversity. But what about other aspects of interviewees' formative years? There is a suggestion in the literature on LiPs that they may be more likely to be difficult or disruptive people.[12] And yet they are also people who continue to go to law. In this respect, an interesting contradiction emerges: LiPs are viewed as being both 'anti' authority, in the sense that they deviate from the rules (particularly relating to how they should behave), and 'pro' authority, in the sense that they continue to invest in the belief that the legal system can deliver justice, whatever that might mean.[13] As I have already suggested in this book, I am dubious about the notion of the 'disruptive' LiP and sceptical of the assumption that this is attributable to an individual's psychology. It seems far more important to consider the circumstances in which one is attempting to act, and the constraints and limits placed on that behaviour, before pathologising it.

[11] H Genn, *Judging Civil Justice: the 2008 Hamlyn Lectures* (Cambridge, Cambridge University Press, 2009) 11.

[12] I Freckelton, 'Querulent Paranoia and the Vexatious Complainant' (1988) 11 *International Journal of Law and Psychiatry* 127; N Bedford and M Taylor, 'Model No More: Querulent Behaviour, Vexatious Litigants and the Vexatious Proceedings Act 2005 (QLD)' (2014) 24 *Journal of Judicial Administration* 46.

[13] How LiPs ought to behave is the subject of ch 5 of this book, and attitudes towards justice are explored in more detail in ch 6.

In this respect, similarly, being 'anti-authority' is surely meaningless if we are not considering what authority is being invoked and what legitimacy that authority possesses. As Phil Scraton notes, when considering childhood:

> The ritualization of childhood … maps the progression of the child through his or her stages of development. At the level of appearances the moments of celebration, from birthdays to prize-givings to religious ceremonies, are child-centred. Yet they function also as adult-defined practices of conformity. Beginning with initiations into familial, community, religious cultural and institutional practices they become profound processes through which children are socialized and conditioned. Deviation from the charted path inevitably leads to condemnation, punishment and even expulsion (from school, from church, from home). Within this context of discipline, regulation and correctionalism, passive or active resistance by children and young people is always defined as negative as a challenge to legitimate authority.[14]

Seeing 'anti-authoritarian' behaviour as implicitly negative, particularly in childhood, is highly problematic. Indeed, given the questionable legitimacy of some institutional authorities, it is arguable that comparison across 'authorities' is also meaningless. But what is of interest here is to think about how LiPs encountered, and understood, legal agents and other individuals who are part of the fabric of the legal landscape, such as the police. While this may not tell us *how* individuals might behave, nor predict that they might be LiPs, it does start to fill in the gaps a little as to what picture of law and legal practice these individuals have, and how they feel about institutions of authority: at the very least, it can fill out the 'horizon of expectations' before they came to law, and such expectations *can* be meaningful in understanding how they felt when they came to law.[15]

Some interviewees, like Marie, had direct experience of police in their lives. This ranged from the serious (Marie's contact was due to the making of a report of the violence she experienced at the hands of her father) to the more mundane (Clive was taken to court and fined in his teens for not having a light on the back of his bicycle). Trevor, a Black British interviewee, recalls that the police repeatedly stopped him when he was growing up. This happened regularly enough for him to discuss it in quite banal terms. When I asked him if he 'ever had any contact with the law at that point when you were growing up for any reason?' he responded 'no, apart from police stopping you, it was the Sus law days'.[16] I asked him to elaborate:

[14] P Scraton, *Childhood in Crisis* (London, University College London, 1997) 163–64.

[15] In this respect, when developing a sense of 'horizon of expectations', this information adds both to an interviewee's sense of 'legal culture', in the sense that Sally Engle Merry called 'the public's attitudes towards the law', and to 'legal consciousness' or 'the extent to which individuals see themselves as defined by the law and entitled to its protection'. See SE Merry, 'What is Legal Culture – An Anthropological Perspective' (2010) 5 *Comparative Law Journal* 43. Legal consciousness and legal culture are concepts both explored further in chs 4–6 of this book.

[16] The term 'sus' ('powers to act on suspicion') refers to the stop-and-search powers used by the police under the Vagrancy Act 1824 prior to enactment of the Police and Criminal Evidence Act (PACE) 1984, which outlined new stop-and-search powers. The sus laws were widely discriminatory and their impact on crime rates minimal, as are the current stop-and search-laws, which disproportionately target Black people and have very low arrest rates. See B Bowling and C Phillips, 'Disproportionate and Discriminatory: Reviewing the Evidence on Police Stop and Search' (2007) 70 *MLR* 936.

> I remember one occasion, this is how long this is going back, we were going to the park, I had a football under my arm bouncing it on the pavement. A police car drives past, again, because remember the area we grew up in was a mainly white location, so, there was someone walking with a football. He stops the car and I've got the ball under my arm now and he said, "Where are you going?' I said, 'I'm going to the park' 'What are you doing round here?' I said, 'I live over that way.' He goes 'Okay, blah, blah, blah, what are you going to do with that then?' and I've got a football under my arm and I'm like, 'I'm going to play football' what does he think I'm going to do with a football; what are you going to do with it? So, there was that time that I got stopped and I mean, he didn't like it that I laughed at him when he said to me, what am I going to do with that, so, he was a bit – he searched me and did the whole thing. There were a few occasions, there was another time when I was ringing the bell of my friend's house and they accused me of knowing who was doing the robberies in the area. I was like, 'I don't know who is doing the robberies in the area, it's my friend's house.' Luckily, his mum came back just as the policeman was about to put me in the car. She said, 'What are you doing?' he said, 'Oh, he's been ringing this bell,' she said, 'It's my house, he's my son's friend, it's fine.' If she hadn't come then they would have taken me to the police station.

I asked Trevor if this made him scared or angry:

> No, I never got angry about it but I could imagine that it would make you – I knew it made some people angry. I never got that angry about it, I never had any really nasty experiences, they were always, in the end, alright. But I know of people that had really horrible experiences when they used to stop them and strip them and strip search and all that stuff. So, I know that it was – but I never had anything, it was literally they would stop me. I was never doing anything, so I didn't really ever feel, apart from that time when I was knocking at my friend's, they had any reason – not that they needed one. So, I was always fairly confident I would say, I never felt scared by them or anything.

Trevor went on to say it 'happened far more to other people' that he knew, and he did not express any animus towards the police or any other institutional authority. If anything, he says the opposite might be true. When Trevor was young, he and his friends successfully lobbied his local MP to stop them from being banned from playing football on the bandstand in the park. They did this by knocking on the MP's door when they were about 11 years old. On being invited in, they related their grievance and the MP intervened on their behalf. As Trevor describes it, 'And so, I always had that thing, I know someone, so, maybe that made me feel more confident, I don't know.' Trevor is one of only three individuals in the sample who acted as a LiP without ever having engaged a lawyer. Believing his matter to be simple, Trevor defended himself when his builder took him to County Court for partial payment of an invoice. As we shall see in the following chapter, it did not turn out to be so simple.

For Neil, on the other hand, the police were an active source of good. Growing up in the North in the 1960s, he recalls the local policeman as part of the community:

> Well we had a local copper, and this was the days when coppers were coppers. And in fact the last time I was back in —— I actually saw him; he's a very elderly gentleman now. And he lived just down the road from us. And he would clip you if we were playing

> football in the road and if we dared be cheeky to him, it's 'come here'. And you would go to him and he would clip you or he would take you back to your parents and then they would clip you. But he knew everybody on the estate. He knew all the kids, his kids went to school with us. He didn't live in a police house, he lived in a, he was in a normal, it was a house like my parents. But no, it was great, he was always walking round, always on the beat. He knew every car, he knew every person, he knew every house, he knew when anybody was on holiday, he used to, he was a proper copper.

When Neil experienced bullying from another boy, the policeman intervened and the bullying stopped. This experience forms part of a general background of what Neil calls a 'happy childhood', where '[we] never got what we wanted but we got what we needed'. When I asked him to elaborate, he said:

> They [Neil's parents] didn't waste money. I don't think they had got a lot of money, they had got three kids. But they wouldn't be able to do it nowadays. I mean there was no shame in going to school with just normal shoes on, nobody had to have the designer trainers. And we had school uniform throughout all the schools from infant all the way through, everybody wore the same clothes. And I seem to remember the only difference was at senior school with the clothes were the rich kids had Barathea blazers with shiny buttons on and we had blazers, everybody else had blazers that were like donkey jackets with just little black buttons on. But no, they brought us up right; they brought us up to respect people. They brought us up to respect the local policeman. We never went without anything, we always had holidays. We never had a new car, we always had second hand cars that sometimes had more body filler in then metal in them. No, it was a nice upbringing. It was a nice upbringing, in a nice area, full of nice people. It was a very happy childhood.

Neil recalls weekly Sunday dinners, including crumble made with blackberries or apples they had picked themselves. Describing himself at times as 'cheeky' when growing up, he does not remember strict rules or being punished regularly, although he was given a 'clip' from time to time. He recalls one such occasion:

> I had a bow and arrow once and I shot a dove that was on the neighbour's bird table. I didn't think I would hit it because I had never hit anything in my life with it that I had actually aimed for. And I felt rather sorry because I had pinned a dove to the bird table. And that was the end of my bow and arrow, that went.

Neil's litigation revolves around allegations of medical negligence, and relates to a vicious beating he experienced at the hands of organised football hooligans and the resulting (what he alleges to be inadequate) medical treatment. He suffers from chronic pain and is unable to leave his house, which is where our interview was conducted.[17]

Peter is even more positive towards authority and rules. Coming from a family who were in the military, he says:

> I think a lot of my ambition was centred around what my father was doing. Although he never really talked about it in any detail, it was all sort of from a military background.

[17] We hear more from Neil in ch 4.

> It's like his, well he was in the navy with his twin brother for a while. Then he went in the army and then the air force after the war. But my other uncle, well my uncle on, my mother's brother he was in the Royal Armoured Corps. So, they have been in the service. My other uncle, my dad's brother, he was in the Royal Artillery. So, they've all been in the service in one form or another. And my uncle, my mother's brother, he also, when he left the army he ended up in the police force. So, there's all this. And I think that sort of shaped me in a way to go. When I was a young lad I wanted to go in the army. And that's what I did.

Growing up in what he describes as a 'rough' area in the West Country, Peter has mixed feelings about the area and its safety:

> The reputation is, it's almost like stigmatised in a way as being a rough area where there's a lot of crime. But in reality, that's not the case, there's some very good people. And I always found it, going through my schooling, I always found, I felt that I didn't belong actually. I didn't belong there. And I used to be bullied. There used to be a lot of bullying going on. And there was a lot of problems. In years later you actually seen the area change and a drugs problem came in. And yes, things did get worse. There was areas within —— that had deprivation. But overall yes, it was a, it wasn't what people thought it was, if you know what I mean. It was actually, there was a lot of I suppose what would be classed as media hype now, that still exists today. Like you've got areas in —— there's these council estates and they get a reputation. But if you actually live there and you actually experience day to day, it's not actually the case.

Peter had a strong sense from childhood of wanting to 'uphold the law'. This meant doing what was right, as he put it, and he joined the army. He recalls being sent to Greenham Common:

> I remember being there the first the Cruise missiles landed. The first Cruise missiles to land in the UK. And it's quite amazing really because you see these peace protestors all over the place down there, and I always remember it, they would take down a mile of fence in one go. And quite amazing. And we had, we were, we put up all this barbed wire and then we were in between the barbed wire and the fence. And they just knocked down this fence and they were whipping horses with razor wire. They were whipping horses with this razor wire in the name of peace this is. And they kicked this police officer, they had him on the floor. And he was out. So we, when the fence went down that's the first thing that we did was grab him, drag him back in and then deal with these people. Like they were just literally being thrown on the lorry and took away to the police, you know, in the background on the airfield, quite amazing.[18]

Peter recalls the hostility he felt from the protestors:

> We ain't murdered anyone. Like what, where are you coming from? And yes, they won't talk to you. They just seen you as a total like sort of beast I suppose. Some sort of killing machine. Shocking really. But they were so fixed in their way, like fixated in their way.

[18] Greenham Common was a women's peace camp established to oppose nuclear development. It is well documented that the protesters were peaceful but endured intimidation and arrest from the police. See R Johnson, 'Alice Through the Fence: Greenham Women and the Law' in J Dewar et al (eds), *Nuclear Weapons, the Peace Movement and the War* (London, Palgrave, 1986) 158.

> And yes. But I do wonder you know, if there was like an element in there that like rent a mob sort of element when things started to get built up and it all kicked off.

Peter's litigation results from a tragic incident where his wife attacked his young daughter: Peter's wife was institutionalised and his daughter was placed in foster care, and Peter has been litigating to regain custody.[19]

Tim, on the other hand, is quite anti-police, and says he always has been. He attributes this to growing up in the 1980s and witnessing anti-Black violence, as well as the police retaliation against workers taking industrial action. He notes he felt solidarity, as a Jew, with other minorities who were discriminated against by the police. He himself was arrested at a demonstration in his early 20s and describes the police violence:

> Yes I got arrested with a placard in my hand, not so much arrested, I was assaulted. This was, there was a particularly famous May Day protest, I think it was probably 2000 or 2001, it was the one where basically they smashed up all the McDonalds and the bus stops and left a grassy Mohawk on Winston Churchill's statue. That was a minority of people out there, truth be told I was protesting at the time because I felt like I needed to protest something, this was going through my socialist phase and you know oh we're protesting, what you protesting today? We're protesting anti-capitalism. Yes, that sounds great wonderful. You know nothing much has changed in the last 15 years to be honest, but so I sort of went down and we had our placards and I can't remember what they said now to be honest but the police got there quite late so when all the reports of things getting smashed came in the perpetrators had already been and gone. So they came after the protesters but they just assumed that everyone who was there was violent and various of us got clocked around the back of the head and thrown in the back of a van. Our arrest was expunged from any record because Liberty got involved. I don't know the ins and outs of that one at all it was just like okay do I have a record on me? No. Great. I got a letter saying apologies, that was it really.

Oliver, conversely, whose litigation has primarily been driven by actions against the police, says he had no pre-existing issues or background with the police prior to their assault on him.[20] He notes that he was frequently stopped for speeding (as was his father): 'The police on the beat, who would stop me in their cars and so on, knew damned well that I believed in their job, the job they do and how important it is.' Oliver now considers police officers in this area corrupt, although he does not believe this to be the case more widely, and in fact at several other points in the interview he went out of his way to emphasise his positive attitude toward the police.[21]

[19] Peter's story therefore has considerable similarities to Marie's, although the circumstances of loss of custody are very different. We hear more from Peter in ch 4.

[20] As mentioned, Oliver has been in and out of court for over 30 years in actions against the police. In the course of his litigation, he has also been convicted of contempt of court and he received what he claimed (with pride) was the 'longest sentence every given for contempt in ——'.

[21] Again, Oliver entertains certain beliefs around police and Masonic influence, although interestingly Masonic membership of the judiciary and police was the subject of the Home Affairs Select Committee Enquiry in 1997: see at https://publications.parliament.uk/pa/cm199899/cmselect/cmhaff/467/46703.htm#n1.

So, what can we make of these experiences? Again, there is too much variety to categorise LiPs as anti- or pro-authority regarding police encounters. We can certainly see a pattern of regular racial discrimination experienced by the Black interviewees in this study, but even here there is a diversity of experience of how this manifested and what impact it had. Attitudes to rules, experiences of punishment and other aspects of their lives we have learned so far do not seem to tell us much about how or why they may have come to be LiPs. So what connections, if any, do interviewees have to the legal profession?

IV. Legal Connections

Talia's father was a magistrate.[22] But in terms of what that meant to her, she says all it perhaps gave her as a child was a 'black and white sense of right and wrong'. She did not have any interest in going into law, although her brother went on to become a lawyer. Talia attributes her parents' lack of ambition for her as gendered; they 'only expected her to get married' and she describes her education as 'patchy':

> It sounds stupid but my parents seemed to think that —— was the brainy one. I was the creative artistic one. And —— was the sporty one. And that's all they had to do and it would just happen. And it's not that cut and dried. Both my brothers are extremely bright.

Talia's legal proceedings revolve around fighting the repossession of her flat. At the time of interview, she was still living in her flat, but she was forced to move out and has subsequently continued to litigate in relation to these proceedings from council-provided accommodation in another county.[23] Beyond her father's work abroad as a magistrate, Talia had no contact or experience with anyone in the law or legal proceedings, beyond observing her parents' divorce proceedings, which she said 'just went on and on and on and on and on'.

Oliver, similarly, says his only family member in a legal profession was a father's cousin who was killed in the war:

> [T]here was no one in the family or relations, anything to do with law. The only one that affected my father was of course his cousin who was killed on D-Day beaches and he was a lawyer from Lincolns Inn I think, yes I think it was Lincolns, yes. And he volunteered to go to war in 1944 for the D-Day landings and he died about four days later around the corner there at the docks.

He tells me, however, that in adulthood, his sister married a barrister. Indeed, family connections to lawyers when the interviewees became adults were not limited to these two. Anna, for example, had a cousin who worked in law, but said

[22] This was in a British colony, not in the UK.

[23] Years after interview, I continue to receive updates from her, telling me of her ongoing attempts to dispute the repossession.

she had no particular interest in that area. Trevor's sister is also a lawyer, but Trevor himself did not ever really see himself as someone who could be one:

> I like all the dramas about law, those things I like, but law itself – I think – Yes, I like the idea of it but I don't know enough about it. I realise it's not just standing up in front of someone and making these speeches, it's not that, well, not only that. I like things with – it would be sort of like with rules that you can manipulate if you know what I mean? These are the rules and you've got to try and find a way – I like that type of stuff, of working out how you can use that to get where you need to be and put your case forward. I like that type of stuff. So, yes, but standing up in front of people might be a bit more difficult for me.

These family connections were nevertheless present only for the minority of interviewees (four out of 15). On balance, it is reasonable to conclude that there does not seem to be much family contact with the legal profession for any of the interviewees prior to their own legal proceedings. Eleanor's experience was typical of the interviewees' limited contact with, and experience of, the law:

> Kate: What about in terms of law, was there anything along the lines of law or anything like that?
>
> Eleanor: Nope, nope in those days there was quite a rigid sort of bunch of A levels and law and you know interesting ones weren't really offered in fact I don't think we had, I don't know anywhere that offered a main A level in law in those days, I can't think of anywhere.
>
> Kate: And did you know growing up anyone who did work in law?
>
> Eleanor: Nope.
>
> Kate: And no one in your family?
>
> Eleanor: Nope.
>
> Kate: So you had no contact, do you remember any one in your family or in your kind of circle of acquaintance having any contact for any reason with someone involved in law or a police officer or anything like that?
>
> Eleanor: My mother used to get arrested every once in a while for bad driving.[24]

The exception to this lack of contact with and experience of law is, of course, Tim, who did a law degree. But even he was ambivalent about becoming a lawyer (and never in fact became one):

> So at school we obviously had to choose the way that our school was kind of gearing us towards university was either you went to Oxbridge and basically became either an academic or you know high echelons of whatever it was you were doing because you were at Oxbridge or you basically chose a degree for the profession you wanted to work in. … [A]nd having spoken to careers advisers they kind of suggested that law was a good way to go. … Then when I actually came to an open day there that became

[24] Eleanor first represented herself as a defendant in a small claims case, and then went on to pursue claims relating to the return of her possessions and her cats as a LiP. We hear more from Eleanor in section VI.

> even more of an argument that you don't choose to do a law degree because you want to be a lawyer. You know you choose to do a law degree because you find the subject of interest and that will help you, then move on to further studies in law … the whole way through everyone said look you do it because you want to do this degree don't do it because you want a job in law. So it's very strange messages we had the whole way to be honest.

So, what can this lack of connection to the legal profession for the majority tell us? Perhaps greater proximity to legal professionals may have influenced attitudes away from acting as a LiP, although this is nothing more than speculation. Trevor commented, in another context, '[t]he problem with getting lawyers involved or people with legal minds, is they see all the problems that can happen'. Not being aware of the difficulties or problems that might ensue may be more likely to encourage individuals to become LiPs.[25]

It also perhaps speaks to the *absence* of 'family connections', which Michael Blackwell identified as a key factor in the career trajectory of senior counsel and judges, who overwhelmingly came from privileged backgrounds with multiple familial connections to the profession.[26] There is a social gap here: a lack of private education and networking that facilitates access to the law and maintains it as an elite profession. Georgina, for example, who does come from a wealthy background and was privately educated, had this to say when I asked her what contact she had with lawyers when growing up: 'I knew one of the top lawyers for King Hussain, Egyptian man, I only ever saw them socialising, you see a very different side of people when you're in a party.' This encounter is part of a series of social encounters Georgina had when growing up in a household where her father held an influential role that involved a close relationship with prominent politicians, meaning her house was a place where the influential and well-heeled gathered. She was quite conscious of this:

> I've known lawyers … let me think … yeah, I suppose because I grew up in a privileged, as they call it, background, especially in B—— in the sixties and seventies, and saw the power that my Dad seemed to have, because everyone was falling at his feet because of who he was in with, the prime minister, I mean I used to go to dinner with the prime minister from B—— in Mayfair in London, for example.

Georgina, by far the most conspiracist of this sample, was the hardest to understand in terms of following her litigation profile. Much of it seems to relate to her company's being declared bankrupt and the potential repossession of her house, but there seem to be multiple other claims that have spiralled out in relation to this, due to what she perceives to be the endemic corruption of the courts. She also entertains extreme antisemitic beliefs.

[25] On a more practical note, lack of personal contact with legal professionals can be limiting in terms of helping LiPs resolve legal problems later: it is notable that Trevor's sister's being a lawyer had a direct impact on his being able to seek help when he needed it. This is discussed in detail in ch 4.

[26] See M Blackwell, 'Old Boy's Networks, Family Connections and the Legal Profession' (2012) 3 *Public Law* 426.

Oliver also had contact with lawyers because his family employed them, and he maintained a relationship with them into adulthood. It is also worth noting that the three interviewees in this study whose siblings married barristers were also all privately educated. The fourth interviewee whose sister became a lawyer, Trevor, went to a state school, but he made an explicit point of saying in his interview that when he went to the comprehensive school, it was the 1970s – a time when state schools were not so demographically separated:

> [M]ost of my friends are through school and in those days, the positive thing was that the state education, because they had just come out of the whole secondary modern thing, comprehensive schools were coming in. There were a lot of middle-class parents who now would be looking to send their kids to private school, which were quite enthusiastic about sending their children. Especially people who were in the arts, or creative world send them to state school. So, actually, I had, in my class at school, I had a full spectrum of people from professional to – all sides of life were in my class. So, I would go to some people's houses and they were pretty well off, and it was completely different to our house … Whereas, the school I went to, it was just up the road here, was really mixed and so, I liked that, and so, my friends were really mixed in terms of their cultural background.

While we cannot push this argument particularly far, given the limited sample, it does suggest there are consistencies with Blackwell's and others' research around connections between access to the legal profession and social privilege.

Another aspect worth noting following from the above is that only a handful of the overall sample went to university. The majority did not, many describing themselves as having had limited educational experiences for an assortment of reasons (primarily financial, but this also includes gendered expectations that limited their options, poor experiences of secondary schooling and lack of opportunity), so we cannot eliminate the possibility that LiPs might also be less likely to have a higher education.[27] Here we have to be very cautious about the limits of any speculation of what difference this makes, as there is no unequivocal evidence, but higher education *may* play a role in enabling individuals to establish effective research and evaluation skills, which could help them as LiPs.[28]

Several interviewees in this study were clear, for example, when asked whether they had considered the law as a profession, that it was out of reach as it was too expensive and/or not for people like them. Charles expresses it thus: '[N]o, I mean law was for rich people [laughter]. We don't … contemplated that. You had to have the right accent, and um, lots of money.' Peter echoes this, stating 'from my own personal point of view um, I would, if I had the money and it is all about money because if I had the money I, I would study law'. Neil similarly notes that given his

[27] It is far from clear that higher education does improve critical thinking or research skills, although this has been suggested in some scholarship. See C Huber and N Kuncel, 'Does College Teach Critical Thinking?: A Meta-Analysis' (2016) 86 *Review of Educational Research* 431.

[28] Certainly Eleanor, with two Masters' degrees, was much less inclined to conspiracist explanations for her experiences and more successful in her dealings on balance.

time again, he would study law, although he had no interest in law at the time he was at school. However, even if he had, as he outlines, it was not an option for him, as he needed to earn money immediately to support himself. As he says:

> All the lads, all the girls and the fellas that went to university, it took them another five or six years before they were earning the same amount of money as I was earning, you know, and they were off at university somewhere and their family were having to pay for them and we didn't have that sort of money either.

At the very least, though, we can be sure that the limited contact with and understanding of the law that we see here for most of our interviewees will undoubtedly make the first experience of litigation potentially more confusing and difficult.[29] And that is what I explore in section V, which considers interviewees' first contact with legal proceedings and the issues to which it relates.

V. First Contact

Charles's first contact with legal proceedings was in the County Courts sometime in the early 1980s. Charles went to collect his son for the day from his estranged partner and she would not let him in. Instead, she called the police. Charles became extremely fearful and upset, as he was working at that time in communications for the police and, as he put it, 'I thought I could lose my job if I got in trouble with the police so for her to do that sort of thing, you know, it was really beyond belief'. When the policeman arrived, Charles was in tears, trying to explain what had happened and also telling him how he could not understand how she could have called the police. Charles decided then, he says, to walk away, to 'walk out of his [son's] life' and he got in his car. But then the policeman knocked on his window and talked to him. The policeman said to him 'don't just walk away', before telling Charles how he had regretted losing a relationship with his own child. At that point, Charles says, 'I decided that I had to fight to make sure that I could get access to him'. This led to his first appearance as a LiP in the County Court, being awarded joint custody of his son.[30] Although his former partner had representation, through legal aid, and he did not, he described himself as 'very confident' going in:

> Like I said, all I'm asking, all I was asking for is, um the opportunity to see my son on a regular basis so I couldn't see, the, the judge had no reason why he would deny me that. He had no reason to deny me that access.

Eleanor's first experience, on the other hand, was as a defendant in the County Courts in 2008. Owning her own business, Eleanor was sued by a subcontractor

[29] This gap between legal knowledge and lay research is explored in detail in ch 5.

[30] The Family Court was created in 2013. Prior to this time, family proceedings were heard in County Courts and magistrates' courts.

who claimed it had not been paid for work done for Eleanor's business. Eleanor attended a £30 fixed-fee interview at a solicitor's firm she had found online in her local area; she said the solicitor 'walked me through what I needed to put into the defence to send back to the court so that's what I did'. Following this, and some further communication from the claimant, she attended the County Court. She describes attending the hearing:

> Well I mean I remember sort of sitting outside S—— County Court, the, you know the court offices, hearing rooms or whatever they're called, um, feeling, you know, my stomach sort of turning somersaults and stuff like that because … no matter how well prepared you are it's still fairly scary, 'cause you, the trouble is with court is you have a, you can go in there with the strongest case in the world and still lose … over a technicality.

Both Eleanor's and Charles's experiences differ again from the experience of Talia, who attended the then Leasehold Valuation Tribunal (LVT).[31] Having used solicitors at the first hearing of this tribunal, she dispensed with them for the appeal, and was thereafter a LiP in almost all of her subsequent legal actions, including the ones she later took to the County Court:

> Um … it was, it was after the[LVT] decision being appealed [that Talia dispensed with the solicitor], I think, well it must have been. Um … without referring to my files, I wanted our solicitor to write a witness statement, I thought that would help, and he said okay, I'll do it for £200 and then like a week before he was supposed to give it to us, he said Oh, I haven't quite finished, I'd like another £200 and I really, uh [laughter], I don't think, think he just expected me to just … and I said 'that's it, okay we won't use it, forget it' [laughter].

Talia first attended County Court in 2007, when she took her freeholder to court for failing to properly insure her property according to the terms of her lease. The freeholder did not turn up, and Talia was successful. Talia then took the order the same day to the freeholder's place of work, but he did not comply with the order or acknowledge it in any way, sending her back to court less than six months later.

These are just three examples of first contact with legal proceedings, but we can already also see the considerable diversity of experience inherent even in the most surface-level examination of LiPs. Charles's first experience relates to family matters, Eleanor's to small claims and Talia's to housing. Both Charles and Talia are claimants, while Eleanor is a defendant. In addition, Charles does his own research and seeks no external advice, and is confident acting as a LiP. Eleanor, on the other hand, seeks a solicitor's advice prior to attending the hearing and is extremely anxious about the outcome. Talia employs a solicitor initially but eventually stops this, and chooses to do her own research, considering solicitors to be individuals who drag out proceedings for their own financial gain.[32]

[31] Now the First-Tier Tribunal (Property Chamber).

[32] This is a view shared by many interviewees, including Charles later in his legal proceedings experience. The lack of trust LiPs have towards legal representatives is explored in detail in ch 6.

At first glance, this disparity between the experiences is hardly surprising, given how different all the interviewees are as well as the inherent complexity of civil justice. Researchers, such as Moorhead and Sefton, as well as John Baldwin, have also argued that the category of LiP captures a wide range of individuals.[33] However, accounts of LiP failures often do not consider the variety of circumstances in which LiPs act, as perhaps they would when thinking about represented actors in civil disputes. What is also important is how substantial these differences are, and the concomitant difficulties this inherent diversity poses, both in terms of practical reform as well as in raising questions about the term 'litigant in person' itself.

First, an obvious example of how this diversity is a practical problem arises when considering how to provide useful guidance for LiPs. In a context where reliable free legal advice has been drastically reduced, how can one, for example, provide written assistance or online information for LiPs when the category itself, even in the County Courts alone, is so broad? While they may attend the same kind of court, LiPs will differ regarding any advice they sought or received, any research they undertook, whether they had representation at any point, how much legal or courtroom experience they may have had, the nature of the dispute itself, and whether their opponent is represented or unrepresented.[34] The LiP may also face an individual, or a corporation or a local authority (all of which are represented in this sample). Alongside this difference in types of proceedings and legal claim, there are of course differences in age, sex, ethnicity, education and language to contend with.[35] These differences clearly raise immense difficulties as regards being able to provide applicable, sufficiently tailored or specific advice. This is also occurring in a context where the limited sources of face-to-face advice, such as the Citizens Advice Bureaux (CAB), are increasingly inaccessible. As Neil comments:

> I found the Citizens Advice Bureau was basically impossible to get in to … uh … and to find one in the locality or to get an appointment to see somebody … well I can't say they're useless because I never actually got there to use them. Um, there are various people like litigants in person help thing on the, uh, like on Twitter and they've got their own website, ah I'm sure you've seen those haven't you, litigant in person help. They may, they may be effective, uh, but I've never seen any evidence of it.

Second, this diversity of individuals and circumstances also draws attention to problems with the term 'litigant in person' itself. It includes those such as Eleanor, who seek legal advice but are not formally represented, people like Charles, who conduct research through legal forums online but do not instruct a solicitor, and those like Talia, who intermittently employ solicitors before dispensing

[33] R Moorhead and M Sefton, *Unrepresented Litigants in First Instance Proceedings* (London, Department of Constitutional Affairs, 2006); Genn (n 1); Baldwin (n 2) 20.

[34] Or they may not: many LiPs will resolve the dispute (or give up) before it reaches the court at all.

[35] In this group of individuals, 13 interviewees were white and two were Black British; 10 were men and five were women; and they ranged in age from 28 to mid-80s. All spoke English as a first language.

with them.[36] It also includes anyone of any background and experience, including, potentially, solicitors and barristers who choose to act for themselves. In this research sample, it includes both Tim, who has a law degree but who did not qualify, being unable to obtain a training contract, and Marie, who was raised in care and left school at age 16.

It is unclear, then, where the role of LiP starts and stops. Is being a LiP a role that is adopted temporarily? Or is it more than that? When does one start to be, and stop being, a LiP? This was something of interest in this study, because it raises the question of whether these individuals *recognise themselves* under such a label. For many interviewees, it was a label for which they did not feel any affinity. For example, as Tim put it:

> I don't, I wouldn't necessarily say that I saw myself … obviously I was, but it didn't sort of occur to me that I was a litigant in person. Um, again part of that is probably for me, that when I was studying [law] that was kind of a, a wild fantasy that someone had that they would actually, you know you could represent yourself absolutely, I think we probably covered it in about five minutes in a lecture once, you know people do, depending on the case, they're either idiots or they're geniuses and that was it basically, but it's a rarity.

Tim went on to note that LiPs are 'kind of looked down on slightly. More than slightly, um but that's largely by the lawyers who would rather be getting paid a lot of money to uh, to, to, to do the case themselves.' This was echoed by Charles:

> I think they look down at us sort of, I think they wa–, they think of us as people wasting their time, wasting the court's time … it's not something that they want. They'd prefer if it didn't exist because, because I mean if you look at the documentation from my barrister for instance and compare it to my documentation, there, there's no comparison [as regards quality].

As both interviewees point out, the label itself has become cluttered with largely negative associations that do not treat the term 'litigant in person' as a temporary role; instead they tend to talk of the LiP as a specific type of person.[37] So although the term technically describes a specific and discrete temporal moment in an individual's life, it is spoken about by many in the legal profession, and *felt* by those who act as LiPs, as something approaching an all-encompassing *identity*: but this is an identity that is troubling for many interviewees, because of all the negative connotations it brings.

Alongside these problematic issues of terminology and identity, however, the current working definition of 'litigant in person' also implies that individuals' experiences prior to entry into judicial space are not relevant. By denoting individuals as LiPs only during a discrete period of time, we fracture the longer narrative that for any individual is relevant to how they come to act as a LiP, and

[36] The category of LiP also includes those who are accompanied by McKenzie friends, paid or unpaid. In this sample, Marie has been using a McKenzie friend for several years, and they have become so jointly committed to her case that they undertake work on her case together, including, notably, this interview.

[37] For example, see D Swank, 'The Pro Se Phenomenon' (2005) 19 *Brigham Young University Journal of Public Law* 373.

that will shape how they inhabit and perform that role.[38] This context of course includes background, education, family, income and so on. It also, crucially, involves any subsequent experience with legal proceedings.

Returning to our three cases, for example, Talia then went on to experience further disputes with her freeholder, as well as her mortgage lender, that spanned a period of 10 years and were still ongoing at the time of writing. She has acted as a LiP throughout this entire period. Charles also went on to appear on two subsequent occasions relating to custody in the County Courts over the next 10 years. In the mid-1990s, Charles started litigation against his conveyancing solicitor that took him to the High Court. Throughout this period, and the subsequent appeals, he was intermittently represented, and at one point he sued the solicitor he employed to bring the case, for negligence. Charles also became involved in a dispute with a contractor. This action started in 2010 and was ongoing at the time of his interview, by which time Charles was employing a direct access barrister. Finally, after Eleanor's initial experience in the County Court, she went on to act as a claimant in two further civil proceedings: one she won, and one she lost. She conducted the majority of these proceedings as a LiP, and did so from prison, where she served three-and-a-half years of a seven-year sentence before being released in 2014.

Looking at the above, then, beyond all the diversity inherent in being a LiP, one area of convergence in this study was that almost all of the LiPs who spoke to me had had multiple encounters with legal proceedings and legal professionals. All but three started their litigation experience by employing lawyers. So it seems key to think about what the relationship is, if there is one, between contact with legal professionals and becoming a LiP.

VI. 'Bad' Lawyers

David used the same high-street solicitor for a number of proceedings. Initially using him for his house conveyancing, he employed him again when he went to an employment tribunal. When the next legal issues arose relating to a fire at his property, he again went back to the solicitor:

David: He was a sheriff and a magistrate.

Kate: Right.

David: I would have thought that would have made him an honest man.

Kate: So up until this point that you hadn't had any questions about his …

David: No, no. I mean I sometimes think that solicitors like to run things out for as long as they can.[39]

[38] Indeed, as I go on to note in this chapter, the inability of a LiP to restrict arguments to one area leads to difficulty.

[39] Remember, Talia also made the same claim and used this as the reason for becoming a LiP.

Dissatisfied with his solicitor's performance, David complained to the Law Society:

> Well I complained about negligence. I said, he hadn't taken it to court, he hadn't followed the evidence, he'd played down certain evidence, cast it aside and he dismissed evidence as if it didn't matter. And so the Law Society said, 'Well you'll have to find another solicitor and bring a negligence case against him.'

David found another solicitor and was given legal aid to sue his previous solicitor for negligence. The Law Society appointed a law firm to represent his solicitor, called Mills & Stephens. David notes, 'We call them Mills and Boon because they like writing fairy stories.' Unsuccessful in this action, David attributes this failure, and his other litigation failures, to Freemasonry.[40]

David is not the only interviewee who sued his solicitor. Charles, too, ended up in court, suing his solicitor for negligence. Charles felt that different solicitors he had employed would take his money and fail to provide the service he had paid for. He spent some time complaining in writing to the Law Society and solicitor representative bodies before going to court:

> Well in terms of, I did, I went through all the complaints procedures with the Solicitors Complaint Bureau and that took a couple of years because they just, they just drag it out because it's, although officially that body is there to kind of help you, they don't do anything for you. They just keep sending you in the wrong direction and when you go, when you pursue that direction you find out you get there and come back to them and that just carries on until it literally drags on for about 24 months before you realise that this is just a waste of time. And I'm not the only one saying this, a lot of people have, I don't know if you have, I did actually have a few links on my site whereby lots of other people have got sites that were actually trying to say the same thing about their frustration after having been ripped off by their solicitor, and finding out that they can't get any justice from anywhere, even the Pro Bono Unit, so I've got details of which I've got in that folder. I was referred to them by the Citizens Advice Bureau at the Grand Court of Justice and when the barrister found out that I was going against my solicitors he basically dismissed it, he didn't want to know.

Charles also attributes his failure to succeed in his claim at least partly due to conspiracy theories.

Similarly, Anna felt the incompetence of solicitors was indicative of their infiltrations by the Masons:

> You know, as part of this I also had my first experience of … ——. I had been using a solicitor in —— for a car crash compensation claim. So I said to him, you know, 'I've got this medical accident claim, what shall I do?' So he referred me to —— Solicitors, to this woman. And these Solicitors are founded by a Grand Master, basically. Anyway, this woman was charging me a lot of money to research and giving me bad advice and undermining my case. So I thought, well this is waste of time, I'm sacking you. I don't like what's going on, I'm sacking you.

[40] David's Masonic conspiracy theories, and his antisemitism, are discussed in more detail in ch 6.

At first glance, the above stories fit our negative expectations of a LiP: these individuals become disillusioned with their solicitors because they do not succeed, and this may not necessarily be related to anything other than the strength (or lack of strength) of the individual's claim or defence. We can perhaps imagine that a solicitor gives this person unwelcome advice, and this is the cause of a rupture. The conspiracy theories these three LiPs rely on underline this tendency here to fall into our lazier expectations of LiPs: that these individuals are simply being paranoid or unreasonable. But I want to pause here to say that it is notable *just how many* individuals in this study were disappointed by their experiences of, and contacts with, their solicitors, including those who were not conspiracist in their claims.[41]

Thirteen out of 15 interviewees in this sample complained about their experiences with solicitors and the other two didn't instruct a lawyer.[42] Neil, for example, much like Charles, David and Georgina, felt that his solicitor failed to listen to him or appropriately take instruction:

> Well that solicitor, well that legal exec, it's the same thing that's been going on for years that they just don't listen. They say well it must have happened, this is what happened, and I say, well no I will tell you what happened because I was there.

This feeling of not being listened to, or not having their experiences sufficiently taken into account, seems to be a common feature in these interviews as regards criticism of solicitors.[43]

Alongside Talia, Charles and David, Eleanor also complained of her lawyer's incompetence ('I had a really bad lawyer') before becoming a LiP. This was in relation to her arrest:

> He was a duty solicitor. The thing is it's ironic. The more you get arrested, the more you understand the game that is played because it is a game that is being played with you. It's not about finding the truth, it's not about justice. It's about playing the game and getting a conviction at all costs a lot of the time and the fact that you have not done whatever it is you're being accused of is completely irrelevant to the process. And as I say bad lawyer and … but the thing is you don't realise the first time you get arrested they call you a solicitor. It's the duty solicitor. You have no idea whether or not they're any good and it's only when you go down the whole process that you discover they're really pants but and also nobody tells you that if you have a really pants duty solicitor you can actually change them. You can go off and find your own lawyer and get aid transferred over. Nobody tells you this so you think you're stuck with the really pants lawyer who's doing a really piss poor job of representing you. And it's actually quite scary because the whole legal process is designed to completely and totally disempower whoever has been accused of the crime.

[41] And it is mostly solicitors: interviewees tended to view barristers more positively. The most likely explanation, I would suggest, is the relatively limited contact interviewees had with barristers compared with solicitors.

[42] The exceptions here are Tim and Trevor, both of whom acted as LiPs without attempting to instruct lawyers beforehand, and who are not engaged in multiple proceedings.

[43] We could make a link here to the literature on procedural justice and the importance individuals attach to having their voices heard. See N Zimerman and T Tyler, 'Between Access to Counsel and Access to Justice: A Psychological Perspective' (2010) 37 *Fordham Urban Law Journal* 473.

When I asked Eleanor why she felt this lawyer was poor, she said:

> Like I'd go and meet him and we'd discuss things like there was evidence available that I was in a completely different place at the time so could not possible have done what I was being accused of. It's basically they advise you not to get that evidence because you could potentially fake, forged, tampered with whatever. They need to get it so you tell them how to get it and then they don't get it. They agree to get it and then they don't.

Leo also had a negative impression of solicitors. Like Charles, he initially chose to represent himself, as he did not feel solicitors were necessary in relation to his first experience of litigation, when he represented himself in a small claims proceeding. However, later in life, when he became involved in legal proceedings relating to his spouse's right to remain in the UK, he did employ solicitors and had this to say:

> Leo: It was early on and I went to the solicitor and said, There are two things I want, and one thing is I want to go to court, present the judge with my financial evidence, and for the judge to consider it, and give an order stating what amount of income he accepts that I have, and what amount of consistent savings he accepts that I have, and various other things – a list, a little list, of the things I wanted to get … The solicitor refused to do this, did something else, and wanted to charge me a fee. It was 500, 700 quid, for not doing what I wanted.
>
> Kate: You're saying that periods of time related to the immigration issue, you've instructed solicitors and they have not done what you have requested?
>
> Leo: They don't. Their job is to have money. They want income. Their job is not to do your legal work. It's not to solve problems. So, why give somebody a load of money? And then, of course, they sued me because I wouldn't pay them some of the money, and I said, 'Well, you haven't done what I asked you to do.'

For Marie, it was her second solicitor that she felt was not doing the job she had asked him to do. After her first legally aided solicitor, with whom she had a good relationship, was moved on, she was put with someone she felt was incompetent:

> He was a bit of a wet lettuce. He'd done one court hearing because obviously, I've had several court hearings. Done one court hearing and he'd done nothing to even argue or fight or anything. And I specifically said I didn't want him, but they just put me … put my case with him. So, I ended up walking away from the firm. Started looking for help on the internet.

It was through the Internet that Marie found an advocacy group including those who acted as McKenzie friends, and it was there she met her advisor, whom she has subsequently retained throughout her experience as a LiP.

These experiences echo the findings of other studies into LiPs. McKeever et al's study of LiPs in Northern Ireland, for example, found that

> many LIPs reported that part or all of their motivation for litigating in person was due to dissatisfaction with the legal services they had received previously. These

> LIPs were not merely objecting here to the limits of the law's power, but to the failure of the legal representatives to communicate in a way that allowed them to be a participant in their case when they were represented, rather than feel frustrated at having their voice excluded. It is this source of powerlessness to which some LIPs in our study objected.[44]

We cannot, of course, assess the truth or otherwise of any of these stories. We can, though, know that this is what LiPs *think* happened, and that alone is reason enough for us to think more about it if we want to understand why people become LiPs. Clearly, negative experiences with legal professionals constitute a reason for many to become so: this seems to be a large and relatively unexplored explanatory factor. This is perhaps attributable to the reluctance to believe LiPs when they complain of poor service. As McKeever et al's study noted:

> Court actors' perceptions of why people self-represent … differed with regard to the reasons for LIPs becoming dissatisfied with prior legal representation. They felt it arose from LIPs not being willing to accept advice from their lawyer rather than from poor communication, a lack of progress in the case or errors being made.[45]

But, as always when it comes to LiPs, before we assume it is *only* down to unreasonable LiPs (which of course it certainly could be), we also need to weigh the evidence we have of poor and incompetent lawyering and the role this may play.

There is, in fact, good evidence to find complaints of poor service plausible. In his 2014 address on professionalism and lawyering, Richard Moorhead revisited three studies he had conducted that looked explicitly at the performance of non-lawyers compared with lawyers.[46] The first study, looking at legal aid help, showed a better outcome for non-solicitors compared to solicitors.[47] Another study conducted in 2004 showed that not-for-profits outperformed solicitors.[48] As he goes on:

> In a third study, we looked at generalist lawyers and sent model clients (or mystery shoppers) with specialist problems. The idea was that they should have sent these clients away because the clients' problems were probably beyond their competence. Some, however, decided to advise the clients and get paid as a result. Levels of incompetent work in those circumstances were very high indeed.[49]

[44] See McKeever et al (n 4) 83.
[45] ibid.
[46] R Moorhead, 'Precarious Professionalism: Some Empirical and Behavioural Perspectives on Lawyers' (2014) 67 *Current Legal Problems* 447.
[47] R Moorhead et al, Quality and Cost: Final Report on the Contracting of Civil, Non-Family Advice and Assistance Pilot (London, Stationery Office, 2001).
[48] R Moorhead and R Harding, Quality and Access: Specialist and Tolerance Work under Civil Contracts (London, Stationery Office, 2004).
[49] R Moorhead and A Sherr, An Anatomy of Access: Evaluating Entry, Initial Advice and Signposting Using Model Clients (London, Legal Services Research Centre, 2002).

On reflection, Moorhead observed across the studies that about 'one in four clients received substandard legal work':

> On the whole, the non-professionals were either no worse or better than the solicitors and they delivered more excellence. There is some good news. Solicitors were sometimes cheaper but that did not explain away the quality differences. There was no evidence that being professionals improved quality. Absolute quality was, I submit, poor. Relative quality was no better. Even if we add in studies that paint a more positive picture of lawyers … we do not get to a situation where we can always be confident about professional quality.[50]

It is important to emphasise here that the 'non-lawyers' referred to here are not LiPs; they tend to be specialist workers in particular areas of law. Indeed, previous studies, such as those by Genn and Genn and Sherr, have also found that it is specialisation, rather than legal qualification, that may determine the quality of representation.[51] However, for our purposes, it certainly should remind us that bad lawyers are a real possibility. It is not a stretch to say that lawyers are not always competent or effective. They also at times overcharge, underperform, fail to communicate, even break the law. As Moorhead notes:

> Let us forget about excellence for a minute. How many cases would we expect a lawyer to handle competently? Out of a hundred? How many? If professions guarantee competence we might argue that the number should be close to 100. Would we be right to? I do not know. I do not know how many clients can be let down before we start to doubt the claim to professionalism. Or maybe we should think of it in relative terms. How much better do professionals have to be for them to make a plausible claim to be a useful regulator of quality? If professionalism is not to be precarious, then should we not see the professions outperform the nonprofessionals?[52]

We cannot ever know how and why these relationships between client and solicitor broke down. We only have unilateral, partial accounts from unreliable narrators. We of course cannot draw clear conclusions here. But I suggest what we can do is to at least remind ourselves that if we are going to concentrate on LiPs and what is wrong with *them*, we equally need to think more about negative experiences with legal professionals and the impact this might have in terms of generating LiPs, because, clearly, there is something significant going on here that warrants further exploration.[53]

[50] Moorhead (n 48) 455.

[51] H Genn and Y Genn, *The Effectiveness of Representation at Tribunals: report to the Lord Chancellor* (London, Lord Chancellor's Department, 1989); A Sherr, 'The Value of Experience in Legal Competence' (2000) 7 *International Journal of the Legal Profession* 95.

[52] Moorhead (n 48) 454.

[53] The connection between failed litigation and loss of trust in legal professionals is explored further in ch 6.

VII. Conclusion

This chapter has suggested that to really understand how and why people become LiPs, we should not just look at their stories and lives; we need to think more deeply about their contact with and experience of legal professionals. Litigants in person are a category created *by* contact with legal professionals, and this chapter bears this out. Varied in all their meaningful life experiences, attitudes and choices, the only commonalities they share are a tendency to have a very limited understanding of or contact with law prior to their proceedings, and the likelihood that they have had a negative experience with a legal professional at some time. In this respect, then, the *first contact* and the relationship and understanding they develop with legal professionals are crucial, and contain within them, perhaps, the potential to create these individuals as LiPs. But what happens once they set off on this pathway? The next two chapters constitute the 'during' section of litigation, where I will explore interviewees' experiences of litigation in more detail and ask 'What's it *really* like to go to law on your own?'

PART II

During Litigation

4

Being a Litigant in Person: Complexity, High Stakes, Vulnerability

I. Introduction

Kate: What impact do you think … going to court has had, on your life? Financially, personally?

Neil: … You can't really put a cost on it monetary wise, well you can, I suppose, it can be a quantum worked out with all the Ogden tables and all the loss of earnings and interest and what have you. Uh, it has cost, from loss of earnings, say, I'd say £20,000 a year. It's uh, not nearly, twenty, twenty-eight years now, so earnings, it's cost me lots of money.

You can add, you probably, it's not a great deal because, uh, there's probably, probably £10,000 worth of paper and ink and printer ink and what have you. And the, the models [medical models Neil has had made] there's a couple of grands' worth of models, postage. Telephones. But that's, that's not, the important thing, the one thing that they've taken from me, and I'm looking up there, that's J——'s grandson, you know that photo, little one, not my son, not my grandson … I'll never have that. There's a grandma, there's a great grandma there, there's a grandma and there's a little grandson and there's all sorts …

Where would you, where would you, you know like, how long have you been, I'm not trying to find out how old you are but what's your … what's your destination in life? Where would you like to be in thirty years' time? Successful, safe, secure? Healthy? Family around you? You know, being able to help your family … well think about, in thirty years' time, that's where you are, right, and then rewind yourself thirty years to now, and think something happens now that prevented you from getting where you want to be, that wasn't your fault, that was somebody else's mistake and then that person, with the aid of a, with the aid of solicitors just lied through their back teeth to stop you from … you might never have gotten to where you were, but you shouldn't, you shouldn't be out of pocket …

Basically, we're talking money aren't we, the ability to earn money, your economic loss, you know, yeah, I'm going to be paying for the rest of my life. But I'm dealing with that. The one thing that I hate is, [beginning to cry] little things. Social life has gone. And that's, that's all to do with money, you know. Being abro—, in my life I've been abroad, well, three times. Three times in fifty-four years. I've never been abroad with mates, I've never been able to afford … [crying]. God. I've never been able to afford to take me mum out

> for … a decent meal … you know, oh, sorry [crying]. God. It's weird [long pause] … I haven't been the brother I would have liked to have been, the son, the uncle, the grandson. Father. The grandfather, great grandfather. Because. Not because I was discharged from hospital by mistake, but because a group of supposedly ethical, intelligent, powerful people decided that they could get away with not dealing with their mistakes and responsibility and … just being unaccountable.[1]

One of the most important findings of this book is that LiPs' lives – and cases – are significantly more complex and challenging than expected.[2] The impact of being a LiP goes deeper than anticipated. The individuals who talked to me in this study, like Neil, quoted above, told me of long, multifaceted cases involving multiple courts that left them financially exhausted and emotionally drained. Some said the experience of pursuing a claim led to their losing their families, and some lost their homes. Many felt the experience had a negative impact on their mental health, with the spectrum covering minor anxiety, depression, severe depression and those who had been, at times, suicidal. The stories told by LiPs demonstrate significant, genuine vulnerability.

So, what to make of this finding? I am not a psychologist and am not qualified to make any judgements on the potential pathologies of interviewees, nor would such speculation be within the ethical boundaries of this research. But I am reluctant to pathologise LiPs anyway – whether diagnosing them as litigious, or obsessive or deluded. The result of this labelling is that we tend to internalise problems within an individual, at the expense of considering the context in which these individuals are acting. The emotional and psychological stress LiPs experience is at least partly, and perhaps even largely, related to the *sheer cost* of pursuing or defending a claim. In other words, a LiP's vulnerability – the vulnerability I am talking about, anyway – is not one embedded in an individual's psychology but is fundamentally connected to the legal proceedings in which that person is acting.

This chapter argues, then, that deeper engagement with LiPs telling their own stories reveals that what we might call the 'outsider' narrative of LiPs involved in multiple proceedings – that LiPs pursue a hopeless claim, come to court, lose their case, and this makes them angry and drives them to more and more fruitless litigation – is reductive, for two important reasons. First, this outside narrative implies that LiPs understand what is happening. And, mostly, they do not. Second,

[1] Neil lives in Northern England and has been in chronic pain and unable to work since he was severely beaten by a group of organised football hooligans. He was sent home from hospital, having been told his collarbone had not been fractured and, according to Neil, not having had it x-rayed. He suffered significant pain and was unable to work; his doctor subsequently told him on examination that he *had* broken his collarbone. For Neil, the hospital's failure meant that he did not receive the treatment he needed to be able to heal sufficiently to return to his livelihood as a floorer. This was the basis for the medical negligence claim he brought in the County Courts, which lasted, in one form or another, for nearly 30 years.

[2] This is partly due to the dearth of literature about LiP stories, but also due to the tendency to see LiPs as individuals navigating discrete cases: this chapter suggests that this may not in fact be the usual case, at least not for more than we think.

the outside narrative also implies that the legal system works efficiently and fairly. Quite often, it does not. This means that LiPs may bring a worthy claim but still lose. They may defend an action well, and still lose. There may be a defence available to the LiP they do not know about. But what is certain about these situations is that these individuals will feel that something fundamentally unjust has occurred in a context of considerable importance to them.[3]

What emerges from this research, then, and what I explore in this chapter and the following two chapters, is not what I expected it to be. To employ a double negative: my research does not demonstrate that LiPs do not behave in the ways ascribed to them. Instead, we might call this section 'Yes, *but*'. Some LiPs *are* involved in multiple proceedings, some *do* suffer from mental-health problems, all *are* confused and unsure of legal proceedings. But from *their* perspective, the situation looks very different. It is this perspective that I want to try to communicate.

I begin by exploring how each interviewee's story demonstrates significant complexity, across cases, courts and time, and the challenges this poses about narratives of LiPs that are orientated around 'single issues'. I then consider the issue of litigiousness by considering the stakes, arguing that, far from voluntarily or enthusiastically pursuing litigation, each LiP in this study felt they had 'no choice'. Finally, I will think about what work the lens of vulnerability can do: seeing things from a LiP's perspective, partial and emotive as it can be, can tell us something of the relationship between high stakes, impact and multiple proceedings for LiPs. And through this, we can learn something of considerable importance: how we treat vulnerable people in the courts and how we show respect for their stories.

II. Complexity

Kate: Do you have any other memories of making a complaint?

Charles: I'm sure there are lots but I can't actually remember at the moment [laughter]. I'm always trying to, always complaining about something to be honest [laughter].

Kate: Why do you think that is?

Charles: No, I, 'cause over the years, once you get, um, once you start complaining, because when you see people have deliberately taken the pee, you can't just, just let it go, you can't just turn your back on it so you tend to try and fight for your rights.

Kate: So in your experience you usually have to be persistent?

Charles: I think you have, because people just deliberately take the mickey because they know that a lot of people won't bother and a lot of people don't know their rights so they just take the mickey.

[3] In this respect, this chapter echoes Didi Herman's findings in her article on vexatious litigants, where she makes a similar point: a 'focus on the litigant's pathologies occludes an understanding of the broader social and political context within which such litigation, at times, arises'. See D Herman, 'Hopeless Cases: Race, Racism and the "Vexatious Litigant"' (2012) 8 *International Journal of Law in Context* 27.

A striking finding of this study was how many individuals were involved in multiple proceedings. In this sample, 13 of 15 interviewees had been involved in more than one case. Of the two who had *not* been involved in multiple cases, one, Trevor, was in the process of preparing to start a second case that arose directly from the circumstances of the first case. This means only one interviewee, Tim, had a single, discrete experience of attending County Court, receiving a judgment (against him) and then ceasing proceedings. Of the 13 who had gone to court multiple times, their litigation spanned from between two to three years (Eleanor) to over 30 years (Oliver). Neil, for example, as outlined in at the start of this chapter, has been pursuing some kind of remedy since the early 1990s. This has taken him to the County Courts, as well as to the Appeal Courts and directly to the High Court. Peter has been to the County Courts, the Family Courts and the Queen's Bench on multiple occasions over the last five years. Leo has participated in proceedings in the County Court, the High Court, multiple employment tribunals and, most recently, the Immigration Tribunal. Marie, in her late 20s at time of interview, has been involved in legal proceedings almost non-stop since the age of 21. At one point, in 2012, she was involved in five different proceedings occurring simultaneously: 'Basically we had cases in the County Court, we had cases in the Family District of the High Court, we had cases in erm, European Court of Human Rights, we basically had cases in every level of court going.'

This complexity cannot, of course, be separated from the methodology of this project. Ultimately, advertising for this project meant seeking interviewees identifying themselves as LiPs, as well as having the available, unpaid time to complete what was a very long interview. My sample is more likely to contain individuals who have been involved in more complex situations, as the average 'one-shotter' LiP perhaps does not consider their story to be sufficiently of interest to a researcher, or does not identify with the label 'litigant in person'.[4] But while this may be a factor in these findings, and we cannot make any assumptions as to how representative this complexity is across *all* LiPs, this finding reminds us that the assumption that County Court cases are simple and discrete belies the potential complexity of any individual's legal history.

So *how* do LiPs come to be involved in multiple actions? In chapter 1, I argued that there was a tendency on the part of the legal profession to conflate all LiPs with high-risk and vexatious litigants. This was at least partially because of the perception that LiPs are more likely to be involved in more than one case. By performing this conflation, the legal profession provides its own explanation as to why individuals pursue multiple cases. As Didi Herman notes, vexatious litigants are

> characterized as falling into one of two groups: those with histories of mental health problems who launch multiple legal actions against diverse targets; and those whose

[4] M Galanter, 'Why the Haves Come Out Ahead: Speculation on the Limits of Legal Change' (1974) 9 *Law and Society Review* 98.

initial legal action, for example (one that recurs often) a complaint of discrimination under the Race Relations Act (RRA; now incorporated into the Equality Act 2010), was resolved against them, and who then attempt to carry on with aspects of that complaint in various ways.[5]

A minority of interviewees in this sample clearly met the latter definition: that is, their multiple actions seemed to spring from obsessively continuing a complaint they felt was wrongly decided, to the point that they had become actively conspiracist in their attitudes towards the legal profession.[6] But the majority of the interviewees did not seem to fit the description. And yet they pursued multiple complaints. So how had this come about? For some interviewees, their multiple different actions were unrelated.[7] But for others, the picture is more complicated: in the stories the interviewees narrated, it often *was* about pursuing other actions relating to an initial injury or wrong. And yet, to characterise these individuals as vexatious is arguably to insufficiently consider the circumstances in which this took place. For example, for one interviewee, the impetus towards starting another complaint was due to bureaucratic errors, where not to continue a 'related' complaint would be not to be able to seek restitution for something that was clearly unfair. This is the case of Trevor.[8]

Trevor was sued by a contractor for withholding some of the money promised to complete a job.[9] Sending away his forms to the central Northampton Claims Processing, Trevor then heard nothing for several weeks before receiving a letter from the court telling him they had lost some of his paperwork and asking him to re-send it. He then did so. A further few weeks passed before the court again contacted him, claiming it had not received his resubmitted paperwork. He then re-sent it a second time, this time ('luckily for me' as he puts it) using recorded delivery. He was then sent a letter explaining that the case had been allocated to

[5] Herman (n 3) 28.

[6] This includes interviewees Anna, Frederick, Russell and Georgina. However, even these stories do not necessarily imply that their original complaint had no merit, or that any of their subsequent legal actions were baseless.

[7] Eleanor is relevant here. There is no relation between her first case as a defendant and her subsequent two civil actions. When Eleanor went to prison, her mother was elderly and unwell but still at home. A decline in her mother's health led to her being moved into care. This meant that Eleanor's property, which she was keeping at her mother's house, including her two cats, no longer had a home. Both of Eleanor's subsequent actions relate to trying to recover her lost property when she was in prison. Similarly, Charles's family proceedings, in the old County Courts, are totally separate proceedings from his civil claims. Leo, too, is currently involved with the Immigration Tribunal as regards his wife's right to remain in the UK; this is unconnected with his previous multiple experiences at the Employment Tribunal.

[8] This also again chimes with the reality of the multiple interlocking problems individuals experience. See P Pleasence, 'Causes of Action: First Findings of the LSRC Periodic Survey' (2003) 30 *Journal of Law and Society* 11; N Balmer et al, 'Worried Sick: The Experience of Debt Problems and their Relationship with Health, Illness and Disability' (2006) 5 *Social Policy and Society* 39.

[9] Trevor never disputed this, but he had deliberately withheld some of the money because the contractor had done a substandard job, some of which he had to employ another contractor to put right. When he received a summons from the small claims court relating to this, he felt confident that he was justified in his actions.

the County Court.[10] He heard nothing after this until he received a letter telling him that because he failed to submit his defence, the judge had found against him ('thrown my case out'). Luckily for Trevor, he had a sister who was a qualified lawyer, who helped him to have the judgment set aside.[11] Unfortunately, in the meantime, the initial judgment resulted in bailiffs being sent to Trevor's door. He had to pay them to leave, and the loss of money from this, as well as what he called the blatant overcharging of the bailiffs (even though they were also not meant to be there), has led to his preparing to go back to court.

Trevor's case demonstrates that simple administrative errors can potentially lead to a LiP's losing a case. While his case is the only example in this study of poor bureaucratic practice that, in Trevor's version at least, leads *directly* to a negative outcome, numerous other individuals in this study talked of similar problems, including not receiving materials from the courts, the courts' failure to send them judgments, missing or incomplete case files and other errors that posed serious problems for them, resulting in delays and additional time and anxiety.[12] Marie, for example, relates the experience of a missing case file:

> I mean it's like um, we nearly ended up with a boycotted he——, first hearing on the contact case because they put the j——, they put the application in front of uh, the judge that had actually been the QC in the previous court contact case, you know what I mean? It's simple mistakes made by the court like that can cause so much, like messing around and everything. The court, the courts are so lackadaisical about things at times. Then you, then you ring up and try and speak to um, a clerk about something and they're like, they don't even know what's going on and then it's like you turn up in court and there's uh, no court bundles, we actually ah, turn up in court and there's actually erm, bundles missing. We had to lend, lend the judge our bundle until erm, the missing bundle which is found at another, was actually found at, um, at the criminal cour–, the criminal court, it was actually found at the criminal court and they had to send a taxi to go [laugh], go and get the files. You know what I mean? It's simple stuff like that make it so much hard work.

Trevor's case, as well as the similar experiences of Leo, Talia and others, illustrates that administrative issues can quite easily lead to mistakes and, potentially, unfair outcomes. This is clearly a relevant concern for LiPs in a context of increased 'efficiency' measures, such as central processing in Northampton, and increasingly limited telephonic and face-to-face contact in the courtrooms themselves due to a reduction of court staff.[13] Interviewees in this study noted the difficulty they

[10] Trevor had also ticked the box signalling his willingness to mediate, but he never heard any more about this.

[11] Eventually Trevor and the contractor came before a judge and decided an amount they both agreed on.

[12] Both Leo and Talia also had considerable problems with the courts not providing information to them on their respective cases.

[13] The repetition of the same complaints of poor administration indicate that this is a key issue for LiPs, and not one generally dwelt on in LiP studies, which usually focus on LiPs' inability to successfully navigate advice or follow instructions. See K Williams, *Litigants in Person: A Literature Review*

had simply trying to speak to somebody at the courtrooms: the central telephone line failed to pick up or would transfer to voicemail. Similarly, emails received an automated response, and there was no way of reaching someone who could assist them as to what to do next. Most enquiries led to their being redirected to the website of HM Courts and Tribunals Service (HMCTS) only, which contains very limited information to assist LiPs.[14] However, what is also important to consider is the impact this may have for the majority of LiPs, who may be unaware of what 'normal' proceedings are like.

Trevor repeatedly stressed during his interview that it was only because he had privileged access to someone legally qualified that he was able to know what to do to redress the situation (although he still ended up £1,000 out of pocket). Most people who act as LiPs will not have such privileged access and were, he stressed, at considerable risk, particularly those who were more vulnerable:

> It's [central processing], it's like half-arsed, to use that, it's not, there, there should be loads of, there should be loads of places that you can go and access information and someone within the court system that you can speak to that's there to help you because you are not legally trained. But there isn't anything like that, you have to find it for yourself and that to me is silly 'cause it's law you're talking, it's, it's, it's still a legal thing, it's still something that can be, can, you know, can have ramifications, you know, and yet it's just left for you to do. And I, you know, that might be alright for some people who are, you know, quite intelligent and fairly, you know, together, but if you're a drug addict or, or somebody not that, you know, academically bright, or can't read very well, or, or all those sorts of things then it's not going to be that easy for you is it?

For those individuals, it would be exceedingly difficult to, first, be able to identify what had gone wrong and, second, be able to rectify the situation.[15] This returns us again to LiPs' feeling of a lack of accessibility to courtroom staff who could help.[16] As Marie puts it, LiPs are considerably disadvantaged compared with legal professionals:

> I've had a hell of a lot of issues filing applications and erm, applications going missing and it seems to happen more if you're a litigant in person than it does for solicitors,

(London, Ministry of Justice, 2011) 1. This issue is picked up again in ch 6 when we look at the future of civil justice litigation.

[14] It is worth reflecting here on Pat Carlen's characterisation of courts as 'theatres of the absurd'. See P Carlen, 'The Staging of Magistrate's Justice' (1976) 16 *British Journal of Criminology* 48. Jacobson, Hunter and Kirby, and Paul Rock also call attention to the 'chaotic' nature of legal proceedings, with Jacobson describing them as 'structured mayhem'. See J Jacobsen et al, *Structured Mayhem: Personal Experiences of the Crown Court* (London, Criminal Justice Alliance, 2015); P Rock, *The Social World of an English Crown Court* (Oxford, Oxford University Press, 1993).

[15] The concern that such individuals might 'give up' is noted by H Genn and Y Genn, *The Effectiveness of Representation at Tribunals* (London, Lord Chancellor's Department, 1989); G Cookson, *Unintended Consequences: The Cost of the Government's Legal Aid Reforms: A Report for the Law Society of England & Wales* (London, KCL, 2011).

[16] This belief is supported by findings from the HMCTS survey into court staff carried out by the Trade Union Congress (TUC), which demonstrates a reduced, deskilled and demoralised court staff. See TUC, *Speak Up For Justice* at www.tuc.org.uk/sites/default/files/Justice_Denied_Report.pdf.

> like solicitors have internal emails and you're given a lot more information if you're a solicitor, you're given you know, more precedence whereas if you're a litigant in person you've got to go through the direct channels, you can't have communications through the court a—, except via a generic email, uh, generic phone, phone number, erm, and uh, solicitors have direct access to the judges you know what I mean? They can email a judge, they can send paperwork directly to the judge, litigant, again litigants in person don't have that power, they don't have, are not, are never, very rarely given that opportunity. I mean, I have once or twice which was pretty lucky to be honest with you but a gen—, as a general rule litigants in person have to go round the houses to get where they're going whereas solicitors are given all the shortcuts.

As Trevor sees it:

> It seems to me that the, the court system is full of error, 'cause, you know, you hear of it all the time, stuff going missing, and getting lost and not having it, people turning up and this not happening and also, it seems from the outside, *sup*er inefficient. It seems. Now there's probably loads of reason why it is like that, you know, but on, on bigger cases I can imagine, you know, there is a lot of bits and they need to come together on a particular day and you only need one of those bits not to be there that you can't proceed with.

For Trevor, court processes are by 'nature' inefficient, and efficiency measures can only undermine any fairness. This situation of administrative error, then, is clearly either far more likely to happen to LiPs in the first place, or far more likely to be more difficult to rectify than it would be for legal professionals. This is assuming, of course, that the LiP is even able to recognise what has gone wrong. If the LiP does attempt to rectify these problems, however, these administrative failures certainly present a persuasive reason for an individual to pursue a further complaint related to their initial proceedings, without its being symptomatic of inherent litigiousness. Here, for Trevor, the transformation from 'one-shotter' to 'repeat player' has little to do with psychology and far more to do with the inefficiency of the legal context in which he was operating, as well as relating to the considerable disadvantage LiPs operate under compared with legal professionals.

Summarising the above, then, it is clear that multiple proceedings can be unrelated, or can be due to court system failures. Any on-the-surface assumption that conflates LiPs involved in multiple proceedings with vexatious litigation purely on this basis can therefore be wrong. If, for example, an assumption is made that *because* LiPs have been involved in multiple proceedings, they are more likely to be vexatious, this becomes a kind of circularity of logic and can detract from the serious hearing of a LiP's claim. However, it would be disingenuous to represent the majority of LiPs' multiple proceedings as down to bureaucratic failure. Although it is a frequent occurrence along the way, such failure does *not* explain the bulk of the interviewees' complex legal proceedings in this sample. Here the picture is much murkier. For the majority of interviewees involved in complex proceedings who spoke to me, these people were pursuing, at times obsessively, claims that proliferated around an initial 'wrong'. This clearly echoes the outline of a typical 'vexatious litigant' that Herman summarises in her article. But even for *these* individuals, as I will argue in section III, to conflate complexity and vexatiousness is to mistake the gravity of the injury that prompted their initial contact with law. It is also, importantly, to potentially misunderstand what these individuals are trying to achieve by going to law in the first place.

III. High Stakes

> So um, I go to court.[17] I leave —— [Peter's wife] at home with —— [Peter's daughter]. In court they're [the local authority] getting thrashed, they're getting thrashed in court. The judge is doing in his nut with them, he's gone ballistic with them because they're saying: 'The judge before, she's corrupt!' I just can't, I was just totally in turmoil, I couldn't believe, I was just, ha, couldn't believe what was going on, they were like absolutely desperate. 'Yeah the judge's corrupt' and I always remember it, the judge he turned around and he said, 'so you're telling me that the judge, the previous judge, is corrupt and they've made the wrong decision?'. 'Yeah, yeah that's right!'. He said 'right, I've never heard nothing like this in my whole career'. He said 'I'm going to adjourn now' and he said 'I want you to seriously consider what you've just been saying' and this is to the local authority. So we adjourn. This is about 11 o'clock in the morning … then five, maybe five minutes later, I stayed in the courtroom, and um, five minutes later, um, my wife's solicitor comes in. Guy. Nice bloke. He, he said, 'uh, I just, I just phoned up —— [Peter's wife] to give her an update'. He said, 'you'd better go home'. I said, 'well why?' 'Oh she don't' sound well'. 'Oh … what do you mean?' 'Well she don't sound well, you'd better go home. Wait until the judge comes in, ask him to leave' and so I did, and I go off home, going, uh, what's going on?
>
> So gets to my, drives home, gets to two streets away down that way, E——. There's a great big police van across the road, I think, what the, what's this? So, they've stopped, 'who are you?' so I told them, so pull up over there and he said 'just wait', and he radioed through and all I could see all the way down the road and our house is at the bottom, is police vehicles. I think what the hell is happening? So, I uh, wait, and this car comes out, green car, with two police officers in it. And they, they say 'oh can you sit, sit in the uh, sit in the back and have a chat'. They said, 'uh, there's been a incident'. I said, 'what, well what incident?' And they said 'oh your wife, uh, she's took a overdose'. Oh my —, … I said, 'well wh—, wh—, what about ——, where, where's my daughter? Where's our daughter?' 'Oh, um, well there's been an incident', and they wouldn't, and I said 'well, wh—, what is it? Oh. I said 'well where are they?' 'Well, your wife's gone to —— Hospital'. I said, 'but where's my daughter? 'Oh well, he's gone to —— [hospital]'. I said, 'well why?' and then they said, 'oh there's been an incident. She's been stabbed'.
>
> And that was it I just [exhaling noise], I just like burst into tear– oh my god. And um, off we go. They race me in the car over to —— hospital A&E and um, I'm sat in the, they said 'wait here', so I'm sat in the car waiting, they rush into A&E. They come out and they say 'right come on in, we're going to the family room'. So go in the family room,

[17] This is Peter talking, and the case for which he attends court is trying to stop the local authority from taking his daughter into care.

> I'm just in like, uh, total, state and um, I get in there and I, I just, a [exhalation], terrible. And um, they say 'social services are outside, we told them to get', oh he said 'we've told them to leave' and they wanted to come in to see me! Like, and I said, 'well what's going on?' Then the surgeon comes in, and uh he says 'oh we're operating on, on your daughter'. They've had operating, lifesaving, touch and go. I, I find out she, she, what happened, she, she tried to kill herself and our daughter. She stabbed her eight times. She, she tried to kill her. And uh, yeah they had three surgeons working on him, and obviously, thankfully they saved her life.

Peter has been in and out of court since 2010, trying to regain custody of his daughter.[18] At the time of the events outlined above, the local authority was already trying to remove Peter's daughter from his and his wife's care because of concerns about Peter's wife's mental health and stability. After the incident, Peter lost custody despite, as he has always argued, there not being any evidence against *him* as an inadequate parent.[19] For him, going to court is, and has always been, a means of trying to be reunited with his daughter. At the time of the interview, his daughter had been in foster care for over seven years, and Peter had had no success in the courts. Peter's case is clearly an extreme and unusual situation, yet it illustrates the point that the clear majority of the LiPs I spoke to only pursued claims that were of considerable significance: indeed, for some, like Peter, the stakes could not be higher. This is also the case for Neil, quoted at the start of this chapter. For him, the alleged failure of the hospital staff, and the subsequent inability to obtain some form of restitution, led to his losing his livelihood and, through this, his means of being able to afford to have his own family. Marie's story also fits this narrative. When Marie was 20 years old, her baby was taken from her care. After assessment in a Mother and Baby Unit, the child was fostered and then, ultimately, adopted. Marie has been fighting in the courts since then, in one way or another, to get her child back.[20]

The above cases might perhaps seem more extreme examples compared with a more 'typical' LiP experience. But of course there *is* no typical LiP experience. And this study suggests that any idea we might have of discrete and straightforward dispute resolution may itself be less normal than experience of the contrary, which, as shown above, is messy, confusing and complicated. Many other LiP experiences in this study also indicate, if not quite as extremely, a similar proportional level of personal significance to the individual in question. This is well illustrated by the case of Eleanor. When Eleanor was in prison, her mother's health

[18] This has mostly been, prior to 2014, the family section of the County Court and, post-2014, the Family Court, although also at times the higher courts as well.

[19] Peter's wife was convicted of attempted manslaughter and is currently detained indefinitely under the Mental Health Act. He has not had contact with her since 2010. Peter's son's foster home is less than two blocks from where Peter currently lives, and as of the time of interview they had regular supervised contact that was soon to shift to unsupervised contact. As Peter puts it, what is most likely to happen is that as his son grows older, he will then have his own say about where he wants to live, and Peter is optimistic that this will result in his son's coming home.

[20] Similarly, Talia has been fighting possession proceedings on her home. As of September 2017 she had been evicted, and to date she still continuing to fight to regain access to the property.

deteriorated, leading to her mother's ultimately going into a care home, eventually passing away. When Eleanor's mother went into care, Eleanor's possessions and her cats, which had all been at her mother's house, went into storage and her cats went into a cattery. Somehow, throughout the course of her imprisonment, the cattery bills were unpaid, and an employee at the cattery took it upon herself to take the cats home. Eleanor then went to the County Courts as a LiP to reclaim possession of her cats. On the surface, this may not seem as significant as fighting for the custody of a child, but from Eleanor's perspective, fighting for return of her cats was as important as any fight in her life could be. As she expressed it:

> It was fairly antagonistic because it's basically sort of 'how dare you walk off with my property and my family', because basically those two are my family and it's like, it's the same as me turning up, you know, deciding I like, I've taken a fancy to your kids and taking them home with me. You wouldn't like that so, you know, it's the same thing.

For Eleanor, her two cats *were* her family, and the case in County Court was essentially, therefore, a custody dispute. As she said:

> It had become a point of honour by that point, just because I'd been in prison doesn't mean you get to help yourself to whatever you fancy of mine with no consequences which was basically the attitude she'd [the employee who had taken Eleanor's cats home from the cattery] taken.

As well as being about keeping together the only family Eleanor had at this point, for Eleanor it was also about retaining a sense of identity. Alongside the case to get her cats back, Eleanor also fought as a LiP in the County Court, to retrieve her possessions, which had been stored in a place she could not access.[21] Essentially, the loss of her possessions and of her cats would mean that Eleanor had no connection whatsoever to her previous existence when released from prison. As it turned out, she managed to win back her cats but not her possessions, and so when she returned to the community her cats were all she had.[22]

These stories remind us that for many LiPs, they are in court, and only in court, to address issues of great importance to them.[23] They would not be there if they did not have to be. As Eleanor says, 'people don't go to court on a whim, they usually go to court as a last resort in a civil matter and, in criminal court, they get no choice and the implications of judgment can have huge consequences for people'. Eleanor emphasises what was expressed uniformly in this study: that is,

[21] As Eleanor tells it, the solicitors [for her mother's estate] involved in this storage refused to move it to a nearer facility that Eleanor could access on day release from prison. Because of this, Eleanor was not physically able to go there to retrieve her things and organise to have them moved. However, she was also not allowed to send a proxy. This meant that eventually, her possessions were disposed of.

[22] The sheer significance of the cats to Eleanor's sense of personhood is evident not just in this narrative but also in the interviewing process itself, which took place at Eleanor's home. Eleanor's cats were present, interview breaks were made around the cats' feeding times and, fittingly, the cats can be heard throughout on the interview tape.

[23] This of course demonstrates the huge amount of emotion involved in these cases versus a civil justice system that does its best, as Paul Rock notes, to keep emotions at bay. See P Rock, 'Witnesses and Spaces in a Crown Court' (1991) 31 *British Journal of Criminology* 266.

that going to law is a last resort. The LiPs in this sample routinely expressed that they felt that they only went down a legal path when they felt they had no other choice. As Tim said, 'I tend not to, as I say, I tend not to complain unless there is something fairly significant to, to complain about'. Charles similarly remarked, when discussing going to court over what he argued was misappropriation of the funds from his property sale, 'I tried to avoid litigation because, um, he's [his opposition] um, he's a barrister, and um I don't know, I don't want to, I didn't want to get involved in that because of the cost, so, um, eventually I had no choice'. This belief that they largely had no choice was echoed by Marie, Talia, Peter, Oliver, Russell, Frederick and others. As Talia put it, it was to be done only in the context of something of the utmost significance: 'It's, it's something that, if you have to do it you have to do it, you, you, um, sometimes the choice is between, between being a litigant in person and losing your, your home or your rights to, um, well any of your rights.'

From the above, therefore, it is clear that many LiPs will only go to law when the stakes are sufficiently high and they feel there is no other choice. There are, however, two things important to note here. First, of course, LiPs' feeling that they had no choice is not the same thing as their actually *having* no choice, and I would not want to mistake one for the other. Second, of course, what is of utmost significance to these LiPs may not be accorded the same significance in a wider context. While Peter and Marie's fights for their children might be recognisably significant, for example, Eleanor's case might seem less so. But what is important is that it tells us about the significant investment and *belief* each LiP has in the case he or she is pursuing or defending, and the seriousness with which he or she takes the decision to pursue or defend a legal matter. It should also, perhaps, give us pause if we do not question the use of litigation in the context of a matter involving significant amounts of money but we are sceptical of litigation over things that are deeply connected to a litigant's identity.

This serves as a reminder of a point frequently returned to in this book: that LiP perceptions of significance frequently differ from legal perceptions of significance. Underestimating the importance of an issue to a LiP can lead to failure to see *why* a LiP might pursue what someone else might consider 'Pretty Boring Stuff'.[24] The gap between these different ways of seeing can lead to a situation where the courts risk trivialising or undermining a LiP's cause, especially where this might result from failure to recognise the relative weight or value a LiP may accord to it.[25] Therefore, LiPs run the risk of being dismissed as vexatious or time-wasting, and can even be financially punished for carrying on, even if the case is of the utmost significance (to them).[26]

[24] D Cowan and E Hitchings, 'Pretty Boring Stuff: District Judges and Housing Possession' (2007) 16 *Social & Legal Studies* 363.

[25] This is, of course, not the case for the Family Court or Court of Protection.

[26] In ch 5 I look at examples where a LiP continuing a dispute can be financially penalised.

Returning, then, to Herman's definition of the vexatious litigant, we now run into some problems. Clearly, as I stated above, some LiPs may consider their case to be significant, but that will not prevent the proceedings from being vexatious. This is seen in those who verge on the conspiracist and who have pursued multiple, increasingly less plausible claims, and who blame their failure on corruption. Others, like Eleanor, are obviously *not* on the vexatious spectrum at all, despite attending court on multiple occasions, but they risk being perceived as potentially vexatious because the 'merit' of their case is untranslatable in the civil justice system.[27] And for people like Peter, Talia, Neil, Marie and others, the situation is even more confusing. As far as Peter is concerned, for example, anything he can do to attempt to win back his daughter, or extend contact with her, is worth the cost and time. This can mean trying in any way he can to have another hearing with a judge. This will always *relate to* the ultimate issue of the loss of custody of his daughter, but the case itself may be clearly of less merit.

For example, once a care order was made against Peter, he immediately appealed the decision as a LiP. This was despite not understanding how the appeal process worked. This resulted in the grounds that he put forward being insufficient. As he says, when he got to the appeal, the judge explained what the problem was:

> He explained the appeal is about, did the judge, the lower court do something wrong. And this is the thing, see. And um, so I ended up going back to court again there. Uh, March the 28th. Um. And then again … what have I got, yeah April 2012, yeah, I must have went three times then … yeah, went three times, yeah, but it ended up he couldn't do nothing. So the care order stayed in place obviously, um, and I couldn't do nothing.

At this point, Peter's appeal was technically without merit. And yet this is clearly because he did not understand how an appeal worked and how narrow the terms of a successful appeal had to be. He himself says 'I must have went three times then', and he is unable to clearly articulate on what legal grounds he felt justified in doing so. From Peter's perspective, then, it seems that an appeal is another chance to explain that he should have custody of his daughter, and to argue that the previous case was decided incorrectly. This is something that may be characteristic of vexatious proceedings, but it is far more understandable if we consider it in the context of the longer narrative. And therefore, the more chances Peter has of doing this, the more chances he has of overturning the initial decision against him.

[27] While Eleanor has gone to court twice, she has been successful once, with the judge clearly finding merit in her argument and in returning her cats to her. Her previous experiences with court proceedings do not interfere with this assessment; none of them bear any relation to obsessive pursuit of any particular target, nor do they evidence any desire to compulsively pursue legal proceedings.

Peter's story, and similar versions of it, is what I heard repeatedly throughout these interviews: individuals who have a central injustice or wrong for which they are trying to seek a remedy. While this fits into what Herman described – the individuals initiate or defend a complaint that 'was resolved against them, and who then attempt to carry on with aspects of that complaint in various ways' (see section II) – this description does not sufficiently get to grips with *why* they might be doing so. This *why* seems to be about seeking a sense of justice and 'rightness'; but underlying it, there seems to be a hope amongst LiPs that going before a judge *one more time* might finally lead to that judge's overturning the original wrong. This is an impossible wish, but one that arguably drives many. So, while Marie might now be pursuing a case against the local authority for their failures to *her* while she grew up in care, underlying it is the belief that these systemic failures materially contributed to the circumstances in which she lost her child. As such, if she were to succeed in this action, then greater scrutiny might be paid to all situations where those raised in care lost custody of their own child. And there is then a perceivable window of possibility that this could result in something changing: perhaps an inquiry, perhaps a scandal, something *else* that could undo what has been done.[28]

Similarly, for Peter, once he had exhausted the appeal process, he kept returning to court looking for other things to help him somehow subvert the care-order decision. For example, he discovered that before the permanent care order was made, the interim care orders (ICOs) were incomplete: that is, there was a 17-day gap that was not accounted for in the ICOs issued. For Peter, this was a chance to prove that his daughter had been detained 'illegally'.[29] It is not difficult to see how this is a 'hopeless case'. However, it is also easy to see that from Peter's perspective, it is about dismantling the initial wrong decision somehow, *anyhow*, and a technicality will do. Peter was hopeful that if this had been found to be so, then retrospectively the ICOs would have been voided, and that therefore the permanent care order could not have been issued.[30] That this is a hopeless belief is apparent to individuals with more knowledge of the legal system, but from Peter's perspective, any action to gain access to his daughter was, and is, worth a try.

I argued earlier that the definition of a 'litigant in person' as an individual involved in a discrete proceeding essentially fractures the longer individual narratives that are essential and relevant to LiPs' understanding of how they came

[28] Herman (n 3) 28. This belief also has echoes of Nobles and Schiff's construction of perceptions of 'miscarriages of justice', where lay and law conceptions of 'justice' fundamentally talked across one another; here we literally have individuals talking across one another in the court. See R Nobles and D Schiff, *Understanding Miscarriages of Justice: Law, the Media and the Inevitability of a Crisis* (Oxford, Oxford University Press, 2001).

[29] This tendency of LiPs to be hyperliteral about legal documents and their authenticity is something I return to in ch 6, which reflects on the undermining of trust and development of conspiracist explanations for failed litigation.

[30] It is interesting to reflect here that this echoes Ewick and Silbey's claim about 'narrative' in how everyday laypersons understand law. See P Ewick and S Silbey, *The Common Place of Law: Stories from Everyday Life* (Chicago, IL, University of Chicago Press, 1988) 29.

to be acting for themselves in any situation. This can create the appearance of vexatiousness in individuals who are pursuing something that, from their perspective, is both significant and quite straightforward. For LiPs, their *case* is about the longer story: restitution for a wrong, the return of their child, the security of their home.[31] In this respect, it would seem that those who are *most* likely to pursue what could be considered vexatious proceedings are those who are pursuing claims of the *greatest* significance – as far from 'time-wasters', from their perspective at least, as is humanly possible.

This fracturing of LiP narrative leads to the potential proliferation of 'hopeless cases'. However, it can also arguably lead to another, related problem, which is the diminishment of the ability of LiPs to effectively represent themselves in court, regardless of the inherent merit of any proceeding. This issue became apparent in this study. It was notable how many interviewees struggled to be able to tell their story coherently during their interview. This was often because, as noted above, the complaint or 'big issue' took the form of multiple different levels of proceedings. For example, Charles went from talking about the case where he took his conveyancing solicitor to court over misappropriated funds put into an investment property (the court termed this a partnership dispute, although Charles vehemently rejected this label), to talking about his negligence claim against his solicitor, heard in the High Court. The sheer difficulty of holding all of this information in one's head was evidenced in the confusing language deployed: 'I think this … this one was actually after my experiences with the, um, with, it sort of goes back now to this case and then that one came up after that.' This was repeated again and again by others, when they were tasked with outlining what each case was about and what happened during it.[32]

The process of asking each interviewee to describe cases one by one causes considerable difficulty; I would argue that this is because, from a LiP's perspective, it is the wrong or the harm that is the central organising feature, and the cases feature secondarily in amongst this. As Ewick and Silbey note,

> one is never before only the law because any legal matter is also a matter about something else … everyday life occurs as interactions among friends, among colleagues, among family members, between consumers and merchants. These relationships are the raw materials out of which disputes and legal cases emerge.[33]

This means the experience of interviewing was frequently about catching individuals in the middle of an experience that for them made no sense without a wider context.

[31] Here we might reflect again on the professional expertise required to identify potential legal problems. See W Felstiner et al, 'The Emergence and Transformation of Disputes: Naming, Blaming, Claiming …' (1980) 15 *Law and Society Review* 631.

[32] This includes Georgina, Talia, Anna and others. Of course, memory and time elapsed since then are factors in this, but even taking this into consideration, the marked confusion between one case and another is suggestive of a real problem for LiPs involved in multiple cases.

[33] Ewick and Silbey (n 31) 284.

This also tells us that if these LiPs are struggling to explain their stories to me in the context of an interview, this probably reflects a similar struggle that occurs when they are in the courtroom. It seems likely that LiPs will similarly be unable to separate out incidents, nor be able to stick only to the relevant matter of a hearing, because the complex nature of their claims means that it is not necessarily clear to them how they can be separable in the first place.[34] This must be a disadvantage for LiPs and add fuel to the perception that they are unable to stick to the point.[35] It also fuels the perception of LiPs as obsessed, returning again and again to what for them is the most important factors, and what for the court is frequently irrelevant.

Yet what this section has demonstrated is that, from the perspective of the LiP, multiple cases are not pursued on a whim, and are only undertaken out of sheer necessity. This problematises the assumption that LiPs who pursue multiple proceedings are necessarily vexatious. While some of the proceedings themselves may be spurious, they do not stem from a frivolous impetus. Until we better understand this gap between perception and reality, and until we recognise the disjuncture between, on the one hand, LiPs' right of access to the civil courts for dispute resolution and, on the other hand, the significant barriers they face, the complexity of LiP experience is likely to be dismissed as anomalous or, at worst, indicative of LiP mischief. The reality for these LiPs, though, is that going to court is far from fun; instead, it has a real, detrimental impact on their lives in a variety of ways.

IV. Vulnerability

It is perhaps unsurprising that the LiPs most involved in multiple legal proceedings were impacted by them the most deeply, but what is notable is that even those involved in only relatively minor or short proceedings spent some time in these interviews emphasising how difficult they found the experience.[36] While it is of course important to emphasise that much of the impact and strain of legal proceedings is clearly inseparable from the actual hurt or wrong that prompts those proceedings in the first place (to blame all of Peter's negative experience on legal proceedings, for example, would of course be to overlook the extremely painful and difficult situation he found himself in), even taking this into consideration, clearly, being a LiP is extremely hard and stressful work.

[34] Felstiner et al (n 32) 648.

[35] The introduction of irrelevant material is highlighted by Richard Moorhead. See R Moorhead, '"The Passive Arbiter": Litigants in Person and the Challenge to Neutrality' (2007) 16(3) *Social and Legal Studies* 405; see also *Jones v Longley and Others* [2016] EWHC 1309 (Ch).

[36] Trevor, for example, as mentioned in section II, was involved in only one case, but bureaucratic errors led to bailiffs' arriving on his doorstep and his losing over £1,000.

I stated in the opening of this chapter that I did not want to talk about vulnerabilities in terms of pre-existing mental health issues. But it is important to reflect on the degree to which a lens of vulnerability may help us understand the disadvantaged parties in legal proceedings, such as LiPs. Vulnerability is much more commonly discussed, and understood, in criminal proceedings than in civil proceedings, with special measures designed to assist vulnerable witness participation having been implemented since the enactment of the Youth Justice and Criminal Evidence Act (YJCEA) 1999. In the criminal context, vulnerability refers to any witness whose 'quality of evidence is likely to be diminished' due to their age (all those aged under 18 are considered vulnerable), disability, psychological disorder or mental-health issue.[37] This category also includes sexual offence complainants. In the civil courts, vulnerability and the need for special measures have been recognised, but such measures have not been implemented through primary legislation. Rather, it is left to the discretion of the presiding judge to offer accommodations similar to those given in criminal proceedings, which includes the use of screens, intermediaries or video-link testimony.[38] Due to this discretionary power, we know very little about how and when such special measures are implemented, and this further evidences the relatively less-well-understood nature of vulnerability in civil proceedings.

But beyond the limited applicability of special measures for civil procedures, the term 'vulnerable' itself largely escapes interrogation in this procedural and legislative context. What do we actually mean by 'vulnerable'? As Munro and Scoular point out, vulnerability tends to 'conflate … many different experiences and positions' and 'fails to dissect and interrogate the multiple and complex causes (both inter-personal and social) of that vulnerable condition'.[39] They go on to note '[w]hat is more, it tends to attach the condition too firmly to the individual herself'.[40] The tendency to label individuals as vulnerable, in other words, is a mechanism by which the vulnerability is internalised, at the risk of failing to recognise the context in which such an individual may be vulnerable. This is something I recognise and feel concern about in labelling LiPs as vulnerable: we are very good, on the whole, at finding fault in these individuals; but as this book stresses, it is the context in which they operate, which is not designed for them, that exacerbates and worsens their experiences. So the label 'vulnerability' can operate to forestall examination of the systemic constraints in which LiPs operate.

But, on the other hand, in a legal context, the roll call of those who may find it difficult to communicate and traumatic to participate is far longer than generally recognised. As Mulcahy points out, in a context in which court proceedings

[37] YJCEA 1999, pt II, including s 22A, added in 2009 to cover sexual-offence complainants. This provision refers to witnesses only, however.

[38] Civil Justice Council, Vulnerable Witnesses and Parties in Civil Proceedings: Current Position and Recommendations for Change (London, CJC, 2020).

[39] V Munro and J Scoutar, 'Abusing Vulnerability? Contemporary Law and Policy Responses to Sex Work in the UK' (2012) 20 *Feminist Legal Studies* 189, 201.

[40] ibid.

(particularly criminal ones) are intimidating and stressful, we should recognise that all witnesses are potentially vulnerable.[41] In this respect, to recognise the vulnerability of LiPs can be to draw attention to the daily difficulties faced by all laypersons attempting to participate in legal processes. Such a label can perhaps be useful without implying some kind of pathological judgement. Here I think the work of Jacqueline Gibbs can articulate a pathway. Gibbs notes that there is a tendency to assume that the label of vulnerability is dichotomous with agency and autonomy, but she disagrees, arguing that we can avoid this and see 'efforts to develop an ontological notion of vulnerability as outside of negative connotations of victimisation'.[42] In other words, being vulnerable does not render the individual a passive victim but still an individual capable of resistance.[43] So we might therefore be able to move from here to think about the stories in this book, with their accounts of trauma and devastation, as not being a result of these individuals' personalities, nor entirely due to their traumatic history, but rather a complex fusion of what happened to them in their lives that led to legal proceedings, in addition to what happened to them when they tried to pursue or defend these claims.

So here, I want to think about this framework of vulnerability to consider how the LiPs themselves felt their encounters with law affected them. We can begin this with returning to the beginning, the case of Neil. In his interview, Neil described the proceedings as costing him a considerable amount of money, both the loss of earnings he would have had, as well as huge costs involved in representing himself. But in addition to these material costs, he talks about the formidable personal costs that have come in the wake of these proceedings. Neil's quest for some kind of restitution has led to his social isolation and his inability to have a family.

For Talia, the sheer anxiety she feels on an ongoing basis, and the sheer *work* involved in staying on top of the paperwork, has led to her rarely leaving her house, except to attend court and walk her dog. As Talia put it:

> It's been very difficult. It's been by turns terrifying, I, sometimes, you know, I mean when you're in court, you're, you're being held up by adrenalin but at other times when an order or a letter arrives from them with some new insanity, it feels as if you've been hit, been hit by a baseball bat and sometimes its felt, literally felt as if my heart would stop, I was so anxious.

[41] L Mulcahy, 'The Unbearable Lightness of Being? Shifts Towards the Virtual Trial' (2008) 35 *Journal of Law and Society* 437. Martha Fineman also argues 'a descriptive account of the human condition as one of universal and continuous vulnerability': M Fineman, 'Vulnerability and Inevitable Inequality' (2017) 4 *Oslo Law Review* 133. Roxanna Dehaghani draws on Fineman's work to consider the positionality of the defendant in the police station. See R Dehaghani, 'Interrogating Vulnerability: Reframing the Vulnerable Suspect in Police Custody' (2020) 30 *Social and Legal Studies* 251.

[42] J Gibbs, *The Politics of Vulnerability: Affect, Relationality, and Resistance in UK Austerity* (Phd thesis, London School of Economics, 2018) 43 at http://etheses.lse.ac.uk/3878/1/Gibbs__the-politics-of-vulnerability.pdf.

[43] This resistance can be seen, I argue, in some of the ways in which LiPs assume and disseminate their own forms of 'expertise' in legal proceedings. I explore this in the following two chapters of this book.

Talia states quite clearly that she does not have the time, or the energy, to pursue anything else outside of this claim:

> It has completely shot up my social life, um, partly because being too tired but it's also the emotional thing as well. There was a, were a few months where I didn't, I, I became conscious that I had no conversation but, but this litigation, this litigation and the litigation against my freeholder. I, I, I don't know how long this is going to go on, and I'm going to have to try to revive my social life because I can't do without my social life.

This is echoed in Oliver's case. For Oliver, pursuing proceedings against the police led to his sectioning under the Mental Health Act, as well as the loss of his wife and family and, eventually, his home:

> Me being sectioned under the Mental Health Act, that took away two–three years of my life, lost my wife and family, my health, wealth and professional qualifications, all in the middle of these proceedings. So I'm working all summer to put that as mitigation circumstances that, that the £1 million or £1.5 million claim [against him] which is currently resting on the table should be struck out.

Currently Oliver travels to stay at friends' houses, but frequently sleeps in his car and is homeless.[44] Anna, too, has been rendered homeless on a number of occasions throughout the pursuit of legal proceedings. Talia was also evicted from her home and had a period of homelessness, although she is now in council accommodation. Both Oliver and Anna are unable to work as a direct consequence of legal proceedings. In Oliver's case, his professional licences, in the two areas in which he could earn money, were taken away as a result of his ongoing litigation and issues with the police. In Anna's case, she simply has no time to run her own business when she is also conducting complex litigation on her own.

Peter, too, lost his job as a direct consequence of legal proceedings. As he explains it:

> And um, tha–, the important part of that is actually through this pro——, these proceedings, um, I lost my job. My company was extremely supportive of me, they never wanted me to leave, they, they, really really, was impressed with my ability to work as a training manager. Um. And it came to the stage where I needed to go back to work but the only way I could do that was, um, to make a proposal, which I did, I made a proposal, not in this hearing but the one going back in the early stages. I put a proposal in, um, to change contact which would allow me to see my daughter on a weekend or the evenings, even at a contact centre if needs be. Um, but it would have freed me up to go back to work and I would have to go back, my, my, I, my work involved Monday to Friday and they even agreed about if I could ease my way back in just a few days at a time and then get back into the rhythm of things because of all the trauma. The local authority, um, in a court session, my barrister was on the phone to my boss, and her words actually to the judge was, and I'm in the witness box … Um 'this man is going to lose his job if the local authority don't agree with this proposal' and it was a reasonable proposal. It weren't nothing, you know, Uh, they turned around

[44] Charles too, had a partner leave him because of the ongoing litigation.

> and said no. That was in March 2012. In August 2012 I lost my job. And they made, basically put, it's either you see your daughter or you have your job [ironic laugh]. I mean, sorry but, just crazy.

This has resulted in Peter's being unemployed and becoming, at times, significantly depressed.

The emotional impact of conducting multiple proceedings is echoed by Marie, who elaborates on the cost of both losing her baby and attempting to get her back:

> Well at the moment, um, I'm under Mental Health Services, I've been in and out of hospital on the mental health side, erm, for the last 18 month, I've been in and out, in and out, in and out, 'cause different things trigger different feelings and erm, and like I suffered severe depression, I've been suicidal, I've been, you know what I mean, I've been through the works really over the last 18 month, um, I mean if you asked me like two, two and a half, three years ago if I'd be under Mental Health Services, been suicidal, not been able to cope with everyday things, I would have laughed in your face, I was a strong person, or so I thought I was, erm and now I'm just like I say, I'm a shell. I'm a shell of what I used to be. I can't cope with normal everyday things. I struggle daily to, to actually find the will to move forward with things and try and find a way forward with things. Erm, I've had to completely change my coping strategies, I've had to completely change, my whole life's changed, but mentally and physically I'm still stuck at the day I lost my daughter because I can't, I can't, I can't bring myself forward, I can't … my whole life, on that side of things, relationship side of things is non-existent and has been since the, the day I lost my daughter. Erm, and like I said, my mental health has deteriorated. I used to be, you know what I mean, I used to be upbeat, I used to be able to cope with things, I used to try and look on the positive side of things but now everything is just black. Everything is just dark. It's always negative and it's very hard to try and pull yourself through each day. And it's hard to convince yourself that it's better off that you are, you are are alive, it's better off that you are here for your child when you've got the feeling that they've not been told they're adopted.

Clearly, the emotional and material costs of going to court are extensive. What is also evident from these examples of cost is that they do not purely represent the cost of the traumatic event that led the litigants to court. For Marie, the emotional impact of the loss of her child and the stress and cost of the proceedings are inseparable, as is the case for most of the LiPs to whom I spoke. And this cost is significant for all LiPs, before even considering the financial cost, which, when roughly estimated by the LiPs themselves, runs into at least £1,000, minimum, to upwards of hundreds of thousands of pounds.[45] There is no doubt, for some LiPs, that mental-health issues pre-existed, or were triggered or exacerbated by the sheer emotional turmoil of the situation in which they found themselves. But even if this was the case, this vulnerability is at least worsened by the experience of going through legal proceedings.

[45] Marie estimates about £15,000.

For others, loss of income, jobs and relationships was a direct result of going to law. This is clearly a result of repeated proceedings, something that may be characterised as 'obsessional'. As discussed earlier, this is due to the emotional significance of the event that may trigger the need to pursue restitution at all costs. But it is crucial not to forget that this obsessive pursuit also occurs in a context where LiPs are not fully able to comprehend the proceedings, and where they are unable to articulate their longer narrative or have it heard: a narrative that for them is central to the reason they are there in the first place.

Going to court has a dramatically disproportionate impact on a LiP compared with a legal professional. The sheer costs of paperwork, the collision between regular working hours and court opening times, the delays and lack of notice, the poor communication by the courts and other technical aspects aggravate a situation that is already the cause of considerable emotional stress, and this can lead to situations where simply being involved in important proceedings can result in the loss of a job for an individual such as Peter. This can only exacerbate the likelihood that the case will become an obsession: because ultimately, the sheer impact of going to law can lead to a point where pursuing the case is all the LiP has left. As Peter expresses it:

> He [the judge] said 'you've been bamboozled by the court system'. I thought yeah, that speaks volumes. Because at no time did they ever, and I've said it before, in no time did they ever consider me, as a person, like what I've gone through or … shocking really.

V. Conclusion

This chapter has argued that the experience of being a LiP is a harder, more complex and more confusing experience than previously considered. The LiPs in this study are often involved in multiple proceedings; and for some, these proceedings have been going on for many years. Their experiences are consequently complicated by the sheer complexity of the cases involved, as well as by the emotional significance of the central issue at stake for each individual LiP. Far from pursuing litigation frivolously, then, the LiPs in this study are very clear that they did not take the decision to pursue or defend a claim lightly: for some LiPs, doing so was the only way to try to save their home, to keep their child or to preserve their sense of identity. And the impact of going to law has been dramatic, with people losing family, losing their jobs and losing their homes.

But what I have also sought to demonstrate is that the difficulties LiPs experience are not simply due to wilful, vexatious obsessions on the part of delusional individuals. Instead, they are also because of the considerable constraints involved in continuing to fight for something the LiP believes is right, in a context where doing so is made disproportionately difficult. In this respect, this chapter has suggested that the civil justice system, while theoretically existing to adjudicate disputes, may in fact exacerbate grievances for LiPs, rather than redressing them. But while I have discussed the impact *of* these difficulties, what exactly are these difficulties themselves? How are LiPs being bamboozled? What are the challenges LiPs face when going to law themselves? How and why is being a LiP a disproportionately more difficult situation than being represented? These are the questions I pursue in chapter 5.

5

How To Be Good

You get people turning up and looking like idiots, when in actual fact they're not, they just haven't been given the, there's no guidance for them to find anywhere.

Tim

And I said … they've just tried to bully me, and I'd got a cassette recording, a cassette in my briefcase, and I picked it up and I said, I remember I felt like Rumpole of the Bailey, 'if it pleases My Lord, I have transcripts made of these telephone conversations and we'll see who said what'. Then uh, Mr Justice Eady said to B——, 'Shall we listen to these tape recordings, Mr B——?' B—— turns round to his solicitors sat behind him and they're like: 'no no no no no!' [whispered], shaking [their heads], 'no, no, no, no!' 'That won't be necessary My Lord, we withdraw our application for costs.' But you know the thing is, if I'd actually put this tape in, I'd got the right box but the wrong tape and if we'd have plugged it in and played it we would have heard a friend of mine called Butty, he's a Black guy, we would have heard Butty's Special Reggae Dub Mix.

Neil

I. Introduction

Why is going to law so difficult for LiPs? In chapter 4 I argued that it was disproportionately *more* difficult for a LiP to go to law than for a legally trained professional. This is not a controversial conclusion to come to; many researchers in the area have argued this to be the case.[1] But why? A number of reasons have been suggested. Some argue that it is because legal training is a prerequisite

[1] See R Moorhead and M Sefton, Litigants in Person: Unrepresented Litigants in First Instance Proceedings, Department of Constitutional Affairs Research Series 2/05 (UK, DCA, 2005); H Genn and Y Genn, The Effectiveness of Representation at Tribunals: Report to the Lord Chancellor (London, Lord Chancellor's Department, 1989); J McFarlane, 'The National Self-Represented Litigants Project: Identifying and Meeting the Needs of Self-Represented Litigants', Canada Treasury's Advisory Group on Access to Justice Working Group Report (nd); J Baldwin, 'Litigants' Experience of Adjudication in the County Courts (1999) 18 *Civil Justice Quarterly* 12; L Trinder et al, *Litigants in Person in Private Family Law Cases* (London, Ministry of Justice Analytical Series, 2014); P Lewis, 'Litigants in Person and their Difficulties in Adducing Evidence: A Study of a Small Claims in an English County Court' (2007) 11 *International Journal of Evidence and Proof* 24.

for successfully participating in any kind of legal proceedings.[2] Others claim it is because it is easier to pursue or defend claims when one has knowledge and experience of the context and environment in which one will be acting.[3] Another suggestion is that the difficulty arises because LiPs are too emotionally attached to their stories to be able to represent themselves coherently and to successfully engage in proceedings.[4] But which is it? All these reasons, or some of them? Or different reasons altogether? In this chapter I seek to address these questions by considering where LiPs *themselves* believe the difficulties to lie, and through examining how these difficulties are manifested in their experiences. I do this by exploring two key areas of potential difficulty that emerge through this study.

First, I look at the gap between legally specialised knowledge and lay understandings of law. As I have outlined in earlier chapters, this gap has been argued by many to be a deliberate and necessary separation, which functions at least in part to perpetuate dependence on the legal profession. The gap manifests in practice in the collision between two ways of seeing: what is common sense to a layperson and what is common sense to a professional. In legal proceedings, any knowledge outside of field-specific knowledge is either diminished in value or inadmissible, unless it can be translated effectively into legal discourse.[5] This means that experiences such as those narrated by the LiPs in chapter 4 must be translated into specialist language to be accepted. This gap also means that the language used by legal professionals is often alien to an outsider and difficult, if not impossible, for LiPs to comprehend. As I will show, in the interviews for this study, LiPs were frequently unable to accomplish the effective translation of their experiences into appropriate discourse, which resulted in their feeling unable to communicate what they believed to be important, leading to frustration that they were not being listened to. In addition, LiPs routinely found themselves unable to understand the language deployed by legal professionals both inside and outside of the courtroom, to the extent that LiPs were unable to understand the proceedings in which they themselves were at the centre. In a number of cases, LiPs felt that this lack of understanding had an active impact on the outcome.[6] The collision between two ways of seeing, then, poses considerable barriers of access for LiPs.

Second, there is the equally large difficulty concerning role play that is less well recognised. In the Introduction to this book, I suggested that inconsistencies exist when it comes to articulating exactly what it is that a LiP is meant to do.

[2] Lewis (n 1); J Baldwin, *Monitoring the Rise of the Small Claims Limit: Litigants' Experience of Different Forms of Adjudication* (London, Lord Chancellor's Department, 1997) 74–75.

[3] Nicholas Crichton, DJ, quoted in G Langdon-Down, 'Litigants in person could struggle to secure access to justice' *Law Society Gazette* (London, 19 January 2012).

[4] T Sourdin and N Wallace, 'The Dilemmas Posed by Self-Represented Litigants – The Dark Side' (2014) 24(1) *Journal of Judicial Administration* 61.

[5] The role of expert witnesses is a moderate exception to this, where there is a degree of recognition of expertise, but this is still controlled by rules of evidence, and such witnesses can be questioned and have their explanations accepted, or not, by a judge.

[6] The two most obvious examples of this are Trevor and Marie.

In this chapter I will consider this in more detail. What behavioural expectations are there for LiPs? How can a LiP perform well, or perform badly? As I will show, LiPs are frequently given contradictory information. They are told, for example, to tell their stories 'simply'. Yet they are also expected to be able to conduct closed questioning, or be able to, on the spot, explain what area of law their proceedings deal with.[7] These inconsistencies of performative demands lead to most LiPs in this study feeling that they do not have a coherent script to which they can adhere. Should they act naturally? Should they mimic the behaviour and language of lawyers? What would a good LiP look like? Interviewees were told at different stages of proceedings to both act naturally and act like a lawyer, sometimes at the same time, leading LiPs to feel they were being punished for failing to perform adequately in impossible circumstances. The significant, and unclear, performative demands placed on LiPs are therefore also a clear source of disadvantage. Ultimately, I conclude that LiP experiences show us that there is no way to 'be good' as long as we see them as aberrant. Until we recognise and conceptualise the role of the LiP as an everyday actor in civil justice, LiPs will be excluded from meaningful participation.

II. Red Herrings

Neil: No disrespect to your colleagues or solicitor friends and stuff [laughing] … All college, no knowledge? Where's the common-sense element? I mean, there's no, there's very little common sense in law. You know it doesn't, it just doesn't make sense, does it? A lot of law.

In 2012, when Marie still had a solicitor representing her, she attended the final hearing regarding the custody of her son. Ultimately, this hearing resulted in Marie's child being permanently adopted. From Marie's perspective, the issue of relevance for this hearing was ensuring that the presiding judge in the case understood that she was in the process of getting an Independent Social Worker (ISW) assessment. Marie believed that if the ISW was positive, it could change the custody outcome. An ISW assessment date had been agreed, but the date was *after* this final hearing and Marie could not get it moved sooner. Consequently, she wanted her solicitor to explain this to the judge so that they could delay the final hearing. Instead, this is how Marie recalls what happened when the judge asked her solicitor about the ISW:

Marie: My solicitor said it was a red herring. Now, at that point in time I had no idea what that meant, but when I found out what it meant I was absolutely livid because basically that comment had allowed the final hearing to carry on.

Kate: So you were present during this final hearing?

[7] This is precisely what happened to Tim, as I will explore in section II.

Marie: Yeah but like I said I didn't know nothing, uh, I didn't even understand the terminology of red herring.

Kate: And so you didn't have anyone else with you? They weren't allowed to …

Marie: No.

Kate: So did your solicitor raise the ISW?

Marie: No as I, he turned around and said it was a red herring, like the appeal and everything about it was a red herring and I was, when I found out what it actually meant I was absolutely livid.

Kate: And when did you find that out?

Marie: Um, yeah, when the appeal happened, 'cause we actually got our transcripts.

For Marie, the language used by her own solicitor was incomprehensible. As she herself says, it was only much later, during the appeal (by which time she was a LiP), that she obtained a transcript and, in consultation with her McKenzie friend, finally understood what the expression 'red herring' meant, and what the consequences of her solicitor's statement had been.[8]

I begin this section with Marie's experience because what happened to her is not unusual in the context of this study, or in the context of other research into the challenges posed to laypersons by certain kinds of language, but it *is* difficult to capture if we assume that 'legal language' refers only to legal vocabulary.[9] As stated in section I, it is a generally accepted fact that legal terminology is inaccessible to an outsider and needs to be explained.[10] There is no doubt that a certain amount of progress has been made in this direction: plain language is advocated by researchers, and guides for LiPs explaining key terms, can now be accessed online and sometimes at courthouses themselves.[11] But in this study, the language that functioned to exclude or confuse LiPs was not limited to specialist legal terms, or Latin or anything else that we might expect to constitute 'legalese'. Instead, the kind of expressions and constructions that confused LiPs frequently encompassed language that was unusual or deceptive.[12]

[8] I want to emphasise here that the impact of this happening is of course still based on Marie's perception, and we cannot be certain what effect the ISW may have had. We can be certain, however, that it had a material effect on Marie's perceptions of fairness in the justice system, and it was a major factor in her becoming a LiP. This latter outcome – how loss of trust in legal professionals can lead individuals to become LiPs – echoes the discussion in ch 3 of this book.

[9] J Jacobsen et al, *Structured Mayhem: Personal Experiences of the Crown Court* (London, Criminal Justice Alliance, 2015) 23. Similarly, see The Law Society, *Litigants in Person: Guidelines for Lawyers* (London, The Law Society, 2015) 6.

[10] Christopher Williams argues that the key features of 'legal vocabulary' are the use of archaic or rarely used terms, a preponderance of foreign vocabulary, particularly French or Latin, and 'obsessive repetition' of terms to avoid obscurity. In addition, this is complemented by the use of long, 'convoluted' sentences and impersonal language. See C Williams, 'Legal English and Plain Language: An Introduction' (2004) 1 *ESP Across Cultures* 111, 113.

[11] For example, the Bar Council's *A Guide to Representing Yourself in Court* (London, Bar Council, 2016).

[12] By deceptive, I mean language that has a double meaning: one within the legal field and one without it. I will return to this idea later in the chapter.

The degree to which such language may be a product of the legal world, even though it is *not* specifically 'legal language', is something that clearly needs to be considered.

To approach how we might do this, it is helpful to draw on the work of Pierre Bourdieu. The smallness of the interviewee sample means that I cannot claim that my interviewees are representative of all LiPs, and I hesitate to make any assumptions about demographics on the basis of this sample. But it *does* seem quite likely that many LiPs, including those in this study, are formally educated to a lesser degree than the legal professionals they encounter in a courtroom.[13] Pierre Bourdieu recognises the importance of this when he argues, in his sociological theory, that all semi-autonomous fields, such as the field of law, operate within and are relatively closer or further away from the field of power. Individuals who work within a field are therefore also part of a broader operation of social power. Those who work in positions of authority or influence within a field are likely to exhibit traits that reinforce their social status and class in all their encounters, and this will be most obviously manifested in encounters with those of lesser authority. This idea is emphasised in Bourdieu's *Distinction*, where he argues that aesthetic choices are determined early on by one's *habitus* and the earliest social influences individuals have through their parents, the kind of people they go to school with and their education.[14] It is clearly also evident in language. As Bourdieu emphasises, language is a function of social power. As he expresses it, when critiquing the neutral or scientific study of linguistics:

> [O]ne must not forget that the relations of communication par excellence – linguistic exchanges – are also relations of symbolic power in which the power relations between speakers or their respective groups are actualised.[15]

The idea I want to take from this is that when talking about 'legal language', we need to go beyond narrow definitions that only encompass technical language. Litigants in person are not only confused by this kind of language, they are also potentially excluded from fully comprehending proceedings by the use of unusual, formal or complex language that goes unexplained to them because it is not recognised to *be* legal language. By failing to see such linguistic constructions, like Marie's red herrings, as part of a broader pattern of social power, we limit the significance of legal language difficulties by saying they only evidence difficulties with a particular kind of transaction in a specific time and place. Laypersons do not understand because they do not have law degrees.[16] But instead, by encompassing a broader understanding of legal language, we can see these transactions more broadly as involving an unequal relationship of power

[13] This was the conclusion reached by Kim Williams. See K Williams, *Litigants in Person: A Literature Review* (London, Ministry of Justice, 2011). See also C Ball, 'Most people in the UK do not go to university – and maybe never will,' *The Guardian* (London, 4 June 2013).

[14] P Bourdieu, Distinction: A Social Critique of the Judgment of Taste (London, Routledge, 1979).

[15] P Bourdieu, *Language and Symbolic Power* (London, Polity Press, 1991) 37.

[16] Although, of course, some of them do, including Tim in this study, as well as Oliver.

that denotes social class and educational differences, and which is common to many such encounters.

The importance of considering the unequal distribution of power in the relationships between LiPs and legal professionals is supported by the work of Larson. The 'professional project' is about the collective pursuit of social mobility for professions that will result in the achievement of 'the desired social position to their occupants'.[17] Specialisms, such as lawyering, are predicated on the development of increasing autonomy based on markers of distinction, and through this distinction enjoying the exercise of financial and social power. As Larson notes, 'The upgrading of an occupation into a profession, or the upgrading of a profession in terms of respectability and social credit, implies the articulation of principles of inclusion and exclusion.'[18] This pursuit of such a 'project' is one where acquiring specialist skills is only one small piece of a much more complex process that is rooted in processes of exclusion: class and educational differences. As Larson points out,

> professions are not exclusively occupational categories: whatever else they are, professions are situated in the middle and upper middle levels of the stratification system. Both objectively and subjectively, professions are outside and above the working class, as occupations and as social strata.[19]

Returning to Marie's story, while 'red herring' may be a common enough expression that other LiPs are not confused by it, we should not underestimate the degree to which use of this kind of language may trip up many more LiPs, because legal professionals may be *more likely* than LiPs to use it in the first place, whether formally or idiomatically, or with reference to aesthetic traditions that are tied to specific social origins and contexts. For us, it means that we cannot ignore the disadvantage that Marie, and other LiPs, may experience by not sharing the same social or educational background as other individuals in the courtroom.[20]

Individuals in this study talked of a general lack of comprehension; and while one can only speculate on the impact complex or formal language constructions can have, in this case at least we know that it meant that Marie was unable to understand how the decision was reached in the most important hearing she ever attended.[21] It also seems likely that this is not an unusual experience for a LiP. Clearly, facilitating access for LiPs also requires addressing ourselves to language differences as expressions of power, not just as evidence that laypersons lack a narrow, specialised knowledge.

[17] MS Larson, *The Rise of Professionalism: A Sociological Analysis* (Berkeley, CA, University of California Press, 1977) 67.

[18] ibid 74.

[19] ibid xvi.

[20] This was not the case for all the interviewees, however, with some coming from a relatively privileged background, such as Oliver, Georgina and Talia, as outlined in ch 3.

[21] This hearing, and the behaviour of her solicitor, had clear consequences when it came to Marie's trust in the legal profession. The impact of solicitor behaviour on shaping LiPs' decisions to forgo representation will be explored in ch 6.

However, Marie's experience also draws attention to what appears to be troubling behaviour on the part of her legal representative. Clark D Cunningham, in his 1992 article on lawyers as translators, notes that he uses the metaphor of translation because

> [t]he metaphor suggests that the meaning of the client's story will 'inevitably' be transformed through the lawyer's representation; no sentence can be perfectly translated from one language to another. Yet if one feels a sense of loss in speaking through a translator, there can also be something gained. By speaking through a translator, one can be heard and understood in places where otherwise one is mute. The translator does not silence the speaker but rather seeks to enhance the speaker's voice by adding her own. The good translator does not alter the speaker's meaning without the speaker's consent, and may even collaborate with the speaker to produce a statement in the foreign language that is more meaningful than the speaker's original utterance. Thus, translation offers both an image of the constraints upon a lawyer's ability to represent fully his client's story and a model for recognizing and managing the inevitable changes in meaning in a way that may empower rather than subjugate the client.[22]

But, as Cunningham points out, 'lawyers routinely silence and subordinate their clients while purporting to tell "their" stories'.[23] Clearly, while the solicitor may not have deliberately or consciously employed the term 'red herring' to evade Marie's understanding, this solicitor, by Marie's account of this event, was not attempting to translate Marie's needs, or to communicate for or with her. At the very least, the relationship between Marie and her representative suggests a lack of 'translation'.[24] Indeed, he seemed in practice to be cutting her out of the communication taking place in court.[25] Eleanor also explicitly referenced this feeling of being ignored when she went to court. When she appeared opposite a represented party, she described it as 'Like being in criminal court, they basically would not let me talk. The judge directed absolutely everything to the barrister, the barrister talked to the judge, they both ignored me.'

It is of course important to stress here that the concept of 'lawyering' is a complex one, and how people 'do' lawyering is matter of historical and contextual specificity, so overly generalised claims should be avoided. Sarat and Felstiner draw attention to the complicated power dynamics existing between lawyer and client. Their 1995 work emphasises the 'dynamic' nature of the power relationship whereby, at different points in time, both lawyer and client feel a relative 'powerlessness', and that the relationship between lawyer and client is much

[22] C Cunningham, 'The Lawyer as Translator, Representation as Text: Towards an Ethnography of Legal Discourse' (1992) 6 *Cornell Law Review* 1298, 1300.

[23] ibid 1300.

[24] Another way of thinking about this failure of translation is to consider that lawyers, as Sarat, Abel and Felstiner argue, see each case as a unit of analysis; Marie's separate application, done without this representative, is arguably something that falls outside the boundaries of this case. See W Felstiner et al, 'The Emergence and Transformation of Disputes: Naming, Blaming, Claiming …' (1980) 15 *Law and Society Review* 631.

[25] Genn and Genn (n 1) 237.

more tightly negotiated than had been previously suggested.[26] In addition, more recent scholarship has consistently advocated for a *more* client-driven focus, with a greater sense of equality in the relationship between the two.[27] Further, there has been an emphasis in some critical scholarship of the ethical imperatives of communicating a client's story.[28] This vision of lawyering, however, is usually limited to the extent that there remains an expectation that lawyers are meant to perform some kind of translation and to be relatively autonomous in taking steps that are in the best interest of their client.[29]

In the context of this study, therefore, it is important to be cautious about any claims made as to how lawyers behave generally. All we can know from Marie's tale is Marie's perspective on one incident. But the story remains troubling, at the very least because it indicates a rather paternalistic narrative of lawyer behaviour.[30] A more critical reading suggests that, while exclusion on the basis of language and behaviour largely takes place on a preconscious level, there may well be individuals within the legal profession who might deliberately and consciously exploit this exclusion; in this scenario, by the lawyer's ignoring what his client was saying and failing to translate it to the judge.[31] Larson points out,

> although the project and its means are collective: it is through the upgrading of an occupation – with the attempts to control the individual members which this involves – that prestige is to be attached to the profession roles, and by extension, to their occupants, making the project 'ultimately individualistic'.[32]

While conscious exclusion may not be applicable to the majority of legal practitioners, Marie's experience suggests that Larson's 'professional project' is an important way to consider the minority of lawyers who may well deliberately emphasise and perpetuate distinction through exclusion. As Larson observes,

> [t]he service orientation is … undoubtedly, part of the ideology and one of the prescriptive norms which organised professions explicitly avow. Yet the implicit assumption that the behaviour of individual professionals is more ethical, as a norm, than that of individuals in lesser occupations has seldom, if ever, been tested by empirical evidence.[33]

In keeping with this, alongside being ignored, interviewees talked about feeling condescended to, or patronised: Eleanor, for example, recalls her barrister

[26] A Sarat and W Felstiner, Divorce Lawyers and Their Clients: Power and Meaning in the Legal Process (Oxford, Oxford University Press, 1995).
[27] See, eg, J MacFarlane, *The New Lawyer: How Settlement is Transforming the Practice of Law* (Vancouver and Toronto, UBC Press, 2008) xiii.
[28] AV Alfieri, 'Reconstructive Poverty Law Practice: Learning Lessons of Client Narrative' (1991) 100(7) *Yale Law Journal* 2107.
[29] R Moorhead et al, 'What Clients Know: Client Perspectives and Legal Competence' (2003) 5 *International Journal of the Legal Profession*, 5.
[30] R Wasserstrom, 'Lawyers as Professionals: Some Moral Issues' (1975) 5 *Human Rights* 1.
[31] This is of significance to LiPs not only when they are periodically represented, but also when they, as LiPs, face represented opposition.
[32] Larson (n 17) 67.
[33] ibid ix.

describing her as a 'silly little woman'; and Russell claims that a judge presiding over a hearing was 'arrogant' and that he said 'What a pity. We have a litigant in person in the courtroom,' before repeatedly telling Russell to 'get a move on'.

Another problem with language and communication that emerged from this study was about what might best be termed 'deceptive' language. This can be seen in the case of Trevor. While awaiting the outcome of the small claim he was defending against the contractor who had initiated proceedings in the County Court against him, Trevor received a letter in the post from the court. As he explains it, 'what it said was, um, Judgment, blah blah blah, Action: None, so I thought, with the first one, I thought well okay so there's, he's found a judgment but he's, I don't have to do anything because it says none.' His sister, a qualified solicitor, then explained the meaning of the letter to Trevor. As he goes on:

> Once they [his sister and friend] read it they understood what it meant, but I as a layman don't understand legal terminology, but they write it all legalese so you're there reading it, trying to interpret something that you haven't got a clue what it actually means. When it says action: none, you think that means no action to be taken … but no, that wasn't what it meant, I can't remember what it meant actually, but it meant something else, something to do with the judgment … and they use legal terminology but yet it's supposed to be [for a] litigant in person. How are you supposed to know legal terminology if you're just a normal person who doesn't operate within the law world, if you know what I mean? You don't, you won't know what those things mean so you won't understand what they're trying to tell you or get you to do.

Trevor's experience is a common one for LiPs, where the language employed by legal professionals is difficult to understand. However, as Trevor himself suggests in the above extract, the problem here is not the use of long or complicated terms that would be easily recognisable as a form of such jargon; it is instead words that are misleading because they have both a legal and non-legal meaning, such as 'action', 'judgment' and 'none'. Moorhead and Sefton draw attention to this issue in their 2005 study, where they note the 'risk' of LiPs' expressing themselves 'solely in social, non-legal terms'.[34]

The collision between what Moorhead and Sefton termed the 'social' and the legal can be seen even more clearly in the experiences of Charles and Paul, who both took their solicitors to court for negligence. This is how Charles recalls what happened during the hearing:

> Well, the verdict didn't take long at all, it was like just about half an hour, he [the judge] prepares a document and he reads through it and then says, um, you know, Mr C, basically judgment goes to Mr C but, um, then he goes and tells you what you've actually achieved in terms of the judgment, what judgment would actually be, um, the, the money that you would gain, I don't even know what the right expression is, what the compensation would be for your losses. But then he says, like £5, and I actually sued them for another case as well and it was £5 for each case, I won on both counts, but then he basically said because I couldn't prove my losses, which was nonsense. Because

[34] Moorhead and Sefton (n 1) 154.

> I'd showed him, demonstrated with documents what my losses were because it was in my statement of claim.

As can be seen above, in Charles's mind, he won this case ('judgment goes to Mr C'). As he says, 'like I said, I did very well because I won the case'. Consequently, the tiny amount of damages awarded to him was a source of significant confusion. This confusion was compounded when the judge went on to order him to pay the other side's costs. As he remembers:

> I did actually win the case, but when you win a case on negligence the judge, what he did was, um, he just gave me, I can't remember the exact word they call it, um, punitive damages and just gave me £5 as compensation, knowing that the solicitors would have made an offer and because they had offered me £15,000 which I couldn't take because I'd already lost over £100,000 because of all the cost and the time, I couldn't take £15,000 so because my judgment was less than what was actually offered to me it means automatically I have to pay the solicitors' costs which was £90,000.

Clearly, in the passage above Charles has confused 'punitive' and 'nominal' damages. However, the major source of confusion is what 'winning' means. From Charles's account of what happened, it seems clear that the judge accepted his argument on at least one of his points, resulting in the awarding of nominal damages. However, from the judge's perspective, this was not a victory, but rather a failure to prove the rest of his case, hence the award of *only* nominal damages. In addition, Charles clearly fell foul of the Civil Procedure Rules pertaining to Part 36 on offers to settle. Essentially, because the solicitors offered Charles a substantial settlement, £15,000, and because Charles failed to obtain a judgment 'more advantageous than a defendant's part 36 offer', he was ordered to pay the other side's costs.

The collision, then, between 'social' and 'legal' meanings here suggests that a LiP cannot even be sure if they have been successful or not. Charles clearly believes he has succeeded because the judge has *told* him he succeeded, or 'won', on at least one or more grounds. However, the fact that the other side was awarded costs tells us he has not 'won'. For Charles to know that, though, he would need to understand *Blackstone's Civil Practice*, paragraph 66.10 of which states:

> A claimant who has claimed substantial damages, but has only recovered nominal damages, will normally be ordered to pay the defendant's costs (*Texaco Ltd v Arco Technology Inc* (1989) The Times 13 October 1989; *Mappouras v Waldrons Solicitors* [2002] EWCA Civ 842, LTL 30/4/2002 … Where a claimant recovers more than nominal damages but only a small proportion of the amount claimed, costs should follow the event unless this conflicts with some other established principle …[35]

As noted above, generally speaking, costs orders to a defendant, where only nominal damages are awarded to the claimant, are commonplace, although not

[35] See S Sime and D French (eds), *Blackstone's Civil Proceedings* (Oxford, Oxford University Press, 2023) para 66.10.

automatic. As a 2013 case, *Clack v Wrigley's Solicitors LLP*, establishes, the judge has a 'wide discretion' to decide the issue of costs. In determining costs, though, it is about who the successful party is:

> There is no doubt that the starting point in all cases is that the party who, looked at practically and realistically, is *the successful party* will be awarded the costs of the action, but equally it is clear that there is a wide discretion to depart from this in appropriate circumstances. The authorities, both pre- and post-CPR, establish that a defendant who is held liable only for nominal damages will ordinarily be regarded as the successful party (unless the claimant had a legitimate reason for seeking to establish liability only), and that in such a case (a) the claimant will not ordinarily be awarded any costs but (b) the defendant will not necessarily recover all his costs, especially if and to the extent that (i) they have not been incurred in relation to an issue which should have been conceded and (ii) they would not have been incurred anyhow in resolving issues on which the defendant has succeeded.[36]

In the eyes of the judge, then, Charles is *not* the successful party. However, the circumstances surrounding how this process takes place do not seem to have been clearly explained to him. Charles is aware that his decision not to settle is what has caused this costs decision, but for him, this is still baffling because he 'won'. The fact that one can 'win' but still lose, by virtue of only succeeding in being awarded nominal damages, is clearly, and unsurprisingly, a site of confusion for LiPs.

Leo narrates a similar story, also in a case where he took his solicitors to court for negligence:

> I had to present the case and he [the judge] later complimented me saying I had presented the case very, very effectively, uh very politely and uh, you know, I, uh, handled it really well. So, he ruled in my favour, he said that the solicitors had been negligent. So, I won at that stage and he awarded me costs, and a very tiny amount … they award certain people huge damages and they award other people tiny amounts! [laughter] They're almost insignificant! Pennies! In relation to them. So, um, I was then needing to get these solicitors to comply with the court order and they were not. And I was having to do my, uh, costing to show what I'd, you know, my genuine costs, and they were difficult. So, I then went back to court saying look, they're not complying with the court order. And the district judge awarded *them* costs for attending that hearing. And their costs were more than my costs and damages.

Here we see an account closely paralleling that of Charles, where Leo succeeds only to the extent of being awarded nominal damages, although in his account, it seems that he was awarded costs, or was at least certainly not ordered to pay the other side's costs. While there are no particulars of the case to refer to in order to be certain as to what exactly happened at the second hearing, it seems likely that at this point the judge intervened, presumably because in the eyes of the courts, Leo was not the 'successful party' in this situation and therefore his taking the

[36] *Clack v Wrigleys Solicitors LLP* [2013] EWHC 413 [18], Nicholas Strauss QC, sitting as Deputy Judge (emphasis added).

solicitors *back* to court may have been perceived as a vexatious action. As Leo summarises it, however, 'I won, but then I lost because the district judge, the subsequent district judge awarded costs against me'.

Common to both individuals in these accounts is their sheer bewilderment as to what has taken place in the courtroom. For them, the judge has said they were right and awarded them compensation (albeit a small amount), and then they have been, as they see it, punished despite succeeding. This is clearly because the concept of 'winning' inside and outside a legal context differs.

However, in Moorhead and Sefton's account, although they concede the situation is 'understandable', LiPs are held somewhat responsible for their own confusion because they do not know how to distinguish between what is socially just and what is 'legally' just. This question of course touches on a complex and much discussed issue in legal philosophy: to what degree should what is legal also be 'just'? There are two paths to think about this question that are relevant here: first, there is the fact that the civil justice system has been transformed from a court-based system, where what is just is what judges pronounce to be just, to one of 'structured negotiation', where settlement is the overriding objective.[37] This transformation impacts on LiPs who do not understand these changes and expect to be heard by a judge.

The second path is the gap between popular justice and 'legal justice': here, the work of Nobles and Schiff in *Miscarriages of Justice* is relevant, pointing to the wide gap between the two conceptions.[38] Either way, for a LiP to fully comprehend the situation described above requires either an intimate knowledge of the Civil Procedure Rules or, at the very least, a judge who is able to explain what has occurred in a way that each LiP can understand. We cannot, of course, be sure what was explained to either LiP or both. It is perfectly possible that the situation *was* explained by the judge and that Charles and Leo stated that they understood, even though they did not. It is also possible the judge did not fully explain the reason for their actions. What we can be fairly certain about, however, is that there was a fundamental miscommunication, arising from what is a clear example of legal language and procedure at loggerheads with a 'commonsense' understanding of the matter to a layperson.[39]

It is also unsurprising that LiPs may experience these kinds of decisions as unjust (in the 'social' meaning of the word). If a LiP pursues a case to court,

[37] For more on this, see S Roberts, '"Listing Concentrates the Mind": the English Civil Court as an Arena for Structured Negotiation' (2009) 29(3) *Oxford Journal of Legal Studies* 457.

[38] R Nobles and D Schiff, *Understanding Miscarriages of Justice* (Oxford, Oxford University Press, 2000).

[39] We can also be certain that there was another serious outcome: the result of these transactions for both Charles and Leo was to substantially erode trust in the judges presiding over their cases. The way in which LiPs choose to make sense of encounters with law that are not effectively explained to them, and how some may resort to conspiracy theories, is the subject of ch 6.

despite all the difficulties detailed in chapter 4, so that a judge can adjudicate on the matter, only to be told that even though they have won, they are somehow at fault, we cannot be surprised that LiPs may be angered or upset by the experience. As suggested in chapter 4, what happens here is that LiPs will feel they are being financially punished for pursuing a claim of importance to them.[40]

Moving beyond what happened in these two cases and returning to the broader argument, then, how can we make sense of these kinds of confusions and their impact on LiPs? As I have argued, Moorhead and Sefton's account suggests this collision is inevitable, if unfortunate. However, I believe it remains important to consider the disparity of power levels between parties, which serves to reinforce and perpetuate a LiP's relatively low status. We must also consider how confusing and unfair the situation is for the layperson. It is therefore, perhaps, more useful to think in terms of sociological theory when pondering LiP disadvantages regarding language and procedure, particularly Bourdieu's theory of *habitus*. Following Bourdieu's argument, then, in these situations it is not the case that the judges or solicitors are deliberately trying to exclude or confuse Charles, Trevor, Leo or Marie. Instead, because of the specialised knowledge legal agents have acquired and naturalised, as well as their broader pattern of class, education and social values, what seems obvious to these individuals is not what is obvious to LiPs. Instead, these two forms of common sense will be fundamentally different and inevitably come into conflict.

So far, I have spent some time in this chapter talking about language. However, the conceptual gap between lay and law can be seen in areas other than legal language. Bourdieu argues:

> The institution of a 'judicial space' implies the establishment of a borderline between actors. It divides those qualified to participate in the game and those who, though they may find themselves in the middle of it, are in fact excluded by their inability to accomplish the conversion of mental space – and particularly of linguistic stance – which is presumed by entry into this social space.[41]

The language Bourdieu employs in this extract is highly suggestive, drawing attention as he does to a 'borderline between actors'. Often, accounts of the gap between the lay and the law tend to focus exclusively on language. Clearly, as noted above, the role language plays is very important; however, it is easy to overlook the equally important role of embodied behaviour. How do LiPs perform in the courtroom, and what kinds of performances are expected of them? This is what I explore in section III.

[40] This policy is also in keeping with the increasing use of the courts to punish those who do not settle, regardless of the relative merit of their case. See Roberts (n 37) 457.

[41] P Bourdieu, 'The Force of Law: Towards a Sociology of the Juridical Field' (1987) 38 *Hastings Law Journal* 814, 828.

III. Acting Up

Kate: Did you do research [on how to behave in court]?

Neil: No, what I, it's probably upstairs, I'd got a book out of the library, I bought a book from Waterstones or something called *Advocacy at the Bar. Advocacy at the Bar* and I read a bit of that. I went down to court and quite, quite funny I just, I wanted to see how the barristers, where they sat in court, and how they addressed the court, and what they did. So I remember, a particularly funny case, there were about six defendants in this one case and each one had got their own barrister and they were all bobbing up and down, they were all sat on the same row all with the wigs and the black thing on, they looked like pistons in a car, bobbing up, bobbing, when one sat down, the other one … in no particular order, it was sort of random bobbing up and down. I found it quite funny. I don't think I learned a lot apart from you've got to call a judge in the High Court My Lord. … [Y]eah I just blagged it, blagged it all the way through.

How should LiPs behave in court? Since the coming into force of LASPO 2012 in April 2013, and the concomitant rise of unrepresented litigants ending up in courtrooms, there has been considerable effort by legal practitioners and other legal service providers to provide guidance and advice on this matter. The Bar Council has released guidance for LiPs, *A Guide to Representing Yourself in Court*, and there are other similar documents and sources, such as AdviceNow's website, which has a page called 'Going to court or tribunal without the help of a lawyer'.[42] These guides, produced by the Citizens Advice Bureau, similar to the guidance produced by the Bar Council, envisage specific scenarios in which and times when LiPs might find themselves in court, and attempt to explain what they should do and how they should behave.[43] One of the first things both the Bar Council and the CAB guides emphasise is that a LiP needs to disregard anything they may have seen on television. As the CAB guide puts it:

> Forget everything you see on the telly. Most court hearings in TV programmes are about crime – and that is not what we are talking about here and anyway they focus on the drama of the story rather than reality![44]

This is echoed by the Bar Council, whose guide advises:

> Keep it simple. Throughout the Hearing, use simple, non-legal language as much as you can. Speak in short sentences. You might be tempted to speak like lawyers speak on television. Resist this temptation. Lawyers do not really speak like that. Some bad lawyers do, but judges hate it. Judges just want you to say what you mean in plain English.[45]

[42] Bar Council, A guide to representing yourself in court (https://www.thejusticegap.com/wp-content/uploads/2013/07/Bar-Council-guide.pdf); Citizens Advice Bureau , *Going to Court* (London, CAB, 2011).
[43] ibid, 1.
[44] ibid.
[45] Bar Council (n 11) 23.

Clearly, the emphasis here is to persuade LiPs that they should not behave like lawyers they have seen on television programmes, because these shows tend to be from the US and depict criminal proceedings and will lead LiPs astray. The repetition of this advice in both guides suggests that this is a genuine problem, and this is arguably supported by the fact that many of the interviewees in this study had a far more intimate knowledge of the law from television than they did from reality.[46] But what this also indicates is that many of these LiPs will not have attended a courtroom before and will have no prior knowledge of what it will be like. So they will be quite likely to have *only* ever seen courtrooms on television. This means that, when considering how they should behave, not only do LiPs lack any experience of the proceedings in which they will be acting, but they are also entering unfamiliar and frequently intimidating environments. As Marie describes, attending a local magistrates' court for a civil hearing:

> The courtroom? It felt like I'd committed a crime. It really, really did, walking in, never been in front of the judge, never been in a courtroom or anything. It was horrendous. It was so, the courtroom themself looked like, well look like they do on TV and that and, and its just like, you know when you see them on TV and you think oh right, whatever, but when you're actually in there it's so intimidating. And like I say, you feel like you committed a crime or something.

Marie's extract suggests that the very fact that LiPs might base their knowledge of courtrooms on television may make them *more* intimidating, as they are more likely to associate courts with criminality, punishment or imprisonment. In this respect, many LiPs may already face a behavioural 'handicap': intimidation and fear.[47]

Putting aside the question of intimidation for now, we might begin this section by asking generally, how can one behave well in a courtroom? For a LiP, an obvious place to start might be to watch and imitate the behaviour of legal professionals. This approach is implied in the above guides, when LiPs are told that when they speak plainly, they are following the strategy of how lawyers 'really' speak, and that this is a desirable phenomenon. This is also what Neil does in the extract at the start of this section; he attends a courtroom and observes the behaviour of legal professionals. But Neil clearly finds the experience largely comical. In this respect, it does not seem to be a helpful technique for him. More

[46] Trevor and Charles acknowledge this openly.

[47] The experience of intimidation is of course one that is well-recognised and discussed in criminal proceedings. Many scholars argue that architecture, procedure, placement of the defendant and other forms of 'segregation' are deliberately employed to intimidate defendants and witnesses before the overwhelming authority of the 'law'. See AE Bottoms and D McClean, *Defendants in the Criminal Process* (London, Routledge and Kegan Paul, 1976); P Rock, 'Witnesses and Spaces in a Crown Court' (1993) 31 *British Journal of Criminology* 266; L Mulcahy, *Legal Architecture: Justice, Due Process and the Place of Law* (London, Routledge, 2011). However, less has been written on the experiences of civil claimants and defendants in this regard. See BA Moulton, 'The Persecution and Intimidation of the Low-Income Litigant as Performed by the Small Claims Court in California' (1969) 21 *Stanford Law Review* 1657.

than this, though, Neil's reception of the behaviour and dress of barristers serves to remind us that there is a significant gap between what he, and other laypersons, would consider normal behaviour in a courtroom and what legal professionals themselves might consider normal behaviour. Neil clearly finds the behaviour of the barristers bizarre, rather than instructive; referring to the 'random bobbing up and down' of barristers, he cannot make any sense of it and cannot use it as a basis for his own behaviour.[48]

So how does this gap between two different normalities of behaviour, between that of the LiP and that of the legal professional, come about? This is arguably because the performance of legality is another example of field-specific knowledge learned through repeated experience.[49] No junior barrister or trainee solicitor enters the courtroom fully embodying the expected behaviour and traits of their role; it is something they learn through rehearsal and repetition. This practice enables these individuals to habituate and naturalise their experiences, including overcoming their initial intimidation and establishing familiarity with other participants with whom they may share a courtroom on more than one occasion. Through the example of their senior colleagues, or mistakes or failures on their part, these individuals will learn how to behave appropriately. But the boundaries of what is 'appropriate' or inappropriate behaviour in a courtroom is not a matter of common sense (or rather it *is* a matter of common sense in the sense that 'common sense' itself is a field-specific construct), which is why it is very different from what Neil would recognise as normal.

A legal professional who performs well in a courtroom, then, is an individual who gives the appearance of acting in a way that seems professional, skilful or persuasive to their fellow legal practitioners. But this kind of assessment of skill – what is good – can only exist in comparison to its opposite: what is bad. Poor performance, in the case of legal professionals, might therefore be any behaviour that seemed histrionic, clumsy or overtly theatrical. But while poor performance is sometimes characterised as 'acting up' or performing, whereas good performance consists of behaving 'normally', a better way of interpreting this behaviour would be to understand it as the juncture, for legal professionals, between 'good acting' and 'bad acting'. Bad acting, on the part of a legal professional,

[48] For an overview of the role of dress in legal process, see A Hunt, *Governance of the Consuming Passions* (Basingstoke, MacMillan Press Limited, 1996); P Goodrich, *Oedipus Lex: Psychoanalysis, History, Law* (Berkeley, CA, University of California Press, 1995); R McQueen, 'Of Wigs and Gowns: A Short History of Legal and Judicial Dress in Australia' in R McQueen and W Pue (eds), *Misplaced Traditions: British Lawyers, Colonial Peoples* (Annandale, NSW, Federation Press, 1999) 31.

[49] The term 'performance' is freighted with multiple potential meanings. Here I am following the work of Richard Schechner, who sees performance as existing on a spectrum from the highly marked to the unmarked, and notes that almost anything can be a performance for someone, somewhere. In this sense, 'behaviour is performance studies' "object of study"' and how lawyers operate constitutes a form of performance. See R Schechner, *Performance Studies: An Introduction* (New York, Routledge, 2002). I have written elsewhere on the performativity of legal process and legal acting. See K Leader, *Trials, Truth Telling and the Performing Body* (PhD thesis, University of Sydney, 2008); K Leader, 'Law, Presence to Absence: The Case of the Disappearing Defendant' in S Rai et al (eds), *Oxford Handbook of Politics and Performance* (Oxford, Oxford University Press, 2021) 73.

is any overtly theatrical behaviour that deviates from what is appropriate. Good acting, on the other hand, is misrecognised as 'natural', but it is what I call *legal naturalism*; a style of performance habituated by legal professionals that mobilises years of learning how to behave, move or speak, in a way in which it seems to be relatively effortless. Key to the concept of legal naturalism is the role of the habituated and the preconscious. As Bourdieu would argue, this acquisition and refinement of *habitus* is not explicitly recognised, and consequently legal professionals will see their own competency as 'natural'.[50]

When a professional attains such skill, this is only possible through forgetting how this transformation took place:

> ignoring the social and cultural conditions underlying such an experience, and at the same time treating as a birthright the virtuosity acquired through long familiarization or through the exercises of a methodical training … for the acquisition of art competence in the sense of mastery of all the means for the specific appropriation of works of art is a self-seeking silence because it is what makes it possible to legitimatise a social privilege by pretending that it is a gift of nature.[51]

Performative competence in a court of law, then, could be argued to be a 'social privilege' masquerading as a 'gift of nature'. The point to take from this analysis is that legal naturalism is of course therefore not obvious to a LiP; it is not even obvious to legal professionals themselves. Because lawyers and judges have habituated these courtroom performance skills themselves, they are likely to underestimate how difficult – or impossible – it is for an outsider to master them.[52] In this respect, imagining that performative skills can be 'put on' by LiPs by following a guidebook conceals the inequality that divides the world of legal professionals from that of laypersons. The reality is that LiPs are clearly not going to be able to learn how to behave like legal professionals without the concomitant experience.

This is of course recognised to a degree by those who work in the legal world: indeed, the guides are quite clear that LiPs are not expected to be lawyers. For example, consider the following extract from the Bar Council *Guide*:

> Sometimes, the other side will make arguments about what the law is. Before the Hearing, you might have tried to understand the law as well as you can. If you feel that you understand it and have a point to make, make it clearly and simply. However, you are not expected to be a lawyer. The judge will try hard to think about the arguments that you would be making if you were a lawyer. The lawyers for the other side should talk to the judge about any law that is damaging to their case (and supports your

[50] For example, Geoffrey Robertson argues in *The Justice Game* (London, Vintage, 1999) that advocacy skills are 'instinctive'. See also E Parry, *The Seven Lamps of Advocacy* (London, T Fisher Unwin, 1923) 72.

[51] P Bourdieu, *The Field of Cultural Production: Essays on Art and Literature* (New York, Columbia University Press, 1993) 234.

[52] This is to varying degrees; there will always be more nervous, or less able, individuals, and I do not mean to imply that there is a blanket competency that descends on all practitioners through rehearsal. See P Moore, 'Longing to Belong: Trained Actors' Attempts to Enter the Profession' (PhD thesis, University of Sydney, 2006) 43.

> arguments). In that way, the judge and the other lawyers will be aware that you are not a qualified lawyer and will make allowances for that.[53]

The above extract emphasises that LiPs are not expected to behave exactly like lawyers, and that allowances will be made for them by other court users. This is echoed in the Citizens Advice Bureau guide, which states 'You don't have to speak in legal language or long words – use plain English.'[54] But the problem here is that what is simple or clear in a courtroom is simply not the same as what is simple and clear outside of a courtroom, so while LiPs are being asked to behave normally, this normality is based on field-specific logics that will continue to disadvantage them. Litigants in person cannot speak simply and clearly without having to translate their experiences into legally accepted ones: this may not be a case of using legal words, but it is a case of being expected to be coherent in a specifically legal way.[55] So LiPs *are* being implicitly expected to behave like skilled professionals, because legal professionals *do not realise that this is what they are asking of them*. Speaking 'simply' masks considerable translation and effort that is disproportionately far more difficult for a LiP.

Beyond the problems caused by telling LiPs to act 'naturally', there is also more explicit inconsistency in what they are expected to do. Both the Citizens Advice Bureau guide and the Bar Council *Guide* on going to court provide advice on how to conduct closed questioning and cross-examination, indicating that these skill sets are expected of LiPs as well. So here we reach a significant difficulty: first, that LiPs are told to speak plainly and naturally, as good advocates do, without recognising that this behaviour is not actually natural; second, that they are simultaneously expected to be able to master, or at least effectively imitate, technical questioning skills. As Marie describes it:

> [B]ut the thing is, you've got to learn about, it's not just about learning what's in the courtroom, it's about learning how to deal with court staff because sometimes you can face nightmares filing applications, it's about learning how to put applications together, how to file it, um, how to do fee remission forms and what evidence you need, uh, putting together bundles, putting together um, arguments, uh, putting together questions, if you, even for a final hearing you got questions to do, it's about linking the evidence to the questions, being able to point out certain areas where you, within the evidence where you can pull them up and say what's this about? What —— Yeah, but you said this and then you've said this, which contradicts, you know what I mean? It's not, it's not just as straightforward as walking into court and saying 'hiya judge'. There's so much more to it and it's a very, very hard thing to actually achieve.

There is clearly a kind of confusion of role here: LiPs are meant to speak plainly and clearly, to *not* be lawyers or pretend to be lawyers, but are still expected to master lawyerly skills. As Marie puts it, you cannot just walk into a courtroom and say 'hiya judge'.

[53] Bar Council (n 11) 23.
[54] Citizens Advice Bureau (n 42).
[55] Williams (n 10) 113.

Compounding this role confusion is the inconsistency of how this role may be applied for each LiP at any time. The Bar Council says that while one might have tried as a LiP to familiarise oneself with the law, it does not matter if a LiP does not, because the judge will assist or explain the law to the litigant.[56] But this does not seem to be what happened when Tim first came to court. As Tim describes it, when filling in his County Court claim form, there was no point in this form, or in the limited guidance relating to it, that asked him to frame the claim in explicitly legal terms; indeed, following the logic above, there is no reason why there would be, as the courts say they do not expect LiPs to be legal experts. Tim therefore filled in the facts as best he could. He describes what happened when he attended the first hearing:

> And it's the first, the first question we got asked when we were in there, which I'm surprised hadn't been asked before, was on what grounds of law we were bringing the claim in the first place. Now I'd never been asked the question previously … Uh, um, and you know we were fairly unprepared in that respect. Um, thankfully thinking relatively quickly on our feet, um, it was, it was breach of verbal contract really.

Tim emphasises that he was only able to answer this question successfully because he just happened to have a law degree and had had previous experience of going to court as a trainee on behalf of his employers. This previous training and education clearly assisted him materially. As he says, 'I was able to go back to my old law school folder, pick it up and work out exactly what made a good witness statement and we'd also looked at, um, counties, magistrates, criminal and the larger civil courts and the different statements that were expected for each'. He emphasises that he was lucky, but that this was clearly a serious problem for a LiP, particularly in a County Court, who might not be expecting such a question:

> Certainly, for the County Courts, or certainly for the small claims, it sells itself on being for the layperson. I guarantee a person walking into that room and gets asked the question we were asked with regards to what area of law we were bringing this on, at no point was there ever any question over we bring this as an area of law. Um. You know, there was no, not even a hint in any of the paperwork, or any of the discussion or anything else that we would have to prepare a legal case for this kind of claim. Um, which I think would be very difficult for a layperson in that respect. To, to, you know what area of law are you doing it on? I dunno. It's kind of why I'm here, I was hoping, you know, hoping someone could tell me. You know, that would be my perceived response.

While we cannot be sure how the judge would have responded if Tim could not answer the question (perhaps the judge may have supplied the answer for him), Tim's experience clearly suggests that not having sufficient knowledge of legal grounds can be a point of issue, even in a context where LiPs are told they do not need to have a legal education.

[56] See The Law Society (n 9) 5.

So, if LiPs *are* expected to acquire some legal expertise (and this does seem to be the case, relating either to technical skills, such as questioning, or to knowledge of the subject matter) then how do they go about it? Something that emerged very strongly from these interviewees is how disproportionately more difficult it was to obtain information for a LiP, because legal knowledge is largely inaccessible to laypersons. As Eleanor puts it:

> The average Joe in the street, even if they want to educate themselves and to find out more and to … you know, be the best litigant in person they can, it's stacked against them, because you simply do not have, you're not allowed access to the information because it's jealously guarded by the law firms and everybody else so you, you can't get access to it. Possibly the only way to do it would be to find a tame law student, and realistically, kind of hanging around on street corners asking everybody if they're a law student is not really my idea of a good way to spend my, you know, my free time.

As many interviewees described it, simply getting the basic legal information required was often difficult and required sympathetic assistance, or slightly devious methods. Neil resorted to sneaking into a law library:

> Uh, the law library up at uh S—— university. … I don't know how I found it … to … to be honest I didn't ask because I really shouldn't have been in the law library, I sort of blagged my way in. Sort of waited while somebody swiped their card and then nipped in with them.

Other interviewees noted that accessing legal knowledge was becoming increasingly *more* difficult in the wake of digitalisation and austerity measures. Paul, for example, used to access the *All England Law Reports* in his local library. However, more recently the library has been shut. As he says:

> Um, no, well you see if you do on ——, if you try and do online research, very often there's a, you have to pay a fee to, to access them. It may be online, but it's not accessible. It's not free, it's not like in the library you could go to the AELR, look at the index and find it you know, and pay for copies.

One of the more successful interviewees in accessing legal knowledge was Neil, and this was through relying on fairly unorthodox methods. As he says, '[i]n 1996, I was spending a lot of time in the pub, but that's where you could catch a barrister'. He explains:

> I used to go in a pub in S—— in the town centre where barristers, it was just, just uh, a place called Paradise Square in S——, and there's all barristers chambers around there, down near the courts, so I made a point of going into a pub that I knew all these barristers, well a lot of barristers used to go in and I used to get, a bit of, you know, legal information off them, 'glass of red wine, Mr Barber?' 'Ah thank you Neil'. [Neil imitates a comically posh accent] What do you think of this then?[57]

[57] This was clearly quite a useful strategy. As he says later in the same train of thought, 'I became aware, after talking to the barristers in the pub, of the 1980 *Limitation Act* that says you've got, uh, three years to bring a, to issue a writ with regard to personal injury cases.'

Clearly, then, LiPs are in a bit of a bind. They are meant to behave naturally, like legal professionals, but legal professionals do not behave naturally. Litigants in person should also not actually mimic legal professionals. However, LiPs are meant to be able to conduct questioning like lawyers do. They are also expected to have some legal knowledge, even though this is far less accessible to them than it is to legal professionals. From the LiPs' perspective, then, it is very difficult to see how they should confidently prepare for their role and easy to see how they might get it wrong. This is, of course, what frequently happens. As Charles describes:

> What I did was I, I did a lot of research at the library, at the law library actually at the Royal Courts of Justice, used all their books apart from I'd bought a lot of books of my own about representing yourself in court and that sort of stuff …

He goes on to note:

> Um, that [questioning] was quite daunting, and I think the judge had to kind of assist me with that because, um, I, I, what I did was, because I had read all the books I was trying to [laughter] do it the way it said in the book, you know, um, use certain terms that they would use in the books or, or what, or what you see on TV where in fact it doesn't actually happen that way [laughter].

By following the advice Charles read in legal texts, he found himself at times behaving inappropriately, or resorting to what he had seen on television, and was again reliant on a judge to assist him. Charles's experience is not unique. Many interviewees similarly attempted to acquire legal expertise, only to be told they had misunderstood, were using the information incorrectly and that they should not be attempting to navigate this kind of information. The result of this is, as noted above, that LiPs feel that they are actively prevented from acquiring legal expertise. There are also several LiPs who feel that when they attempted to present their hard-won legal expertise, their information was not accepted, through processes of conscious or unconscious discrimination. This, too, was a significant factor in undermining trust, and led a small proportion of LiPs to turn to conspiracy theory to explain to their different treatment.[58]

What is more likely to be the reason for LiP failures, however, is not a corrupt judge so much as that the litigant's performance was deemed to be a kind of 'bad acting'; that LiPs had misunderstood what legal expertise or behaviour was, and that this is what was held against them. But what is important to note here, in the light of these findings, is that we cannot be surprised that LiPs make mistakes, because their role is so inadequately defined. This poor conception of role means that *even repeated practice* will not assist LiPs. This is at odds with Marc Galanter's influential article, 'Why the Haves Come Out Ahead', where he argues that laypersons in court proceedings are disadvantaged compared with

[58] These conspiracy theories and the circumstances in which they come about will be explored in ch 6.

legal professionals unless they are what he calls 'repeat players' (or RPs).[59] In Galanter's thesis, individuals who are repeat players (such as defendants who have been on trial on multiple occasions) will be able to acquire certain skills and knowledge that will assist them that is not available to 'one-shotters' (OSs). However, what emerges from this study is that while it is certainly the case that some LiPs report *feeling* more confident in attending court through repeated practice, and there is a degree to which some may get better at conducting questioning or knowing where to stand, for example, many instead seem to end up repeating what might best be understood as *bad* acting.

Essentially, LiPs cannot really know what to do when they attend courtroom because a series of inconsistent expectations are placed upon them, failure at any of which can result in their being penalised, and because these performative accomplishments are misrecognised as easily acquired when they are not. Repeat player LiPs, then, often do badly with greater experience. This is because in their pursuit of attempting to acquire legal skills, which is not available to them, they instead rely on a form of mimicry. This takes the form of attempting to memorise and cite legal rules, particularly the Civil Procedure Rules, or to adopt 'formal' modes of address that may be incorrect. Most tellingly, such mimicry leads to a lot of paperwork. Watching the reliance of legal professionals on bundles leads LiPs to develop their own extensive bundles of paper, but this is mistaking what the file is and does. Thomas Scheffer argues that the case file brings together the 'organised memory' of the case. As he puts it, 'The circulation of case-information relies on the file's completeness. Everything that enters the file is supposed to remain in it. As a result, it swells with each file-work session. The file as archive does not forget.'[60] As Scheffer argues, however, the file constitutes a locus of specialised knowledge and activity: knowing how to use the file, access the file and so on, relies on a specific legal skill set. Litigants in person, who do not understand how a bundle is used, only see the materiality of the file – an ever-growing bundle of paper – and they therefore accumulate paper, mistaking the 'materiality' of it for the 'materiality' of what it is to be a legal professional.[61]

This means that each repeat LiP will develop a peculiar 'LiP' skill set, which appears on the surface to have traces of the legal professional but is in fact a product of inaccessibility of knowledge, inconsistency of performative demands and lack of understanding of the embodied skills of legal professionals. While all LiPs will not behave alike, it is likely that such individuals will generate a lot of paperwork, cite legal rules extensively and struggle to understand why this way of behaving is ineffective. It is therefore a role of failure. However, I would

[59] M Galanter, 'Why the Haves Come Out Ahead: Speculation on the Limits of Legal Change' (1974) 9 *Law and Society Review* 98.

[60] T Scheffer, 'Materialities of Legal Proceedings' (2004) 17(4) *International Journal for the Semiotics of Law* 356.

[61] And this leads to the 'plastic bag wielding' image of LiPs (see ch 1, n 51). Neil himself relates carrying his large bundle of papers in a hessian bag with 'Fit as a Butcher's Dog' marked on the side.

argue that this is simply because there is no clearly defined way to be a good LiP. Indeed, this study seems to suggest that for LiPs, what is appropriate or inappropriate is instead largely a discretionary matter for the judge.

Take the extract from Neil's interview set out at the start of this chapter. Neil describes positive experiences, because he and the judge clearly got along rather well. He is obviously not behaving 'normally', in the sense that, as he himself puts it, he is acting like Rumpole of the Bailey. But the judge is willing to listen to him and indulge him, and finds him sufficiently personable or interesting.[62] This seems, in fact, to be Neil's technique throughout his court proceedings; to deliberately distinguish himself from legal practitioners to signify his difference and his (social meaning of the word) normality:

> He [the opposing solicitor] got up and did his little bow, and it was in the district registry. It was in, just like an office really, with a great big desk and we were sat on these little desks up here, and uh, district, oh, mister, Judge H——, he said 'very nice meeting you Mr ——'. And I walked around the table and I said 'very nice meeting you as well sir, thank you very much', I reached over to shake his hand and as he is shaking my hand, he says to me, I would be very interested to see how this progresses' so I said oh, well, do you want me to keep you informed? He said 'I'd appreciate that yes. Thank you Mr H——'. And this uh solicitor for the hospital or whatever he was … he's saying 'You can't do that! I said 'What?'. He said 'Shake the judge's hand'. I said 'I just have done'. But yes, but 'You can't do that'. It's like, 'I've done it, you know, you were there, you saw me'. 'Yes, but you can't do it'. Maybe you can't do it, but I'm doing it out of respect. You can't do it because you're scared of him.

But the success of this strategy is dependent on a judge's deciding that this form of behaviour is charming, rather than offensive or inappropriate. And different judges will behave in different ways. Take this piece of advice from the Citizens Advice Bureau guide:

> People often think that the Judge will run the hearing; that the Judge will ask the other party questions, give them a hard time or unpick the evidence to get at the truth. This is not what happens. If it is your claim, you have to take the lead. Judges vary in how they start a trial. The Judge may invite you to speak, or not. They may just expect you to stand up and start. If you are not sure what to do, just stand up and say something like, 'Would you like me to start now?'[63]

So where does this leave LiPs? While it is a positive indicator that judges are encouraged to intervene and assist LiPs, it is troubling that LiPs are so dependent upon them for a positive reception.[64] Finally, to return to where we started, this very short analysis of the disadvantages for LiPs in role play does not even consider

[62] As Neil tells it, after these proceedings, where he threatens to put on what was in fact a reggae tape, Justice Eady's clerk approached him afterwards to tell him that this was one of the most entertaining days at work Justice Eady had ever had, and the clerk gave him the courtroom notice as a memento.

[63] Citizens Advice Bureau (n 43) 6.

[64] It is also burdensome for the judge, as Genn and Genn point out, noting that in tribunals, lack of legal representation means the judge's task is significantly more difficult. See Genn and Genn (n 1).

the question of intimidation or high stakes, and how they may impact on a LiP's ability to perform. As Talia puts it, 'I'm one of those people who is much better on paper than on my two feet, especially when I'm petrified and someone is trying to take away my home'. There is no doubt, then, that the inadequately conceptualised role of the LiP is a significant source of disadvantage for LiPs, and that it is currently insufficiently addressed by those involved in legal proceedings and those attempting to assist LiPs.

IV. Conclusion

In summary, then, the question I asked at the beginning of the chapter perhaps needs to be changed. Instead of asking 'Why is going to law so difficult for LiPs?', perhaps we should be asking 'How is it even possible for LiPs to go to law successfully? And if it isn't possible, is it their fault?' To begin with, as this chapter has illustrated, LiPs face significant difficulties in communication and comprehension. They frequently feel that they are not listened to. But such gaps in communication and comprehension speak to the preservation of the necessary gap between the law as a professional field and the layperson. Such a gap is not accidental. In addition, no matter how hard they try, LiPs are unable to improve, with success being an exception not the rule. But as I have argued here, this is because there is no such thing as a good LiP: to be a LiP is, by its very definition, to fail. There is simply no straightforward way for LiPs to do well.

In addition, the current policies in place, such as a lack of legal aid, rising court fees and minimal assistance, clearly serve to discourage LiPs' presence as much as possible through indirect means, if not actively direct ones. It seems, perhaps, that LiPs are simply not wanted. Or, to rephrase this in a more nuanced way, LiPs are not significant enough players to warrant further assistance or attention in a belt-tightening environment. However, it should come as no surprise that LiPs themselves feel unwanted.

And it is this idea that leads to the concerns explored in chapter 6: trust and the belief in conspiracy theories. In that chapter, I will examine how the cumulative, largely negative experiences LiPs have can come to affect their beliefs about lawyers, about the legal system and about justice. As I will show, this erosion of trust in the legal system leads some LiPs to entertain conspiracist theories. But while the conspiracist conclusions LiPs may reach may be ill-conceived or disproportionate (and, at times, offensive), I argue that to dismiss these individuals as simple cranks overlooks two essential tenets of conspiracy theories that pertain to LiP experiences in the civil justice system: first, 'Bad Things' certainly happen to good LiPs; and, second, 'even paranoids have enemies'.

PART III

After Litigation

6

The Afterlife of Going to Law

Kate:	Is there anything else we haven't discussed?
Trevor:	No, you've pretty much got my whole life story there.
Kate:	That was the intention. Nothing else you want to say about your experience of [being a] litigant in person?
Trevor:	Not really, I think we've got it down, I just feel that there wasn't the backup there, I think that was the main thing that there wasn't – you're kind of on a high wire without a safety net underneath you, it felt a bit like that. As long as you walk to the other side you'll be fine, [but] if you fell you would be in trouble.

I. Introduction

So, what happens to LiPs after they go to law, and what impact does it have on them? For some LiPs, of course, there is no 'after': many interviewees in this study continue to be involved in multiple proceedings with no end in sight.[1] Some had finished one set of proceedings and were contemplating undertaking more.[2] Others had walked away, not planning on going to law again.[3] This, of course, is a finding in itself: we clearly cannot divide LiP lives neatly into before and after litigation; lives (and lawsuits) are messier than that. But the fact that many interviewees were still participating in legal proceedings at the end of this study tells us something about their experience, although it is hard to know exactly what that is. Perhaps we can say that whatever negative experiences LiPs have, it is not enough to put them off coming back to law. They come back because they still believe they can achieve a positive outcome in the civil justice system, and the value they attach to seeking a remedy is strong enough to overcome any negative experiences they

[1] Oliver, Georgina, Talia, Anna, Clive and Charles were all mid-proceedings when the interviews concluded. Charles was employing a direct access barrister, but the others were acting as LiPs.

[2] Leo was awaiting an Immigration Tribunal hearing; Marie was initiating proceedings against the local authority; and Trevor was considering taking action against the debt enforcers who came to his house.

[3] Tim had no intention of going to court again, and neither had Eleanor. Martin had decided against pursing any further issues and instead was working on assisting other LiPs, as was Russell. Peter had lost his care proceedings battle for custody of his daughter who remained in foster care.

may have had. We can say that this is a positive finding. Despite all the negative experiences detailed in this book, these individuals still feel hope.

But as with so many aspects of LiP experiences, there is another, equally persuasive way of reading this. We could instead say that LiPs are coming back because, despite routinely failing in their proceedings, many are simply not accepting the judgments made against them, returning to court with unmeritorious claims, taking up more time and, at worst, becoming the litigious bogeymen they are sometimes made out to be.

Here, this chapter can only suggest that, as with all the complex realities of being a LiP, the answer is both interpretations and neither of them. The LiPs in this study were profoundly disillusioned by their contact with legal proceedings. Many had idealistic visions of justice that, in the context of their failure, materially damaged their capacity to trust legal professionals, and legal institutions. For them, coming back perhaps has less to do with faith and hope, and more to do with necessity: pursuing a dogged belief in the *right* of their claims in the face of poor odds. These people indeed at times verge on the side of the obsessive and litigious. But at the same time, the impact of the litigation itself cannot be discounted in shaping what a LiP does next. The sheer magnitude of *loss* experienced by the individuals in this study is profound. There is the material loss: loss of money, income, loss of family, loss of homes, friends and marriages. There is also the loss of faith in the capacity of legal institutions and legal professionals to achieve justice. As Trevor said in the extract opening this chapter, LiPs operate without a safety net. So, for some interviewees at least, after all this loss, perhaps they come back because litigation is all they have left.

And what is left is what this chapter thinks about, considering the afterlife of litigation and trying to gather up the threads of interviewees' experiences. What impact has going to law had on the LiPs in this study? How has it affected their lives and their beliefs? Overall, the impact of litigation is overwhelmingly negative. But LiPs also talk of the broader impact their experiences have had on their perceptions of the future, both their own and that of the civil justice system more generally. So, while the stories told here are sometimes hard to hear, they remain valuable. These experiences generate insight into what effect the civil justice system has on individuals trying to pursue a remedy. And if the future is looking bleak, we need to try to understand why.

II. Loss

Marie: And then later on when the court cases had finished and there's nothing else that you can do, it all comes back and it causes so much emotional turmoil. It affects your mental health; it affects your physical health. It makes- it does make you seriously ill. I mean I'm in between – I've actually got to go hospital later on this … well, later on, you know what I mean? I'm – I've had so much ill health in the last … I've never had more ill health than in the last

> two years than ever before. And that's both physically and mentally. It drains you; it absolutely drains you of every coping resource that you've built up in your life. Them coping resources, once you hit a certain point, they're not there. And even the slightest thing can set you off.

This book has already detailed the negative impact of litigation on interviewees. We heard in chapter 4 about the consequences of going to law for many LiPs: I do not propose to rehash those experiences in detail here. But it is worth remembering to what extent loss is a key theme that unites almost all my interviewees in their accounts of litigation. In terms of the cases themselves, this is not that straightforward. Eleanor got her cats back. Trevor successfully reached a settlement with his builder (although even he ended up out-of-pocket due to a bailiff visit). But most other litigants in this study tended to lose: if not at every stage, still most failed to achieve the remedy they were seeking. Indeed, as we saw in chapter 5, even those who thought they had 'won' had sometimes lost, but did not realise it. And, of course, loss goes beyond the cases themselves. Interviewees in this study did not just lose their cases, they lost other things as well: family, homes, income and self-confidence. Neither Marie nor Peter had managed to regain access to their children by the conclusion of interview: while Peter remained hopeful that as his son grew older, he might return to his care, Marie's child has been formally adopted and Marie has no ability to reverse this decision.

Talia, Anna, Oliver and Clive were all at different times fighting the repossession of their properties. None of them succeeded. Talia is now in council housing, far from the flat she lost, and she continues to try to pursue a remedy for what she argues is an unlawful repossession of her property (and possessions).[4] Anna and Clive live in rented accommodation. Oliver, after 30 years of attempting to pursue a remedy for alleged police misconduct, has been homeless for several years now, and alternately couch-surfs and sleeps in his car. Oliver also lost his family due to his (self-admitted) obsessive litigation. Talia says going to litigation has isolated her completely. For Neil, the litigation (and his injuries) has prevented his having the resources, time or wellbeing to start a family, and he rarely leaves his home. The impact on mental health for litigants is also significant. Both Neil and Marie suffer from depression, with Marie describing periods of feeling suicidal.

But, of course, not all interviewees are in such a dark place. Eleanor, out of prison, reunited with her cats and lives an independent life in her rented flat. Charles continues to litigate, while having a successful career and caring for foster children alongside his own in his large house. Trevor, tempted to litigate again because of the impact of the bailiff visit, also lives in his own house with his family and has a steady job. Tim, who never wanted to be a lawyer, now works in a job he enjoys in health administration and has no interest in going to law again. Others, though, are in the middle: Leo is in limbo regarding his wife's visa status, which

[4] Talia did her interviews at the LSE because, although she still had her flat at the time of interview, she said it was so full of court documents as to be unusable. Oliver also did his interviews there as he had no home.

threatens their ability to stay together as a family. He continues to record music, however, and has a stable home life in other respects. Georgina, fighting possession proceedings (amongst other legal issues), was still living in her house at the conclusion of interview. Martin and Russell, disillusioned with their own experiences as LiPs, work in different ways to assist others, and remain hopeful that those who litigate with similar issues (bankruptcy proceedings, primarily, and the connected repossession proceedings) will be more successful than they have been.

I said at the beginning of this book that the intense nature of this study with its use of life stories attracted mostly serial litigants, and it is true that this means that we cannot generalise based on these experiences. Not all LiPs will lose, and many will not experience loss to the same extent. And emphasising loss in this sample paints an overly negative picture: LiPs can, and do, also succeed. But we can still perhaps fairly say two things: first, that loss is a common experience for many LiPs, and that the impact of that loss is highly dependent on the circumstances of the individual, including their capacity to accept a judgment, and whether they have other things in their lives alongside this litigation. It also depends on the overall value of the issue: it is hardly surprising that Marie and Peter would obsessively return to litigate, and less surprising that people like Trevor and Tim can carry on with their lives easily. Second, though, we can say that their chances of success, of *not* losing, are materially damaged by being a LiP: LiPs simply are not given equal capacity and opportunity to succeed. And this means that even those who have come out of this process relatively unscarred, find that their experiences of litigation negatively impact their trust in legal professionals and institutions.

III. Trust

Anna: So I took them both down there, to the M—— County Court for what was going to be my first experience down there in many, many years, in the belief that I had a strong case, judges are decent, honest people, wise people who dispense justice and wisdom. That was my perception of what was going to happen.

Most litigants in this study were left profoundly disillusioned by their experiences of civil justice. For many interviewees, like Anna, their initial optimism about the possibility of justice in the courts was diminished by actual contact with legal proceedings. This shift from idealism to cynicism was common. You may recall Eleanor's comments from the opening of this book:

> Basically, you are sold a myth that the British judicial system is the finest in the world, that it is fair, just, reasonable and concerned with finding out the truth. That is a load of fucking bollocks, pardon the French.

Eleanor is not alone in this. Peter narrates a similar account:

> Well it's got to if we're going to have a justice system, I mean how I really feel is like the UK like Great Britain led the way in judiciary, it led the way, it even not instigated, it actually encouraged and formed the legal system in America you know. We're the world leader in judiciary you know the Old Bailey and all this, you know the scales of justice and it seems to be on its backside now. It's gone to the dogs in a lot of areas and it's sad, it's really sad.

Georgina, too, observes that she believed very strongly, prior to embarking upon legal proceedings, that every individual was 'equal before the law, uh, blah blah blah', before going on to note:

> As far as I am concerned it is all just words because they know very well there's no way in the rea—, reality of the set up that you can get a, a fair hearing in British courts across the board unless your, you get lucky. I think the courts in Britain are run like a lottery.

These beliefs are echoed by Martin, who says:

> Well I knew I had a case, and I knew I was right. And I knew I'd been turned over and maybe naive, I actually believe in British justice [laugh] so I thought if only I can get it together correctly and right, with the ability to show it, I will win.

Litigating, for these interviewees, leads to a loss of trust, or belief, in the capacity of the civil justice system to operate fairly. This can play a role in shaping litigant attitudes and behaviours, and result in the development of negative perceptions of legal institutions and the legal profession. But how can we understand what the significance of trust is for litigants, and what the consequences are when it is undermined?

It is here that the work of Tom Tyler becomes particularly useful. Rooted in psychology, it concentrates on trying to understand how perceptions about justice and legitimacy are shaped or understood for laypersons in both civil and criminal processes. Tyler's 1990 book, *Why People Obey the Law*, explores the conditions under which individuals accept or perceive laws to be legitimate, as well as the conditions under which this acceptance or perception might break down.[5] As such, this book, and his subsequent research, is particularly valuable to this study in helping to flesh out how the experiences of LiPs may alter their beliefs and attitudes to civil justice, and to 'the law' as they perceive it.[6] Tyler argues in *Why People Obey the Law* that the dominant paradigm for how authorities generally understand obedience to the law is based on an instrumental perspective; that is, people obey the law because they fear the consequences if they do not. However, Tyler argues that this overlooks the

[5] T Tyler, *Why People Obey the Law* (Princeton, NJ, Princeton University Press, 1990).

[6] See also E Allan Lind and T Tyler, *The Social Psychology of Procedural Justice* (New York, Springer, 1988); T Tyler and Y Huo, *Trust in the Law: Encouraging Public Cooperation with the Police and Courts* (New York, Russell Sage Foundation, 2002).

importance of the normative arguments as to why people might obey the law. As Tyler expresses it:

> Normative commitment through personal morality means obeying a law because one feels the law is just; normative commitment through legitimacy means obeying a law because one feels that the authority enforcing the law has the right to dictate behaviour.[7]

This concentration on the normative perspective is useful for this study, as it is notable that interviewees expressed strong beliefs or perceptions about justice that, after negative encounters and experiences, began to erode their faith in 'justice' more generally, and this affected their behaviour. This led to an undermining of the belief that said 'authority' had the right to dictate any kind of behaviour.

Of course, the normative perception of justice is very broad, and such a category covers up a great many differences in perspectives. However, as Tyler points out, while there are several ways in which we can understand this, 'distributive justice' (caring about the fairness of the outcome) and 'procedural justice' (caring about the fairness of the process) are useful approaches to understanding what may constitute legitimacy for laypersons. Procedural justice, a term originated by Thibaut and Walker in their 1975 study, *Procedural Justice: A Psychological Analysis*, emphasises the importance of the fairness of processes alongside the fairness of outcomes.[8] In other words, it is not as simple as saying that litigants only find the process unfair when they lose: how they are treated during the process can be of equal importance. Zimerman and Tyler note, following Thibaut and Walker's research:

> What law has summarized under the 'due process' rubric, social scientists capture as a bundle of interests, needs, or wants described in a variety of ways – vindication, attention, accountability, information, accuracy, comfort, respect, recognition, dignity, efficacy, empowerment, [and] justice. Research on litigants … reveals a group of individuals who seek something in addition to money.[9]

Indeed, this study underlines that litigants have a complex range of desires when it comes to litigation, beyond only winning. In their 2010 study, Zimerman and Tyler set out to consider the experiences of *pro se* litigants in the US, and in particular to think about how not having representation may or may not affect 'access to justice'. In going about this, Zimerman and Tyler conclude that there are four key aspects of 'procedural justice' that play a strong role in shaping perceptions of legitimacy for litigants: 'voice', where litigant are able to tell their stories; 'neutrality', a belief that those arbitrating litigation are fair and treat people equally; 'respect', where litigants are taken seriously by professionals; and finally 'trust', that is, whether litigants perceive that authorities are listening to them and trying to do what is just.[10]

[7] Tyler (n 5) 3–4.

[8] J Thibaut and L Walker, *Procedural Justice: A Psychological Analysis* (New York, Elrbaum, 1975); T Tyler, "What is Procedural Justice?: Criteria used by Citizens to Assess the Fairness of Legal Procedures' (1988) 22 *Law & Society Review* 103: 103–36; Lind and Tyler (n 6).

[9] N Zimerman and T Tyler, 'Between Access to Counsel and Access to Justice' (2010) 37 *Fordham Urban Law Journal* 473.

[10] ibid 487–89.

If we reflect on accounts in the previous chapters of this book in relation to these categories, we might recall, in regard to 'voice', that Marie was unable to speak and unable to understand her lawyer. In terms of 'neutrality', we might also recall the accounts of Eleanor, Peter, Charles and Tim, outlining situations where they tell us judges and opposing legal professionals demeaned or insulted them. In terms of 'respect', we might recall the experience of Talia's frustration in getting anyone to respond to her or take her intensive study of civil justice procedure seriously. In this respect 'trust', the final factor listed in Zimerman and Tyler's framework, must surely be diminished by LiPs' inability to get anywhere when they seek a remedy.

Of course, the expectations held by the interviewees in this study are idealistic, not realistic: they are rather in keeping with many laypersons' understanding or beliefs about legality as understood in a 'remote sense', as noted by Ewick and Silbey in *The Common Place of Law*. As they observe, 'one story' told about law by their interviewees is where law is

> Removed and distant from the personal lives of ordinary people. In this story, law is majestic, operating by known and fixed rules in carefully delimited spheres. The law exists in time and places that put it outside of, rather than in, the midst of everyday life.[11]

This description emphasises that those who have minimal to no experience *of* legal proceedings are far more likely to entertain idealistic notions of courts and legal proceedings. Such individuals also formulate ideas of justice that are arguably not related to the kinds of justice that may or may not be possible as an outcome of legal proceedings (here we might reflect on Moorhead and Sefton's 'legal' versus 'social' meanings, outlined in the Introduction to this book). Indeed, the interviewees in this study are arguably *more* positive towards the legal system prior to commencing their claim than members of the public identified in Genn's *Paths to Justice*.[12]

So the problems arise when litigants encounter legal proceedings and find that justice does not operate in 'carefully delimited spheres'. And it is not practically accessible. As noted in chapter 5, LiPs sought to attempt to obtain legal information against great odds. When they did acquire it and attempt to use it (which is likely to be incorrectly), this hard-won knowledge was overlooked or disregarded by the judge. As Talia said:

> Um, I didn't, there are other things I didn't expect. I didn't expect some judges not to, uh, implement the Civil Procedure Rules which are rules, I mean they're, they're laid down in law, um, I really didn't expect them, um, not to implement at all or only to implement the ones that favoured the over-mighty claimant. If, if a litigant in person as I'm finding just makes, you know, fails to comply with something or other, the other side will exploit it to the nth degree but the, certainly in my case, the other side has completely ignored timescales in a way that prejudices my uh rights in law, and no one has pulled

[11] P Ewick and S Silbey, *The Common Place of Law* (Chicago, IL, University of Chicago Press, 1998) 28.

[12] See H Genn, *Paths to Justice* (Oxford, Hart Publishing, 1999) 249.

> them up at all! And in two cases, they've submitted their, um, their claim, um, at less than 28 days, I should have 28 days to respond provided I put in the acknowledgement of service, and they cut a week off that by being late and nobody pulls them up on it.

As she goes on to say:

> I have, I have really scrupulously told the truth all the way through and I've been completely fair to them to the extent of my ability, to the other side. And they've lied and lied and lied and it's broken the rules and taken advantage of their, um, greater bargaining power and resources and when it comes to decide whether to believe them or me, judges believe them.

Here we might also think of the work of Sally Engle Merry. In Merry's examination of low-value civil and criminal proceedings in the US in 1980s and 1990s, she found that legal professionals referred to lower-value claims as 'garbage' or 'junk' cases. Merry pointed out that whilst access to justice for all was preserved in the rhetoric of the courts, in practice, practitioners clearly felt that some cases (the minor ones) were a waste of time. As Merry argued, '[litigants] are both invited and encouraged into the court and, at the same time, denied legal handling'.[13] This rings true for LiPs. They have the right to access the courts, but when they get there they find that they are not wanted or are considered nuisances. In a sense, then, we can say that LiPs are doubly marginalised in the civil justice system: first, they are marginalised through their positioning as outsiders; but they are then marginalised again through the positioning of their behaviour as aberrant. This double marginalisation alienates LiPs from the institutions in which they had believed they had a right to operate.

But we need to push this even further. A diminishment of trust in legal institutions following litigation is, of course, not necessarily particular to LiPs. It is a common experience. But what *is* particular is the specific disadvantages LiPs labour under. As Moorhead argued, LiPs tend to experience worse outcomes, irrespective of the merit of their case. He suggested that, on balance, LiPs experience a 'strong perceptual cocktail of unfairness'.[14] This has been supported by research in the US, which similarly demonstrates that legal professionals are biased against LiPs and that this has an impact on their outcomes.[15] This means, then, that negative experiences of LiPs are rooted in systemic disadvantage. It is not just about 'procedural justice', and it is not just about trust or perceptions of fairness. Loss of trust and disillusionment might partly be based on idealisation to begin with, but they are also indicative of systemic inequality for LiPs in the civil justice system. Litigants in person are not getting any kind of justice, procedural or otherwise, and this failure becomes another loss that piles up for them.

[13] S Engle Merry, *Getting Justice and Getting Even: Legal Consciousness Among Working Class Americans* (Chicago, IL, University of Chicago Press, 1990).

[14] R Moorhead, 'The Passive Arbiter: Litigants in Person and the Challenge to Neutrality' (2007) 16 *Social and Legal Studies* 405, 410.

[15] B Levin, *The Times* (London, 30 November 1976).

IV. Conspiracy

For some interviewees, their loss of trust in legal professionals or institutions led to conspiracist thinking. For example, Russell has this to say about his experience in court:

> The barristers are behind you and they've got a nice big space, desks and everything like that. They've got you at the front, you're sitting there, you've got about that much room to sit in, your knees are up against the front of it. There's a desk there, little, about that wide in front of you like that to put your papers on. So, if you've got to stand up and address the judge, you can't do it without tipping the thing up and all your papers fall on the floor. Deliberate this is, absolutely deliberate.

Alongside Russell, roughly one-third of the participants in this study expressed ideas linked to conspiracy theory. These were most commonly to do with Freemasons, antisemitism and perceived corruption in the courts. The Freemasonry and antisemitic conspiracy theories heavily overlap, underscoring what Bernard Levin suggests:

> Freemasonry hysteria … is paralleled to the same principles as those of anti-Semitism, and indeed it has often been to a very considerable extent a stalking-horse for the more ancient vileness. It could hardly be otherwise; attacks on suspect Jewry have almost always been inextricably entwined with anti-freemasonry. Hitler lumped them together without distinction of any kind. [16]

Russell claims that

> [a] freemason, if he is in difficulties, say in a court, and you see it in a court, they go up like that, I just don't know what to do your Honour, so he's saying (finger signals) I'm a widow's son, see that's a fraud, you see, passing themselves off as something they're not. Yeah, they do all sorts of other tricks like you know, turn their head away and that means it stinks, this case stinks.

Similarly, Georgina suggests that

> there's a lot of Machivalean [*sic*] cults like Freemasonry for example, I know that a lot of the things they do, they swear allegiance to each other even above their own families and to me that's highly dangerous, I know an awful lot of the bad things that are happening are in, through … they're in the same lodge, for example members of the police force, members of the legal profession, even judges. I've seen judges shaking like a leaf in terror, probably because they've been threatened if they go against the agenda.

Anna, following similar lines, says:

> Yeah, there's the odd case where suddenly somebody is selected, probably a freemason, to win a landmark case, yeah? Like that actress who got, similar to an MRSA claim, can't remember what her name was but she got huge compensation for something very similar to me, what was it she had, what was her name, quite a famous actress but anyway

[16] Bernard Levin, *The Times*, 30 November 1976.

> she had something similar to me, but oh! It's all over the newspapers. Is it Leslie Ash? Leslie Ash, I think so. All over the papers. I thought oh yeah, she's probably a freemason.

Such Freemason perceptions hinge on the classic conspiracy theory of a controlling cabal or elite that manipulates events and controls outcomes. The antisemitic conspiracy theories expressed in the study by Anna, Russell and Georgina ran along parallel lines. Russell says 'And of course the Jews believe in the bible that, that they are citizens of the world, the world is theirs, that is what they're striving for.' Georgina, similarly, says 'I'm not in any way sexist or racist. David Icke talks a lot about Zionists. It's a particular breed of Jews who are the money changers. They are the ones in the central banking system.' This 'not all Jews' antisemitism was most succinctly expressed by Anna:

> [A] lot of the scandals in the country, like Shipman's obviously a Jewish freemason scandal, but certainly there are a number of Jewish people involved in both my scandals. The medical one in particular, so I thought, because of the Jewish influence that I needed a decent Jewish judge to stand up for what is right because you know, because I'm aware that there are some thoroughly decent Jewish people who have got great family values but I'm also aware from personal experience and what my mother has told me that there are others.[17]

I do not want to suggest any misplaced sympathy for these individuals or the hateful nature of these beliefs. Indeed, this was easily one of the most upsetting aspects of the study, and I want to emphasise again that these views were expressed by a minority of LiPs. Additionally, there is no evidence that LiPs are any more likely than anyone else to be conspiracy theorists. But I do want to suggest that there might be value in thinking about how and why people turn to conspiracist beliefs. Conspiracy theory is, of course, a complex area, and a thorough excavation is beyond the scope of this work.[18] But a unifying theme in much conspiracy theory lies in its explanatory power: people believe conspiracy theories because it helps them explain something they otherwise cannot comprehend.[19] And I suggest here that what LiPs cannot comprehend is why they cannot (easily) succeed.[20] As I outlined in chapter 5, serial LiPs, unlike the 'repeat players' outlined in Galanter's thesis, do not necessarily get better, and their failure to improve despite their efforts is something that they struggle to understand. So I suggest that inability to explain their losses can tip some LiPs towards conspiracist theories. Such conspiracy theories are highly offensive, of course, but they are also rooted in genuine differential treatment. As we have

[17] Here, as Levin suggested was often the case, we see Anna explicitly linking Jews and Freemasons.

[18] I have written elsewhere in detail about conspiracy theory and LiPs. See at https://papers.ssrn.com/sol3/papers.cfm?abstract_id=4277751.

[19] D Aaronovitch, *Voodoo Histories: How Conspiracy Theory Has Shaped Modern History* (London, Vintage Books, 2009) 5.

[20] This argument chimes with Didi Herman's, who suggests that vexatious litigants 'can be read as passionate actors exhibiting high degrees of positive agency and oppositional or alternative rationalities'. See D Herman, 'Hopeless Cases: Race, Racism and the "Vexatious Litigant"' (2012) 8 *International Journal of Law in Context* 27, 43.

seen, LiPs have worse outcomes than represented parties, and legal professionals can display bias towards them both unconsciously and consciously. We can therefore potentially say that conspiracy theory is a result of a scenario in which LiPs are both 'invited' into court and 'denied legal handling'.[21]

Of course not all LiPs become conspiracy theorists, and I would not suggest that litigation *alone* can explain such a development. But there are a few important lessons in here for us. First, we need to understand the degree to which litigation may foster or aggravate this kind of thinking, rather than seeing it as solely down to an individual's psychology.[22] As with so much of being a LiP, when we treat LiPs' difficulties as emblematic of their personalities, we fail to consider the circumstances in which they act. How we treat LiPs in the civil justice system has material consequences. And the more negative experiences LiPs have, the likelier it is that some may turn to conspiracy theories to provide explanations for *why* they cannot succeed. And while LiPs might not be more likely than others to be conspiracy theorists, the absence of adequate explanation and information *for* LiPs means making sense of loss so much harder.

These individuals who are attracted to conspiracy theories are also often the ones who cannot give up and who pursue obsessive actions. Perhaps, then, we need to think a bit more critically and consider that this may demonstrate the degree to which the civil justice system has failed them. Indeed, Herman suggests this explicitly in her study of vexatious litigants:

> While this persistence could be read as further evidence of their pathology, I prefer to see their continued failure to give up in a more positive light – as evidence of their commitment to the ideals of justice.[23]

As Herman expresses it, critiquing Hazel Genn:

> Genn argues that the civil justice system 'contributes quietly and significantly to social and economic well-being' (p 3) and that 'the civil courts publicly reaffirm norms and behavioural standards for private citizens' (p 3).[24]

Too often, the default position is that the civil justice system functions in a mostly positive way: LiP experiences are exceptional. But is this a sustainable claim, if so many litigants have terrible experiences of litigation? Herman suggests we need to cast a critical eye over any claims about 'wellness' and the functionality of civil justice, and not assume that minority examples tell us only about that minority. As she puts it, 'exploring how VLs [vexatious litigants] are judged to be obsessive, hopeless and unhappy tells us something about the relationship between injury and English law itself'.[25] Here I can only echo Herman, saying that understanding

[21] Merry (n 13).
[22] M Butter and P Knight, 'Bridging the Great Divide: Conspiracy Theory Research for the 21st Century' (2015) 62 *Diogenes* 17.
[23] Herman (n 19) 43.
[24] ibid 32.
[25] ibid.

how and why LiPs are treated the way they are, and the experiences they have, can also tell us something bigger about who and what we value (and do not value) in the civil justice system. As Herman says:

> Is continued litigation pursuit of a 'delusion'? Arguably, it is not that VLs cannot grasp reality but that they refuse to accept reality's presumptions … perhaps the 'rationality' of hope – the likely prospect of any particular hope's realisation – is not the question. If hope involves longing, dreaming … is in some sense 'utopian' … and seeks to bring about that which is hoped for, then perhaps these 'race campaigners' are not 'hopeless cases' at all.

Herman goes on to say:

> Those without mental health evidence in their case reports are often accused of having similar perceptions and behaviours to the 'delusions' that the 'ill' people are diagnosed with: an obsession with being 'right'; and a belief in a conspiracy out to get them. It is thus not at all clear from the case reports which came first, the 'illness' or the experience of the legal process.

While we may fear the 'difficult' LiP or the LiP who expresses conspiracy theories, what we perhaps need to take more seriously is the possibility that we are at least partly responsible for creating them. And what these LiP stories have shown us is, all too often, 'the gradual, Kafka-esque deterioration of a litigant as they proceed through the civil justice system'.[26]

V. The Future

In the previous sections of the chapter, I have outlined how the theme of loss unites many LiPs in this study, and how this loss has undermined trust in their perceptions of the legal profession. I have also considered how the more extreme beliefs that may be fuelled by these losses, conspiracy theories, tell us that there are real consequences for LiPs who are unable to understand what is happening to them in a civil justice system that theoretically permits them full access but in practice makes it impossible to succeed. But, finally, where does all of this leave our LiPs? What do they think about the future, their own and that of the justice system? What would they say to others who wanted to be LiPs? This is a question I asked explicitly at the end of the interviews.

For Talia:

> I suppose I would say to other litigants in person, you need to be aware that when you go into this, you may not be able to come out of it for a very long time; it may go on much longer than you think. It's something that – if you have to do it, you have to do

[26] ibid 34.

> it, sometimes the choice is between being a litigant in person and losing your home or your rights to – well, any of your rights, I suppose

Talia emphasises here that sometimes being a LiP is a matter of necessity, regardless of consequence: this is keeping with the fact that she continues to fight in the hope that she can regain her property long after the final decision was made. For Tim, left more unscathed by proceedings, he is still cautious about advising other people about being LiPs:

> I think it's, it's a brave person who takes a step to represent themselves. It's not a decision anyone should take lightly, and I think it's a process that can be very hard but very rewarding. Dare I say if you have to more than once don't feel disheartened if the first time didn't go down the way you hoped it would.

Eleanor provides a typically bracing answer here:

> Kate: So what do you think you would say to someone else who is contemplating being a litigant in person?
>
> Eleanor: Erm if the other party is a litigant in person, go for it. If they're not, think long and hard. Purely and simply because you will not get a fair shake from the courts if you are a litigant in person and your opposing side is not, they got representation you will get screwed because it's not about the law in those circumstances, it's about who's got the most toys and who can do the best performance and who's got the best, who's better at winning the game, because that's one thing I've learned through all of this … is the law is a game.

For these interviewees, then, being a LiP is extremely difficult, may be necessary, is brave but is fraught with risk (again, we might think of Trevor and his reflection on the lack of safety nets for LiPs). But for other LiPs, much of the problem with being a LiP is not just about individual capacity or lack of equal treatment, it is about systemic underfunding and policy initiatives that are degrading the civil justice system. Peter expresses it like this:

> So it has changed me but I've seen it, I've seen in the system there has been, it's been not neglected it's been diluted and eroded away because of austerity as well, it's not just one thing, it's austerity cuts, cut backs on policing, more pressure from the Ministers on the judicial system saying for example, right a family law case has now got to be 26 weeks which I think is crazy, dangerous I think, dangerous because what it's doing is forcing people into, it's corralling people into a decision making sort of process it's pushing them, pressurising them into making decisions quick when maybe there is some work that needs to be done, some support which shouldn't even be in court maybe. Instead, it's pushing them in the wrong direction and meanwhile you've got Legal Aid being cut and everything else being cut so in the end, it's almost like anarchy. Dare I say it.

The legal aid cuts, as well as other austerity measures, had a profound impact on these interviewees in terms of their capacity to communicate with the courts and be understood. It has long been recognised, of course, that the systems of communications in courts are generally poor. In the Lord Chief Justice's Report of 2015, Lord Thomas noted:

> Although in common with many other European states the number of court buildings has been reduced through closure, the failure to invest has meant that many of the courtrooms have not been modernised and lack modern means of communication to provide for better access to justice.[27]

He went on to point out:

> Outdated IT systems severely impede the delivery of justice. For example, the reforms to civil justice which were intended to implement the report of Lord Woolf were introduced in April 1999 only on the promise of modern IT; none was ever provided.[28]

The courts post-LASPO 2012 are facing considerable challenges. The Ministry of Justice cut £157 million from its budget over the period 2010–11 to 2015–16, and although the reductions have slowed a little (in 2019–20, the total Ministry of Justice budget was around 25 per cent lower than in 2010–11), these are still swingeing. Achieving these savings has also involved cutting 22 per cent of staff overall.[29] In addition, half the courts in the country have closed. All these austerity measures have led to a dramatic decline in service quality. This is something explicitly emphasised by court staff themselves in the TUC's publication, *Justice Denied: Impacts of the Government's Reform of Legal Aid and Courts on Access to Justice*, published in October 2016, which drew on interviews with 141 staff members from HMCTS.[30] The report found that 'the majority of respondents (90 per cent) viewed budget cuts to court services and the Crown Prosecution Service as being detrimental to the effective delivery of justice and this in turn was seen as diminishing access to justice'.[31] In addition it noted:

> More than half of those surveyed (57 per cent) feel that their workloads have increased since 2010, and in many cases this was attributed to cuts to staffing combined with an increase in the volume in their work areas … Changes to staffing and workloads over the last two to three years have resulted in, for example: the loss of experienced and permanent staff and an increase in the use of agency and temporary workers or staff on fixed-term contracts; an increase in stress, pressure and unpaid work; and an increase in errors, with quality of work affected.[32]

A single email address serves as a communication point for all matters relating to each County Court; the LiPs are therefore reliant on someone responding to them in good time, which frequently does not happen, due to a combination of poor IT systems and understaffing.[33] In addition, staffing cuts have had an impact on

[27] Judiciary of England and Wales, *The Lord Chief Justice's Report* (London, Judicial Office, 2015) 5.
[28] ibid.
[29] There has been a concomitant significant rise in the costs of hiring temporary and contract staff, going from £3.7m in 2010 to £50.6m in 2017. See O Bowcott, 'UK courts service spending sees tenfold rise since 2010' *The Guardian* (London, 21 July 2018).
[30] Trade Union Congress, *Justice Denied* (London, TUC, 2016).
[31] ibid 5.
[32] ibid.
[33] ibid 6.

how able LiPs are to get any assistance. Trevor commented, when in the midst of attempting to get the court decision stayed:

> I, I felt sorry for the lady in um, B—— because, you know, it's literally just one lady behind a window. There's, there was obviously more people at one stage, because there was lots of windows but there was only this one person and it is, it was all a bit, she can't give you any information or doesn't know anything …

Trevor is sympathetic towards this individual, but his extract also notes that this is a new development; there used to be more windows, and more people to help you, but budget cuts have led to fewer staff. In addition, the woman who is at the window is not equipped to respond to the questions. For Trevor, obtaining help or assistance to clarify what to do next is the prime requirement of being a LiP:

> Who can you speak to? Is there someone? Do they provide some sort of back up, even if it's just a, even if it's just a website, you know, is there a website you can go to that you can, you know, ask a question and get some sort of answer … you know, I mean I know you can be, the problem with that could be is that it gets completely jammed and everyone is asking legal questions to a, you know, a young eighteen year old who is just there for his Saturday job [laughs].

What is interesting here is that Trevor clearly assumes that the individuals who are assisting LiPs are not people who will have the requisite experience or expertise; instead, they are increasingly likely to be 'eighteen year olds' on a 'Saturday job'.[34] The implication is that increasing responsibility in the context of rising numbers of LiPs is being put on the shoulders of those who are not sufficiently trained and who are inadequately remunerated. Many individuals who work at the court therefore *cannot* help a LiP, either because they do not know how to do so, or because it is beyond their job description.[35]

While many of the measures imposed on the courts have an austerity rationale, that of saving money in the face of enormous budget cuts, the results are an increasing inaccessibility of services and assistance for LiPs. It is hard to reconcile this with the concept of 'access to justice', something Lord Thomas himself draws attention to when criticising the rise in court fees and LiPs.[36] The point I want to make here is that while these measures might be posited as unfair or unfortunate, there is arguably an ideological shift being undertaken through such policy initiatives. The reduction of face-to-face assistance, the move to central processing of claims and the closure of windows, the rise in court fees and many other related measures, all also serve to minimise or deflect any accountability government policy may have towards impeding access to justice for LiPs.[37]

[34] This is supported by staffing changes at HMCTS: ibid 16.
[35] ibid, 19, 27.
[36] *Lord Chief Justice's Report* (n 26).
[37] Whether or not the coming online courts will aggravate or improve this remains to be seen. I reflect on some of the technological developments in the Conclusion to this book.

If a LiP does not receive an answer to an email, there is no one to whom they can appeal or complain. If the single staff member at the window has too long a queue then a LiP may not be able to get an answer in time to respond to a claim. If the court fees rise substantially in tandem with a cutting of legal aid, many LiPs will not make it to court at all. But all of these patterns of experience and decision making cannot be directly attributed to any individual or institution's specific failing; instead, they will be attributed, if at all, to the failure of the LiP to sufficiently 'work' with the system. The systems being put in place that cause difficulties for LiPs are not perhaps simply unfortunate; they are an indirect but arguably useful means of reducing certain kinds of court users, while also reducing any accountability for lack of access to justice.[38]

Trevor outlines the collision between austerity and fairness, explicitly reflecting on his own experience:

> Because what I mean is, if a thing is, by its nature going to be inefficient, if you, if what the law is about is getting to the truth, if that's what it's about, it's about giving people the hon—, the honest, as close to the truth as you can get about stuff, um, then it's gonna take, you've got to give that thing time, it can't be done quickly. If you're trying to make it quickly at some, somewhere down the line someone's going to lose out, something's gonna get missed because you're doing it quickly and if it can't be done quickly, then it can't be done quickly. There's no point in trying to make something into something that it's not, that's my point. Is that, if that's the case, that there is efficiency is going to have to be, you can either be efficient or you can be correct, then which, it depends which way you're going to go, whether you want to be correct or you want to be efficient, and then if you want to be correct then obviously you're going to have to put the money in to make sure that you can be correct, you can't, you can't have both, I don't think, I'm not an expert. It seems to me you're trying to save money in something that, where actually, you can't really save a lot of money. All you can do is make things less fair, less right, and then you save money but then you don't get the right result. So, that's what I think about the court system from my experience.

To follow Trevor's line of thinking, then, cost-cutting measures clearly result in disproportionately unfair experiences and encounters for LiPs. But beyond this, we can argue that what is increasingly being put into place through government policy initiatives, is a court system where saving money is the key motivator; and, most importantly, that the implementation of this savings policy is done through decreasing human contact, or recourse to assistance, even if this was not the primary or conscious aim.[39] By achieving savings through outsourcing, or decreasing workplace skills, one can also neuter the possibility of any complaints

[38] M Fouzder, 'There was no money: MoJ called in consultants to help control spending' *Law Society Gazette* (London, 19 October 2016).

[39] This includes, of course, the technology being introduced in the Court Modernisation programme, which aims to move all low-value civil litigation either online or to on-the-papers evaluation. For more detail on this programme, see at www.gov.uk/guidance/the-hmcts-reform-programme.

that may arise: the courts remain theoretically open, but are increasingly impenetrable, expensive and inconsistent. It is no wonder, then, that LiPs find navigating legal proceedings so challenging. First, LiPs are excluded from procedures through a lack of understanding of legal language and behaviour; second, their own role is not conceptualised clearly; and, finally, crucially, LiPs are operating in a system that was never designed for them and that, increasingly, favours privatisation and outsourcing, which serves to disadvantage them further but for which there is very limited accountability when things go wrong.

However, I want to end on a slightly more optimistic note. It is clear we need to address the role and purpose of LiPs in a more coherent and systematic way. Perhaps, then, there is a possibility that some of the more negative experiences recounted in these pages might be avoided. And that is what I will explore in the Conclusion to this book: what we can do with these LiP stories.

Conclusion

This book has tried to understand more about what it is like to be a LiP. In the first two chapters I explored how LiPs are viewed by the legal profession and scholarship, considering why LiPs often have a negative reputation, and how they came to acquire this pejorative baggage. I then turned, through the interviews I conducted, to flip perspectives and consider how LiPs themselves describe their experiences of litigation, and their attitudes towards legal professionals and process. As I conjectured at the outset of this research, a vast divide separates these two different perspectives: misunderstanding upon misunderstanding, deliberate, accidental, useful, detrimental, and all these issues continue to throw hazards in the path of clear communication, eroding trust and accumulating like mounting debris on a highway. It is therefore quite difficult to see beyond the rubble or, to borrow imagery from writing about LiPs, to think about after the 'flood'.

As I set out in the chapters 1 and 2 of this book, distrust and dislike of LiPs is deep-rooted and longstanding. And what LiP perspectives tell us is that this distrust cuts both ways: LiPs in this study have deeply negative experiences that lead them to dislike and distrust legal professionals in their turn. So much of this distrust and dislike is grounded in gaps between ways of seeing. It is also rooted, as I have sought to argue, in the lack of *place* for LiPs. They do not belong. They are made to feel that they do not belong. This perpetuates not only their own negative experiences, but also the very likelihood of their being received in a hostile environment. And so a distrustful cycle carries on. In this conclusion, then, we find ourselves at something of an impasse. Litigants in person are badly and inadequately accommodated in the civil justice system. And more LiPs are coming into this system that has no clear place for them in terms of resources, attitudes and the workings of civil justice itself, which seems to preclude, or at least limit, recognition of LiP needs or desires. The dimension of the problem is vast, and seemingly intractable.

However, while the future for LiPs looks bleak, what I hope to have achieved here is not simply laying out the scale of the problem, but to also provide at least a partial corrective; some small steps or adjustments that may indeed be possible and which may, in a small way, make a difference. To return to Clifford Geertz, 'it is not necessary to know everything in order to understand something'.[1] I might paraphrase this by saying that it is not necessary for me to solve anything, but that does not mean that I cannot make some contribution towards that end. And so

[1] C Geertz, *The Interpretation of Cultures* (New York, Basic Books, 1973) 20.

that is what this conclusion seeks to do: not just to summarise the problems, but also to start to think about what we might do.

What are the problems? As chapter 1 sought to demonstrate, there is a widely disseminated negative perception of LiPs. At different times, and in different jurisdictions, people representing themselves have been described as time-wasters, difficult, 'crazy', obsessive and so on. The emphasis in such writing is on the difficulty LiPs cause others; through taking too long, through lacking legal skills, as well as through what is often conjectured to be fundamentally down to their psychological makeup or troublesome personality. Inherent in these kinds of descriptions is an instinctive association between LiPs and vexatious litigants, and between LiPs and compulsive litigants. There is an implicit assumption in much of this writing that LiPs are there out of choice, in much the same way that criminal rational choice theorists perceive crime: criminals choose to commit crimes, and LiPs choose to 'commit law'. Ultimately, this paints a picture of LiPs as an overriding *problem*, the impact of which needs to be managed or controlled.

Compounding this unflattering portrait of LiPs is the current context in which we find ourselves: 10 years after the cuts to legal aid, which left those pursuing or defending civil claims almost completely without access to free advice or representation. As I have laid out in chapter 1, this has engendered something of a crisis when it comes to LiPs. Attention focused on LiPs has expanded exponentially because the expected rapid increase in numbers has caused considerable concern: how the courts will deal with the influx of LiPs, what legal professionals can do and whether their roles will be expected to change, and a host of other unanswerable questions. At times, this concern is elevated to the status of an explicit threat, evident in claims about potential LiP violence and abuse of others, including court users, court staff and legal professionals.

This threat seems to be rooted in the worry that in the wake of LASPO 2012, there may be *too many* LiPs to be adequately controlled, or dealt with safely in the context of limited resources and funding cuts to court services. This concern is also made explicit in the literature that draws diluvian analogies talking of flooding, tsunamis and waves; apocalyptic and catastrophic imagery to symbolise just *how* problematic LiPs are perceived to be by some practitioners and scholars in civil justice. But as chapter 1 set out, and as this book has maintained throughout, this conceptualisation of LiPs as a threat can only exist through positioning LiPs as outsiders. Fundamental to the negative conception *of* LiPs, therefore, is that they are conceived of as outside of normal legal practice: LiPs are fundamentally aberrant.

Of course, this is not uniformly the case. As I laid out in chapter 1, there have always been sympathetic scholars and practitioners who have tried to assist LiPs, notably the influential and important work of Hazel Genn, Rosemary Hunter, Mark Sefton and Richard Moorhead, John Baldwin, Elizabeth Trinder and others. This book would not be possible without the illuminating work of these scholars, including the difficult groundwork of finding and interviewing LiPs, testing presuppositions, and tracking policy developments and their effects at a time when LiPs were being largely ignored in research. It is also important to emphasise that there is a growing body of scholarship that seeks to understand the LiP. This includes the work of the Civil Justice Council and its Litigants in Person Working Group, the work of Bob Lee and Tatiana Tkacukova at the University of Birmingham, and the work of Bridgette Toy-Cronin in New Zealand, Julie McFarlane in Canada, Grainne McKeever at Ulster University and Jess Mant at Monash. Such literature has attempted to better understand LiP experiences and to offer suggestions for how to improve them, as well as how to minimise the impact on the courts.

There has also been a wave of guidance, research and policy about the LiP since LASPO 2012. Such materials have been produced by the High Court, the Supreme Court, the Bar Pro Bono Unit, the Law Society and numerous others. Networks of research and collaboration have also formed, including the LiP Network, doing important work in finding ways to better assist LiPs. I would therefore not wish to minimise the important work that has recently been done and is continuing to be done in the area. However, this more recent work, while useful and illuminating in some ways, still has certain limitations. First, whilst such work is important and growing, it remains constituted by a relatively small group of researchers. Second, such scholarship is made challenging by the almost total absence of data about LiPs; as I mentioned earlier in this book, figures for LiPs have only been published since 2014, and these are far from robust. This means that much of this research, including my own project, remains preliminary in the absence of better data.

Lastly, though, this book also sets out to argue that a limitation of at least *some* of this guidance and assistance for LiPs is that it is mostly concerned with the future and status of the legal profession; the effect the cuts will have on the future of legal representation. Such motives of course do not preclude a meaningful effort at assistance, but they do reflect the primacy of legal representation as the ultimate objective. Essentially, such scholarship largely seeks to find ways of expanding or obtaining advice for LiPs. This is important, but the solution *here* is always: get a lawyer. And this poses a problem. First, this is because the clock is not being turned back post-LASPO 2012. While over the course of writing this book there have been certain about-turns in conditions for lay litigants, such as the Supreme Court defeat of the raising of employment tribunal fees[2] (and in the criminal sphere, the defeat of the criminal courts charge), and while there are continuing discussions and proposed Green Papers about Family Court fees and access to legal aid, this simply is not the case for civil justice more widely.[3] We are heading towards a general election in 2024 that may see a Labour government in power for the first

[2] See R (on the Application of UNISON) (Appellant) v Lord Chancellor (Respondent) [2017] UKSC 51.

[3] The criminal courts charge was a system of fixed fees of up to £1,200 that essentially would penalise criminal defendants should they be found guilty of a criminal offence. It was introduced in April 2015 under Secretary of State for Justice Chris Grayling. The next Justice Secretary, Michael Gove, scrapped the charges after a Select Committee report highlighted the widescale problems with and protests against such a charge. See House of Commons Justice Committee, *Criminal Courts Charge: Second Report of Session 2015–16* (HC 586, 2015).

time since 2010. But as the Bach Commission Report outlines, published in late September 2017, Labour's vision for legal aid advocates restoration of such aid to certain spheres but does not propose reinstating it for non-family civil matters.[4] So no one at a senior level in government or opposition is proposing the restoration of legal aid for anyone within these pages. This means that 'get a lawyer' is not a good enough answer.

In addition to this issue, however, this book has tried to hint at a deeper one; a fundamental contradiction that exists between the theoretical 'right' to self-represent and a civil justice system that makes this extremely difficult in practice. So how did we get here? Why are LiPs outsiders? As I outlined in chapter 2, this history is quite a specific one. The idea that people who represented themselves were always seen as aberrant is simply not the case. It was common for individuals to act without legal representation for hundreds of years, in multiple different kinds of proceedings, such as manorial courts and in the Courts of Request. But such a landscape was one in which there were forums not dominated by the legal profession.

The coming of the professional, and the professionalisation of the new County Courts, is a story of attorneys fighting for recognition and distinction in these new courts. But these developments limited self-represented litigants from being able to pursue or defend claims without legal expertise. By the end of this process, legal expertise and formal procedure had become the norm in civil proceedings. Being a 'LiP' therefore meant something different from self-representation; it signified the moment when self-representation became aberrant. To be a LiP was to occupy a role arguably defined by lack of judgement and lack of skill: the obverse of the legal professional. This meant that LiPs existed in conceptual opposition to the mastery, colonisation and normality of the legal profession for resolving disputes. From this moment, self-represented parties were outsiders, and there was no place for them in this new, post-Judicature Act world.

It is important not to overstate the point: as mentioned above, LiPs are increasingly becoming a fact of life in multiple courts, and there are many people within the profession who actively seek to assist them. But they remain, *conceptually* at least, outsiders. And this 'outsider' status does something useful and productive: it emphasises the competency of the profession. One troubling question that arises from this study, then, is how LiPs can succeed. How can we ameliorate or improve LiP experiences in a legal world that, unconsciously or not, relies to some degree on their shortcomings? This odd positioning is ultimately echoed in some of the literature that demonstrates *fear* of the LiP: a situation where LiPs are 'normal' is a situation where legal professionals are giving way to another group in an area that they dominate. This issue surely provides some illumination as to why research on LiPs can be limited in what it can do: because it tends to

[4] The Bach Commission on Access to Justice Interim Report, *The Crisis in the Justice System in England and Wales* (Fabian Society, London, 2016).

reproduce the scenario that retains the LiP as outsider. It also explains the most significant research gap identified by this book, and which was noted by John Baldwin 20 years ago: much of the research into LiPs, including more recent and sympathetic scholarship, focuses on the impact LiPs have on the courts. What about the impact of the courts on LiPs?

This is what this book set out to consider. What can we find out by talking to LiPs? Not in concert with legal professionals, nor with the aim of reconfiguring LiP comments into previous frameworks, but unilaterally, *in their own words*? To do this, of course, I argued we need to go 'without the law': find other ways of reaching LiPs that could, if not completely escape, at least partially avoid falling into the potential trap of seeing LiPs as a problem, or of assuming that the solution ought to be legal representation. Most importantly, I argued that we needed to find out more about the impact going to law has on the LiP: what is it like to pursue or defend a claim? As I contended throughout the book, the answer is, for these 15 interviewees at least, 'It's mostly terrible!' Interviewee after interviewee expressed the deep and negative impact these experiences had had on them, including loss of family, loss of jobs, loss of homes, loss of social lives and loss of identity. For some interviewees, their claims became all they had.

It is important to emphasise that this study is of a very small sample and, as such, I do not want to overclaim based on these findings. However, at the very least, I argue the results of this study potentially rebut the idea that LiPs are choosing to 'commit law': no interviewee acted out of choice as they understood it; rather, they felt compelled or obliged to fight for something they perceived to be important in circumstances that were extremely difficult. In addition, whilst the significant and negative impact going to law can have for LiPs is perhaps to some degree recognised in family proceedings, this study has suggested it is not necessarily only those involved in the more obvious 'worthy' claims who have difficult or challenging experiences. No LiP in this study went to law for fun, and the negative impact experienced by interviewees was considerable. This finding suggests, I would argue, that we need to concentrate more on understanding this negative impact when researching LiPs in civil justice.

Finally, this study problematises the distinction between 'worthy' and 'unworthy' litigants: it has suggested that the complex individual histories of litigants often involve a development of litigious behaviour, or a development of distrust. The long-term narrative challenges the valency of a distinction between 'worthy' and 'unworthy' litigants, and suggests that much of this distinction is being made based on assessments of financial or legal merit that do not bear any relation to the relative value to the individual claimant or defendant. So, this book suggests that overall it is arguably a false distinction; at the very least it is unhelpful.

But what this study also found, beyond the depth of difficulties experienced by these LiPs, is that so many of these difficulties are not because of them but arguably embedded within the practice of civil justice itself. Interviewee after interviewee narrates scenarios where access to justice is made disproportionately *more* difficult, whether because of access to legal materials, inaccessibility of language, incomplete understanding of required behaviour, restrictive opening times, limited access to advice and more. This all points to a scenario of differential treatment. This study suggests, therefore, that LiPs are in practice being held to many of the same standards as legal professionals, without the skills, privileges and networks that the latter possess. And they are, at times, blamed for these failures.

So how can a LiP be good? We are very familiar with the bad LiP from the literature: it is clear what it means not to succeed. But what does a good LiP look like? The lack of consistent guidance or a clearly conceptualised role for LiPs results, in this study at least, in the experience of individuals who are being told that they have a right to self-represent, only to find the odds stacked against them when they set out to do just that. In this respect, at least, it is arguably far more likely that they will fail than succeed. And fail many do. With some exceptions, this study largely records and discusses experiences of failures. Litigants in person in this study fail to communicate what they want, they fail to provide the right documentation, they fail to succeed in their claims and they fail to get the right information to the right person at the right time.

There is no doubt that, amongst these failures, there are overblown expectations, perhaps some poor preparation and other difficulties that are due to the LiPs themselves. In addition, of course, all this study has is *stories*: we do not know 'what happened'. But the stories that emerge are deeply troubling because this failure often seems to be attributable to things that the LiP simply does not understand or will struggle to do anything about. Worryingly, an important finding from this study is that one of the worst, and least recognised, aspects of being a LiP is that LiPs are at such a disadvantage when things go wrong: how will they know how to deal with this? As Trevor said, to be a LiP is to operate without a safety net. In the end, then, this study suggests not only that LiPs often fail (which we already knew), but that they often fail *and they do not know why*. This is troubling on a basic level, suggesting we need to do a great deal more to understand what is happening here. But there are also significant consequences to these experiences of failure.

As chapter 6 sets out, LiPs in this study understand failure in particular ways, and for some of them, the only way to understand why they repeatedly fail, despite the effort and *work* they put in, is through the erosion of trust in the legal profession and legal institutions themselves. For some, too, this can tip into conspiracy theory. But while such claims tend to reinforce the negative attitudes some have towards LiPs, what this study suggests is that this disillusionment is a response to the situation that LiPs find themselves in: where they are given theoretical access to the courts, but where they cannot easily succeed, and where it is extremely difficult – if not impossible – to learn how to improve. The differential treatment LiPs in this study experience, the systemic exclusions they face, are symptomatic, I argue, of their fundamental lack of place in the legal system. It is this collective, systemic experience that gives rise to distrust and, for some, to conspiracy theories, rather than aberrant psychopathology. But of course when such individuals come to court and express these ideas, this serves to reinforce negative impressions of them and undermine their claims.

Clearly, we have multiple problems of significant scale. So what can we do? The findings in this study suggest some deep-rooted systemic problems that need addressing. This initially involves recognising the implication of the courts and legal professionals themselves in LiP experiences: how their practices and assumptions serve to reinforce and perpetuate the certain issues with LiPs. This includes considering how the failure of the LiP is linked to the success of the legal professional. How this is done is something for future study and research, but at the very least this study has demonstrated how much more we can understand about LiPs if we speak to them outside of the assumptions we place on them. If we do not do this, we will always fail to understand.

But I want to end on a more positive note. While the issues that this study points to are deep-rooted, there are surely ways to do small things to assist. First, we desperately need more and better-quality data. It is absurd that we still do not have more accurate figures for those acting as LiPs, and it means we are unable to understand the scale of the issue despite all our collective angst about it. The lack of data collection is hardly particular to LiPs: there are numerous failings that the Ministry of Justice needs to redress, as outlined by Natalie Byrom's most recent report.[5] Second, providing clearer, explicit training for legal professionals would surely help. This might involve things like continuing professional development sessions, explaining to them the distrust LiPs feel when they see lawyers and judges gathering and conversing together without them. If legal professionals were more explicit about how and why this took place, or if they refrained from doing it, this could improve LiP experiences. Judicial training would also be valuable as a regular event for all those involved in tribunal and court adjudication (including district judges and lay magistrates sitting in criminal proceedings). Part of this goal of training the profession is a commitment to saying that it is not simply the LiP that has to learn how to behave, it is also the job of legal professionals to learn how better to accommodate and support them. And of course, when LiPs get to court, it seems clear that better explanations are also called for. While many judges of course try extremely hard to explain situations to LiPs, these explanations would work better earlier on in the process. Some of the worst experiences in this study came from LiPs' failure to understand the financial consequences of not settling. This is surely something that can be built on in the mediation process, so that the consequences are made more explicit than they currently are.

Another mooted next step to assist LiPs is the coming online of courts. The Court Modernisation Programme, building on Lord Justice Briggs' Report in July 2016, proposes to move all small claims online.[6] In this proposed process, litigants would go through three stages: early 'triage' to identify problems through an automated system; arbitration with an appointed mediator, which would also

[5] N Byrom, Digital Justice: HMCTS data strategy and delivering access to justice: report and recommendations (London, Legal Education Foundation, 2019).

[6] Lord Justice Briggs, *Civil Courts Structure Review: Final Report* (London, Judiciary of England and Wales, 2016).

take place online; and, finally, only if necessary, a judicial decision if litigants cannot agree. Arguments in favour of an online court cite its greater accessibility for litigants, being online and circumventing the need to attend court.[7] In addition, this would also mean litigants could upload documents rather than sending them to a claims processing centre. While details have not been finalised, simplified proceedings are intended, including the online court's *not* being subject to the Civil Procedure Rules.[8] Such developments may indeed greatly assist in bypassing 'gatekeeper' issues referred to repeatedly in this book: the paper-bound nature of civil justice currently undoubtedly causes difficulties for LiPs.

However, there are areas of concern we need to consider before embracing such a court. Lord Justice Briggs suggested that the UK follow the example set by British Colombia in Canada, where they have already introduced such an online court, but so far this does not seem to be the case.[9] The automated triage system means that litigants will not have any human contact until the arbitration process. The 'triaging' relies on a system that can categorise disputes. But this book has already raised the problem with these kinds of categorisation: LiPs rarely have only one issue, and struggle to separate them out. It is hard to see how an automated system will optimise this process, and the risk is that, once again, it may simply fail to comprehend the complexity of litigants' cases.[10] The presumption built in here is that individuals have discrete problems, but this research contradicts this, as other research has done before.[11] It is also hard not to see this drive towards online courts as another means of pushing litigants out of the courts into alternative proceedings, creating a 'second-tier' system, where litigants would no longer have the 'right' to access the courts. I have argued that this right, in practice, is largely a rhetorical one, but this online court potentially takes this further by removing it altogether. This is compounded by the recent County Court Small Claims pilot, whereby claims of low value would be eligible to be heard on the papers only. As I have argued elsewhere, there are good reasons to be concerned about developing a tiered system whereby perceived low-value claims are driven out of the court altogether.[12]

Technology could, however, vastly improve the experiences of LiPs by making legal information more accessible. Expecting LiPs to do research on their own without being able to access paywalled information puts them in an impossible situation. Bailii, the free case-law resource, is limited in what it contains, and this

[7] ibid 36–52.

[8] ibid 52.

[9] The Civil Resolution Tribunal is available at https://civilresolutionbc.ca.

[10] Most of the suggestions Lord Woolf himself made in 1996 about necessary IT developments never took place, with the system still entirely paper-dependent. This leads to other concerns about the poor history of IT development in the courts.

[11] P Pleasence, 'Causes of Action: First Findings of the LSRC Periodic Survey' (2003) 30 *Journal of Law and Society* 11; N Balmer et al, 'Worried Sick: The Experience of Debt Problems and their Relationship with Health, Illness and Disability' (2006) 5 *Social Policy and Society* 39.

[12] K Leader, 'The Small Claims Pilot: Filtering out the County Court's Garbage Claims' *Modern Law Review* at www.modernlawreview.co.uk/leader-small-claims-pilot/.

inequality of ability to access data needs to be resolved. The use of online free resources could be significant in assisting LiPs.

It is clear, regardless, that technology on its own cannot solve another fundamental problem, which is that we also need to think about what a good LiP might look like. The lack of clear role as it currently stands leads to considerable inconsistency, leaving LiPs unable to know how to behave, and unable to improve. This is a significant source of resentment for them. Is there a way of providing useful guidance that might better lay out the role? Can we make the role a positive one, one that contains within it the possibility of competency rather than signifying its lack? The difficulty we face here, of course, is that to be a LiP is to *not* be a legal professional, and it is therefore hard to imagine how LiPs can ever be 'good'. At the very least, though, admitting such inconsistencies as exist now would be a positive step.

Finally, this book has argued throughout that, whilst there has been a significant improvement in research and the attention paid to LiPs, we are still at the very beginning of the process: we still have trouble understanding LiPs and their experiences. This difficulty forestalls any long-term improvements in LiP experiences. We need to understand why LiPs come to law, and the challenges they pose, instead of seeing them as problems. To make any long-term difference, such education needs to move us beyond any lazy, pejorative assumptions we still at times make about LiPs: it needs to be predicated on a greater understanding of LiP experiences. We need to hear more of the kinds of stories told in this book.[13] And this means we must keep listening.

[13] The former Personal Support Unit (PSU), now Support Through Court, used to provide a workshop as part of the Bar Professional Training Course (BPTC), though I am unclear if this is continuing. I did find a privately run course for lawyers on dealing with LiPs, the subheading of which read 'Develop strategies for managing your interactions and deal with your own response to stress'. See at https://kinchrobinson.com/courses/managing-litigants-in-person/.

BIBLIOGRAPHY

Aaronovitch, D, *Voodoo Histories: How Conspiracy Theory Has Shaped Modern History* (London, Vintage Books, 2009).

Alfieri, A, 'Reconstructive Poverty Law Practice: Learning Lessons of Client Narrative' (1991) 100(7) *Yale Law Journal* 2107.

Allan Lind, E and Tyler, T, *The Social Psychology of Procedural Justice* (New York, Springer, 1988).

Andrews, RW, *The Supreme Court of Judicature Acts, and the Appellate Jurisdiction Act 1876: With Rules of Court and Forms to May, 1880. Annotated So As to Form a Manual of Practice. Adapted Chiefly to the Chancery and Common Law Divisions* (London, Bibiobazaar, 2015 [1880]).

Applebey, G, 'Justice Without Lawyers: Litigants in Person in the English Civil Courts' (1997) 18 *Holdsworth Law Review* 109.

Arthurs, HW, *Without the Law: Administrative Justice and Legal Pluralism in 19th Century England* (New York, Buffalo, 1985);

Assy, R, *Injustice in Person: Revisiting the Right to Self-Representation* (Oxford, Oxford University Press, 2015).

Bailey, E et al, *A Handbook for Litigants in Person* (London, Courts and Tribunals Judiciary, 2012

Baker, JH, *The Legal Profession and the Common Law: Historical Essays* (London, The Hambledon Press, 1986).

Baksi, C '"Litigant in person" back as judges U-turn on terminology' *Law Society Gazette* (London, 4 March 2013).

——, 'Litigant in Person Punches Wife During Hearing' *Law Society Gazette* (London, 21 October 2013).

Baldwin, J, 'Litigants' Experience of Adjudication in the County Courts (1999) 18 *Civil Justice Quarterly* 12, 20.

Ball, C, 'Most people in the UK do not go to university – and maybe never will' *The Guardian* (London, 4 June 2013).

Balmer, N et al, 'Worried Sick: The Experience of Debt Problems and their Relationship with Health, Illness and Disability' (2006) 5 *Social Policy and Society* 39.

Bar Council, *A Guide to Representing Yourself in Court* (London, Bar Council, 2016).

Bedford, N and Taylor, M, 'Model No More: Querulent Behaviour, Vexatious Litigants and the Vexatious Proceedings Act 2005 (QLD)' (2014) 24 *Journal of Judicial Administration* 46.

Bentham, J, *A Protest Against Law Taxes* (London, J Debrett, 1795).

Berger, J, *Ways of Seeing* (London, Penguin, 1972).

Bernard, HR, *Research Methods in Anthropology: Qualitative and Quantitative Approaches* (Lanham, MD, Rowman Altamira, 2011).

Bevan, C, 'Self-Represented Litigants: the Overlooked and Unintended Consequence of Legal Aid Reform' (2012) 35(1) *Journal of Social Welfare & Family Law* 43.

Blackwell, M, '"Old Boys Networks", Family Connections and the Legal Profession' (2012) 3 *Public Law* 426.

Bottoms, AE and McClean, D, *Defendants in the Criminal Process* (London, Routledge and Kegan Paul, 1976).

Bourdieu, P, *Distinction: A Social Critique of the Judgment of Taste* (London, Routledge, 1979).

——, 'The Force of Law: Towards a Sociology of the Juridical Field' (1987) 38 *Hastings Law Journal* 814.

——, *Language and Symbolic Power* (London, Polity Press, 1991).

——, *The Field of Cultural Production: Essays on Art and Literature* (New York, Columbia University Press, 1993).

——, *Pascalian Meditations* (Stanford, CA, Stanford University Press, 1997).
Bowcott, O, 'UK courts service spending sees tenfold rise since 2010' *The Guardian* (London, 21 July 2018).
Bowling, B and Phillips, C, 'Disproportionate and Discriminatory: Reviewing the Evidence on Police Stop and Search' (2007) 70 *MLR* 936.
Brand, P, *The Origins of the English Legal Profession* (Oxford, Blackwell Publishing, 1992);
Brooks, C, *Lawyers, Litigation and English Society Since 1450* (London, The Hambledon Press, 1998)
Brooks, C and Lobban, M (eds), *Communities and Courts in Britain: 1150–1900* (London, The Hambledon Press, 1997).
Butter, M and Knight, P, 'Bridging the Great Divide: Conspiracy Theory Research for the 21st Century' (2015) 62 *Diogenes* 17.
Byrom, N, 'Cuts and the Lawyering Identity Crisis' in A Flynn and J Hodgson (eds), *Access to Justice and Legal Aid: Comparative Perspectives on Unmet Legal Need* (London, Bloomsbury, 2017) 221.
Cameron, C and Kelly, E, 'Litigants in Person in Civil Proceedings: Part II Solicitors' Perspectives' (2003) 33 *Hong Kong Law Journal* 313.
Carlen, P, 'The Staging of Magistrate's Justice' (1976) 16 *British Journal of Criminology* 48.
Citizens Advice Bureau, *Going to Court* (London, CAB, 2011).
Cowan, D and Hitchings, E, 'Pretty Boring Stuff: District Judges and Housing Possession' (2007) 16 *Social & Legal Studies* 363.
Cowan, D, Mulcahy, L and Wheeler, S, 'Introduction' in *Law and Society* (London, Routledge, 2014) 1.
Cunningham, C, 'The Lawyer as Translator, Representation as Text: Towards an Ethnography of Legal Discourse' (1992) 6 *Cornell Law Review* 1298.
Dehaghani, R, 'Interrogating Vulnerability: Reframing the Vulnerable Suspect in Police Custody' (2020) 30 *Social and Legal Studies* 251.
Dorset, S, 'Destitute of the Knowledge of God: Maori Testimony before the New Zealand Courts in the Early Crown Colony Period' in D Kirkby (ed), *Past Law, Present Histories* (Canberra, ANU E-Press, 2012) 39.
Duman, D, 'The Creation and Diffusion of a Professional Ideology in Nineteenth Century England' (1979) 27 *The Sociological Review* 115.
——, 'Pathway to Professionalism: The English Bar in the Eighteenth and Nineteenth Centuries' (1980) 13 *Journal of Social History* 622.
Dryden, BR, 'Technological Leaps and Bounds: Pro Se Prisoner Litigation in the Internet Age [comments]' (2008) 10 *University of Pennsylvania Journal of Constitutional Law* 854.
Ewick, P and Silbey, S, *The Common Place of Law: Stories from Everyday Life* (Chicago, IL, University of Chicago Press 1998).
Felstiner, W et al, 'The Emergence and Transformation of Disputes: Naming, Blaming, Claiming …' (1980) 15 *Law and Society Review* 631.
Fineman, M, 'Vulnerability and Inevitable Inequality' (2017) 4 *Oslo Law Review* 133
Finn, M, *The Character of Credit: Personal Debt in English Culture, 1740–1914* (Cambridge, Cambridge University Press, 1993).
Foucault, M, *The Archaeology of Knowledge and the Discourse on Language* (New York, Pantheon Books, 1972)
Fouzder, M, 'There was no money: MoJ called in consultants to help control spending' *Law Society Gazette* (London, 19 October 2016).
——, 'Bundles guidance "highlights litigant-in-person struggles"' *Law Society Gazette* (London, 22 April 2022).
Freckelton, I, 'Querulent Paranoia and the Vexatious Complainant' (1988) 11 *International Journal of Law and Psychiatry* 127.
Frisch, M, *A Shared Authority: Essays on the Craft and Meaning of Oral and Public History* (Albany, NY, State University of New York Press, 1990).
Galanter, M, 'Why the "Haves" Come out Ahead: Speculations on the Limits of Legal Change' (1974) 9(1) *Law & Society Review* 95.

——, 'Justice in Many Rooms: Courts, Private Ordering and Indigenous Law' (1981) 13 *Journal of Legal Pluralism and Unofficial Law* 10.
Geertz, C, *The Interpretation of Cultures* (New York, Basic Books, 1973).
——, *Local Knowledge: Further Essays in Interpretive Anthropology* (London, Basic Books, 1983).
Genn, H, *Paths to Justice* (Oxford, Hart Publishing, 1999).
——, *Judging Civil Justice: The 2008 Hamlyn Lectures* (Cambridge, Cambridge University Press, 2009) 133.
——, 'Do-It-Yourself Law: Access to Justice and the Challenge of Self-Representation', speech delivered at lecture *Assisting Unrepresented Litigants*, Sydney (15–17 April 2014).
Gibbs, J, 'The Politics of Vulnerability: Affect, Relationality, and Resistance in UK Austerity' (PhD thesis, London School of Economics, 2018).
Goodrich, P, *Oedipus Lex: Psychoanalysis, History, Law* (Berkeley, CA, University of California Press, 1995).
Graham, C, *Ordering Law: The Architectural and Social History of the English Law Court to 1914* (London, Routledge, 2003).
Greenwood, J, 'Letters: Legal Aid: Children Suffer' *Law Society Gazette* (London, 22 July 2013).
Greiner, DJ and Pattanayak, CW, 'Randomized Evaluation in Legal Assistance: What Difference Does Representation (Offer and Actual Use) Make?' (2012) 121 *Yale Law Journal* 2118.
Griffiths, J, 'What is Legal Pluralism?' (1986) 18 *The Journal of Legal Pluralism and Unofficial Law* 3.
Halliday, S and Morgan, B, 'I Fought the Law and the Law Won? Legal Consciousness and the Critical Imagination' (2013) 66 *Current Legal Problems* 1.
Hastings, M, *The Court of Common Pleas in the 15th Century* (Ithaca, NY, Cornell University Press, 1947).
Herman, D, 'Hopeless Cases: Race, Racism and the Vexatious Litigant' (2012) 8 *International Journal of Law in Context* 27.
Huber, C and Kuncel, N, 'Does College Teach Critical Thinking?: A Meta-Analysis' (2016) 86 *Review of Educational Research* 431.
Hunt, A, *Governance of the Consuming Passions* (Basingstoke, MacMillan Press Limited, 1996).
Hunter, R, 'Adversarial mythologies: policy assumptions and research evidence in family law' (2003) 30 *Journal of Law and Society* 156.
——, 'Exploring the "LASPO Gap"' (2014) 44 *Family Law* 660.
Hyde, J, 'Judges call for urgent overhaul to cope with surge of LIPs' *Law Society Gazette* (London, 5 July 2013).
Jacobsen, J et al, *Structured Mayhem: Personal Experiences of the Crown Court* (London, Criminal Justice Alliance, 2015).
Jauss, H, *Towards an Aesthetic of Reception* (Minneapolis, MN, University of Minnesota Press, 1982).
Johnson, P, 'Creditors, Debtors and the Law in Victorian England' (1996) LSE Economic History Working Papers 31/96.
Johnson, R, 'Alice Through the Fence: Greenham Women and the Law' in J Dewar et al (eds), *Nuclear Weapons, the Peace Movement and the War* (London, Palgrave, 1986).
Jones, MP, *Justice and Journalism: A Study of the Influence of Newspaper Reporting upon the Administration of Justice by Magistrates* (Chichester, Barry Rose, 1974)
Judicial College, *Equal Treatment Bench Book* (London, Judicial College, 2013).
Kritzer, HM, *Legal Advocacy: Lawyers and Non Lawyers at Work* (Ann Arbor, MI, University of Michigan Press, 1998).
Langbein, J, *Origins of Adversarial Criminal Trial* (Oxford, Oxford University Press, 2003).
Langdon-Down, G, 'Litigants in person could struggle to secure access to justice' *Law Society Gazette* (London, 19 January 2012).
Larson, MS, *The Rise of Professionalism: A Sociological Analysis* (Berkeley, CA, University of California Press, 1977)
Leader, K, 'Trials, Truth Telling and the Performing Body' (PhD thesis, University of Sydney, 2008).
——, 'From Bear Gardens to the County Court: Creating the Litigant in Person' (2020) 79 *Cambridge Law Journal* 260.

——, 'Law, Presence to Absence: The Case of the Disappearing Defendant' in S Rai et al (eds), *Oxford Handbook of Politics and Performance* (Oxford, Oxford University Press, 2021, 73).
LeCluyse, E, 'The Spectrum of Competency: Determining a Standard of Competence for Pro Se Representation' (2015) 65 *Case Western Reserve Law Review* 1239
Lee, E, 'Shut the Flood-Gates: The Litigants are Coming!' (2013) 38(3) *Alternative Law Journal* 190.
Levin, B, *The Times* (London, 30 November 1976).
Lewis, P, 'Litigants in Person and their Difficulties in Adducing Evidence: A Study of a Small Claims in an English County Court' (2007) 11 *International Journal of Evidence and Proof* 24.
Lobban, M, 'Preparing for Fusion: Reforming the 19th Century Court of Chancery, II' (2004) 22 *Law and History Review* 565.
MacFarlane, J, *The New Lawyer: How Settlement is Transforming the Practice of Law* (Vancouver and Toronto, UBC Press, 2008).
MacLean, M and Eekelaar, J, 'Legal Representation in Family Matters and the Reform of Legal Aid: A Research Note on Current Practice' (2012) 24 *Child and Family Law Quarterly* 223.
Mant, J, 'Neoliberalism, Family Law and Access to Justice' (2017) 39 *Journal of Social Welfare and Family Law* 246.
——, *Litigants in Person and the Family Justice System* (Oxford, Hart Publishing, 2022).
Marshall, TH, 'The Recent History of Professionalism in Relation to Social Structures and Social Policy' (1939) 5 *The Canadian Journal of Economics and Political Science* 325.
Marx, K and Engels, F, *The Communist Manifesto* (London and New York, Simon & Schuster, 2013).
McKeever, G et al, *Litigants in Person in Northern Ireland: Barriers to Legal Participation* (Ulster, Ulster University, 2018).
McQueen, R, 'Of Wigs and Gowns: A Short History of Legal and Judicial Dress in Australia' in R McQueen and W Pue (eds), *Misplaced Traditions: British Lawyers, Colonial Peoples* (Annandale, NSW, Federation Press, 1999), 31.
Merry, SE, *Getting Justice and Getting Even: Legal Consciousness Among Working Class Americans* (Chicago, IL, University of Chicago Press, 1990).
——, 'What is Legal Culture – An Anthropological Perspective' (2010) 5 *Comparative Law Journal* 43.
Meyler, F and Woodhouse, S, 'Changing the Immigration Rules and Withdrawing the "Currency" of Legal Aid: The Impact of LASPO 2012 on Migrants and their Families' (2013) 35 *Journal of Social Welfare and Family Law* 55.
Moore, P, 'Longing to Belong: Trained Actors' Attempts to Enter the Profession' (PhD thesis, University of Sydney, 2006).
Moorhead, R, 'The Passive Arbiter' (2007) 16(3) *Social and Legal Studies* 405.
——, 'Precarious Professionalism: Some Empirical and Behavioural Perspectives on Lawyers' (2014) 67 *Current Legal Problems* 447.
Moorhead, R et al, 'What Clients Know: Client Perspectives and Legal Competence' (2003) 5 *International Journal of the Legal Profession* 5.
Moorhead, R and Pleasence, P (eds), *After Universalism: Re-engineering Access to Justice* (Oxford, Blackwell Publishing, 2003).
Moorhead, R, Sherr, A and Paterson, A, 'Contesting Professionalism: Legal Aid and Nonlawyers in England and Wales' (2003) 37 *Law and Society Review* 765.
Moses, L, 'Helping out Litigants in Person' *Law Society Gazette* (London, 15 July 2013).
Moulton, BA, 'The Persecution and Intimidation of the Low-Income Litigant as Performed by the Small Claims Court in California' (1969) 21 *Stanford Law Review* 1657.
Mulcahy, L, 'The Unbearable Lightness of Being? Shifts Towards the Virtual Trial' (2008) 35 *Journal of Law and Society* 437.
——, *Legal Architecture: Justice, Due Process and the Place of Law* (London, Routledge, 2011).
——, 'The Collective Interest in Private Dispute Resolution' (2012) 33 *Oxford Journal of Legal Studies* 59.
Munro, V and Scoutar, J, 'Abusing Vulnerability? Contemporary Law and Policy Responses to Sex Work in the UK' (2012) 20 *Feminist Legal Studies* 189.
Nobles, R and Schiff, D, *Understanding Miscarriages of Justice: Law, the Media and the Inevitability of a Crisis* (Oxford, Oxford University Press, 2001).

Parry, E, *The Seven Lamps of Advocacy* (London, T Fisher Unwin, 1923)

Pleasence, P, 'Causes of Action: First Findings of the LSRC Periodic Survey' (2003) 30 *Journal of Law and Society* 11.

Polden, P, *A History of the County Courts: 1846–1971* (Cambridge, Cambridge University Press, 1999)

Quintanilla, V et al, 'The Signaling Effect of Pro Se Status' (2017) 42 *Law & Social Inquiry* 1091.

Ridley, MK, 'The Right to Defend Pro Se: Faretta v California and Beyond' (1975) 40 *Alabama Law Review* 425.

Reed, L, *The Family Court Without a Lawyer: A Handbook for Litigants in Person* (Bath, Bath Publishing, 2023).

Reyes, E, 'Litigants in Person Numbers Soar' *Law Society Gazette* (London, 13 October 2011).

Roberts, S, '"Listing Concentrates the Mind": the English Civil Court as an Arena for Structured Negotiation' (2009) 29(3) *Oxford Journal of Legal Studies* 457.

Robbins, IP and Herman, S, 'Pro Se Litigation – Litigating Without Counsel: Faretta or For Worse' (1975) 42 *Brook Law Review* 63.

Robertson, G, *The Justice Game* (London, Vintage, 1999)

Rock, P, 'Witnesses and Spaces in a Crown Court' (1991) 31 *British Journal of Criminology* 266.

——, *The Social World of an English Crown Court* (Oxford, Oxford University Press, 1993).

Sarat, P and Felstiner, W, *Divorce Lawyers and Their Clients: Power and Meaning in the Legal Process* (Oxford, Oxford University Press, 1995).

Saunders, Z, 'How Can Lawyers Learn to Love Litigants in Person?' *The Lawyer* (London, 11 April 2013).

Schechner, R, *Performance Studies: An Introduction* (New York, Routledge, 2002).

Scheffer, T, 'Materialities of Legal Proceedings' (2004) 17(4) *International Journal for the Semiotics of Law* 356.

Scraton, P, *Childhood in Crisis* (London, University College London, 1997).

Sherr, A 'The Value of Experience in Legal Competence' (2000) 7 *International Journal of the Legal Profession* 95.

Sime, S and French, D (eds), *Blackstone's Civil Proceedings* (Oxford, Oxford University Press, 2023).

Smith, S, *Maverick Litigants: A History of Vexatious Litigants in Australia 1930–2008* (Melbourne, Maverick Publications, 2009).

Sourdin, T and Wallace, N, 'The Dilemmas Posed by Self-Represented Litigants – The Dark Side' (2014) 24(1) *Journal of Judicial Administration* 61.

Sunderland, E, 'The English struggle for procedural reform' (1926) 39 *Harvard Law Review* 734.

Swank, DA, 'The Pro Se Phenomenon' (2005) 19 *Brigham Young University Journal of Public Law* 373.

Taggart, M, 'Alexander Chaffers and the Genesis of the Vexatious Actions Act 1896' (2004) 63 *CLJ* 656.

Taylor, M, 'Querulent Behaviour, Vexatious Litigants and the Vexatious Proceedings Act 2005 (Qld)', conference paper delivered at the Australasian Institute of Judicial Administration, Assisting Unrepresented Litigants – A Challenge for Courts and Tribunals Conference, Sydney, 15–17 April 2014.

Thibaut, J and Walker, L, *Procedural Justice: A Psychological Analysis* (New York, Elrbaum, 1975).

Tkacukova, T and Lee, R, *A Study of Litigants in Person in Birmingham Civil Justice Centre* (Birmingham, CEPLER, 2017).

Toy-Cronin, B, 'I Ain't No Fool: Deciding to Litigate in Person in the Civil Courts' (2016) 4 *New Zealand Law Review* 723.

——, 'A Defence of the Right to Litigate in Person' (2017) 37 *Oxford Journal of Legal Studies* 238.

Tucker, P, 'London's Courts of Law in the Fifteenth Century: The Litigant's Perspective' in C Brooks and M Lobban (eds), *Communities and Courts in Britain: 1150–1900* (London, The Hambledon Press, 1997) 29.

——, 'What is Procedural Justice?: Criteria used by Citizens to Assess the Fairness of Legal Procedures' (1988) 22 *Law & Society Review* 103.

Tyler, T, *Why People Obey the Law* (Princeton, NJ, Princeton University Press, 1990).

Tyler, T and Y Huo, *Trust in the Law: Encouraging Public Cooperation with the Police and Courts* (New York, Russell Sage Foundation, 2002).

Wasserstrom, R, 'Lawyers as Professionals: Some Moral Issues' (1975) 5 *Human Rights* 1.
Wilding, J, *The Legal Aid Market: Challenges for Publicly Funded Immigration and Asylum Legal Representation* (Bristol, Bristol University Press, 2021).
——, 'The Legal Aid sector is collapsing and millions more may soon be without access to justice' *The Conversation* (London, 7 June 2023).
Williams, C, 'Legal English and Plain Language: An Introduction' (2004) 1 *ESP Across Cultures* 111.
Zimerman, N and T Tyler, 'Between Access to Counsel and Access to Justice: A Psychological Perspective' (2010) 37 *Fordham Urban Law Journal* 473.

Reports

Advice Services Alliance, *Proposal for the Reform of Legal Aid in England and Wales, Consultation Paper CP12/10* (London, Ministry of Justice, 2011).
Amnesty International, *Cuts That Hurt: The Impact of Legal Aid Cuts in England on Access to Justice* (London, Amnesty, 2016).
Bach Commission on Access to Justice, *Interim Report, The Crisis in the Justice System in England and Wales* (Fabian Society, London, 2016).
Baldwin, J, *Monitoring the Rise of the Small Claims Limit: Litigants' Experience of Different Forms of Adjudication* (London, Lord Chancellor's Department, 1997).
Bar Council, *The Legal Aid, Sentencing and Punishment of Offenders Act 2012 (LASPO): One Year On* (London, Bar Council, 2014).
Briggs, M, *Civil Courts Structure Review: Final Report* (London, Judiciary of England and Wales, 2016).
Byrom, N, *Digital Justice: HMCTS data strategy and delivering access to justice: report and recommendations* (London, Legal Education Foundation, 2019).
Civil Justice Council, *Access to Justice for Litigants in Person: A Report and a Series of Recommendations to the Lord Chancellor and to the Lord Chief Justice* (London, CJC, 2011).
Cookson, G, *Unintended Consequences: The Cost of the Government's Legal Aid Reforms: A Report for the Law Society of England & Wales* (Department of Management, School of Social Science and Public Policy, November 2011.
Dewar, J et al, *Litigants in Person in the Family Court of Australia* (Canberra, Family Court, 2000).
Genn, H and Y Genn, *The Effectiveness of Representation at Tribunals, Report to the Lord Chancellor* (London, LCD, 1989).
Gill, B, The Right Honourable Lord, *Report of the Scottish Civil Courts Review* (Scotland, RR Donnelly, 2009) 240.
Judiciary of England and Wales, *Judicial Working Group on Litigants in Person Report* (London, July 2013).
MacFarlane, J, 'The National Self-Represented Litigants Project: Identifying and Meeting the Needs of Self-Represented Litigants' Treasurer's Advisory Group on Access to Justice Working Group Report, 2013.
MacFarlane, J and C Sullivan, 'Tracking the Trends of the Self-Represented Litigant Phenomenon: Data from the National Self-Represented Litigants Project 2019–2021' (Windsor, National Self Represented Litigants Project, 2021).
Moorhead, R et al, *Quality and Cost: Final Report on the Contracting of Civil, Non-Family Advice and Assistance Pilot* (London, Stationery Office, 2001).
Moorhead, R and Harding, R, *Quality and Access: Specialist and Tolerance Work under Civil Contracts* (London, Stationery Office, 2004).
Moorhead, R and Sefton, M, *Litigants in Person: Unrepresented Litigants in First Instance Proceedings*, Department of Constitutional Affairs Research Series 2/05 (London, Department of Constitutional Affairs, 2005)

Moorhead, R and Sefton, M, *Litigants in Person: Unrepresented Litigants in First Instance Proceedings* (London, Department of Constitutional Affairs, 2005).

Moorhead, R and Sherr, A, *An Anatomy of Access: Evaluating Entry, Initial Advice and Signposting Using Model Clients* (London, Legal Services Research Centre, 2002).

Otton, P, *Interim Report of the Working Party Established by the Judges' Council into Litigants in Person in The Royal Courts of Justice London* (RCJ, London, 1995).

Plotnikoff, J and Wilson, R, *A Study of the Services Provided under the Otton Project to Litigants in Person at the Citizens Advice Bureau* (London, Lord Chancellor's Office 1998).

Trade Union Congress, *Justice Denied* (London, TUC, 2016).

Trinder, L et al, *Litigants in Person in Private Family Law Cases* (London, Ministry of Justice Analytical Series, 2014.

Williams, K, *Litigants in Person: A Literature Review* (London, Ministry of Justice, 2011).

Woolf, H, *Access to Justice: The Final Report to the Lord Chancellor on the Civil Justice System in England and Wales* (London, Stationery Office, 1996).

INDEX

www.ingramcontent.com/pod-product-compliance
Ingram Content Group UK Ltd.
Pitfield, Milton Keynes, MK11 3LW, UK
UKHW022210051026
15624UKWH00001B/99